Los Angeles 5000 km
Honolulu 2000 km
Washington 8000 km

P A C I F I C

O C E A N

TOKELAU

WESTERN
SAMOA
Savai'i   APIA
          Upolu

AMERICAN
SAMOA

TONGA
Tongatapu

COOK ISLANDS

Rarotonga

P O L Y N E S I A

M E L A N E S I A

F I J I

Bora
Bora

SOCIETY
ISLANDS
(TAHITI)

Tahiti

Nuku Hiva
Hiva Oa

TUAMOTU ISLANDS

Mururoa

Santiago 6000 km

Cape Horn 7000 km

N

0   250   500   750   1000 km

Author's Route:

→———————→———— Ship
– – – → – – – → – – – Plane

Transit of Venus

Transit of Venus

Travels in the Pacific

Julian Evans

Pantheon Books   New York

All rights reserved under International and Pan-American Copyright Conventions.
Published in the United States by Pantheon Books,
a division of Random House, Inc., New York.
Originally published in Great Britain by Martin Secker & Warburg Limited, London.

Library of Congress Cataloging-in-Publication Data

Evans, Julian, 1955–
    Transit of Venus: travels in the Pacific/Julian Evans.
        p.   cm.
    ISBN 0-679-41637-4
    1. Oceania—Description and travel—1981–
    2. Evans, Julian,—1955– —Journeys—Oceania.   I. Title.
    DU23.5.E93   1992
    919.504—dc20   92-54117

Manufactured in the United States of America

First American Edition

2 4 6 8 9 7 5 3 1

For my mother and father

'All things of the sea belong to Venus;
pearls and shells and alchemists'gold and
kelp and the riggish smell of neap tides, the
inshore green, and purple further out and
the joy of distances and the roar of falling
masonry, all these are hers, but she doesn't
come out of the sea for all of us.'

John Cheever

1
The Occidental Hotel

Somewhere in Sydney, a water-city with a gothic heart and an unquenchable thirst, there is a fat man with a sunburnt face called Norman.

He was in his mid-seventies, at a guess. He was wearing a pale grey suit and a boater with a purple hydrangea in the hatband. A transparent polo shirt stretched over his stomach like pork muslin; his rough, mottled face gave him the look of an old stockman who had spent his life under the sun. His hands were raw at the knuckles: the left clenched the knob of a blackwood cane which he tapped at with the palm of the other, revealing the impatience beneath his courtesy.

But the most striking thing about him was his eyes. They were a hazy grey-blue, like the colour of far hills, unnaturally bright. The rest of his appearance made him faintly comical. His eyes had a suggestion of lunacy.

The pubs in Sydney are not places to strike up casual friendships. Full of raw-faced men in tiny shorts, they have an air of fuddled calculation. If Australia were still a prison colony, these drinkers would be working out how many days and years they had left. As it is, they work out how far they can escape with drink, and take out their discontent on strangers. In a pub by the docks where they had strippers every lunchtime, a wharfie leaned over and hissed in my ear: 'Er you a fuckin pom? Yer all fucking pisspoor, except for Missis Thatcher.' An hour later, at a hotel in the business district, a blond man with the soused features of a fallen angel said: 'Dontyer hate fucking wogs?' He stuck his chin out and wheedled for the answer he wanted. His cousins in South Africa wrote to him regularly, extolling the virtues of apartheid. To underline that his oratorical powers were undiminished by alcohol, he added, 'Oyve drank twenny-five Heinekens,' but his coordination was so poor that as he said it he was pouring the twenty-sixth over his shoes.

I thought I would be safe in the Occidental Hotel, a sedate place of echoing bathrooms and recent immigrants. I ordered a brandy and soda. When it came, a Sydneyite down the bar with delicate red ears stood up unsteadily.

'Isn't our beer good enough for you?'

I shrugged and said yes and waited for the fight to develop, deciding I would only have one chance to hit him before the whole bar was on me. I was aggrieved enough to hit him, and persecuted enough to think the bar would take his side. But suddenly he thought better of whatever he had had in mind. 'Fucking snob,' he said – it was a change from fucking poms and fucking wogs, at least – 'I've had enough.' Then he staggered through the double doors, still holding his beer glass, and I heard the glass smash in the street outside.

Norman had witnessed the third encounter. I saw the boater and the hydrangea and the steady, bright stare and thought: Another madman. But he bought me another brandy and soda and said, 'You don't want to take any notice of that. It's only your accent.' He fished a card from the breast pocket of his jacket. 'Anything I can do. You only have to let me know.'

The card said, 'Norman Garvey, Hon. Order MBE, Chairman, City Construction Ltd', and gave his office and home phone numbers. There was no address.

Norman fixed his pale gaze on me. 'What are you doing in

Sydney?'

For ten days, I said, I had been trying without success to get a passage on a ship to the western Pacific. The answer was always the same. At one shipping office the clerk in charge of the schedules looked up and said bitterly, 'I've worked here for fifteen years, and if I can't get a passage you certainly can't.' At Darling Harbour a Yorkshireman just in from Auckland, drinking cheap Scotch with a woman whose powdered breasts jostled at her neckline like puppies in a sack, gestured around the narrow, dark officers' mess: 'It's all cargo, cargo, cargo now.'

Norman hoisted himself onto a stool and began to complain about his rheumatism.

If he had been younger he would have taken me there himself. 'I went to sea at thirteen, had my master's ticket at twenty and a half.' He was staring over my shoulder. I turned round. A blonde girl in a white teeshirt stared defiantly back. The hydrangea wobbled as Norman raised his boater to her and said, 'You're a very beautiful young woman.'

To me he said, 'You should give it another try. Go back and ask for the bloke who signs on the crews. And remember, anything I can do.'

Norman's restlessness had got the better of him. We walked to the door of the hotel.

'What were you trading? Copra?'

'In a way,' he said. 'I was with the Nobel Explosives Company for fifteen years.'

He raised his cane as he stepped out into the street. Immediately a taxi stopped and he lowered himself in.

The following morning I asked the woman who had been serving in the bar the night before if she knew who Norman was. She looked surprised at the question. He owned buildings all over the city, she said; he was one of the richest men in Sydney.

It was pure coincidence that later in the day, in a second-hand bookstore on George Street, I found a copy of Nicholas

Halasz's biography of Nobel. It was a strange mixture of hagiography and disapproval, the kind of book written by one incomplete man about another. But it made me think: Everyone should read their own obituary.

On 12 April 1888, in a villa on the Côte d'Azur with a magnificent view of bougainvillaeas and the Mediterranean, Alfred Nobel's elder brother Ludwig died. (Seeing his brother shortly before, Alfred's reaction to his suffering had been to invent an automatic device by which, inserting a special coin, the sick man could procure a fatal electric shock for himself and simultaneously summon the gendarmes. The gendarmes however had denied him a permit for the machine.)

The French newspapers had their accounts ready, but somewhere along the line they mistook Ludwig for Alfred.

The inventor of dynamite, the man nobody knew, was stunned. The obituaries dismissed him as 'the dynamite king', a merchant of death and an international capitalist who had amassed a huge fortune from the sales of increasingly devastating weapons.

What overwhelmed him was not the failure to recognise his scholarly achievement, his seriousness, his abilities as a chemist, the polyglot and philomath. (He was also in his spare time a remarkably bad poet.)

Reticent, untrusting, and melancholy, Alfred had had two hopeless affairs. To Countess Bertha Kinsky, one of the women who might have become his wife, he had once confided his life's true intention. He was working on a new version of dynamite, an improvement on the combination of nitro-glycerine and kieselguhr (the fireproof fossil earth used to build the dome of Saint Sophia). He had stumbled on it by accident after cutting himself on a splinter of glass and applying collodion to the wound; unable to sleep, he had decided to try the collodion in solution with nitro-glycerine. With the addition of eight per cent guncotton, the safe mixture, 'blasting gelatine', was half as powerful again as dynamite.

For the self-effacing, reclusive dynamiteur even the success of blasting gelignite was not enough. He said to Bertha: 'I wish I could produce a substance or machine of such frightful efficacy for wholesale devastation that wars should thereby become altogether impossible.'

It was Alfred's idealism that the obituarists had missed.

2
First journey

Lying like fly-specks on the equator, just west of the Pacific Date Line, the Japanese-held Marshall Islands were a gift to America after the Second World War. The first thing it did, in February 1946, was evacuate the inhabitants of Bikini atoll, 'for the good of mankind,' the Navy officers – inhabited by the spirit of Nobel – told the islanders, 'and to end all world wars.' Between 1946 and 1958, twenty-three nuclear blasts in the atmosphere were detonated there.

It was the decade of stereophonic sound, and fridges and t.v.s for everyone: no one could accuse the Fifties of lacking promise. When I was a baby my father was offered a slice of this promise, a junior diplomatic posting to Australia. Early in 1956 he took the family to Queensland.

In Brisbane my father was a celebrity. Every speech he made for the High Commission was reported in the *Courier Mail*, and the Brisbane establishment came to his cocktail parties to hear the first stereogram in the state and help themselves to the duty-free whisky posted at the four corners of the billiard room. (I came to the parties, uninvited and usually naked.) He rented a huge house that stood next to a banana plantation near Eagle Junction, where the cattle trains of the north Queensland

railway left the reek of hide and tallow on the air. At Eagle
Junction at the age of four I had my first taste of fear, waiting by
the track for the double headlamps and the forty stockcars of the
inbound freight to tread down the ballast and roar through the
curve, the ghostly pennants of cattle-smell fluttering behind it. I
kept lizards in my shorts and only wore shoes on Sunday, when
my mother clipped a bowtie around my neck to take me to the
Methodist church. She could not stand the heat or the sermons,
and I remember her chatty affection disappearing on the walk
home as she fell silent, her chin set under the wide brim of her
hat.

Queensland was a sort of hell for genteel emigrants. My
great-aunt Kate, married to a commercial artist called Harry
Leahy, had come out before us to run a hotel. Fastidious and
culturally superior – she was an ex-headmistress, he designed
publicity material for cigarette manufacturers (these were the
days of 'Craven A, for your throat's sake') – they were both
chain-smokers and had furnished their house in Dorking with the
proceeds from their cigarette coupons.

When the last pouffe was purchased, they became restless
and decided to emigrate. But they misjudged the farming
communities of the Darling Downs and found that the 'hotel' for
which they had given up their teashop near Dorking was a pub
that swarmed every afternoon with the stockmen's six-o'clock
swill. Their bungalow was a tin-roofed shack.

They lasted a year. On their return they went to live in
isolation in a caravan in Sussex, where Harry's remaining consolation, before he succumbed to lung cancer, was to take local
girls into the bluebell woods outside Mayfield for 'painting
lessons'.

Six years after we arrived we turned round and came home
again. Afterwards I hardly thought of Queensland. But I dreamt
about the surface stuff of childhood: the scorching roads that
inflicted puffy blisters; the mosquitoes that hung like rain on the

nets at night; the smell of calamine lotion; the snakes in the banana plantation; the cool smell of the earth under the house; refusing to come in out of the rain, and lying on the shore of the ocean in leopard-spotted swimming trunks.

In south London, when I was scared, huge cockroaches clattered into my bedroom. When I wasn't scared, I dreamt of the last Christmas holiday and my first experience of sex. I was five, and the object of my desire was seventeen. It was high summer on the New South Wales coast. She threw me into the sea, and afterwards on a long empty beach I sat on the sand by her wet head and she propped herself up on her elbows and laughed as I stared and stared at the soft shadow, dusted with salt, between her breasts.

There was a record they played that year that was the first song I remember. Patricia – that was her name – danced to it with me in the evening, round about barbecue time. Sweet surrender: I held her around the hips and pushed my head against her soft stomach which trembled with her giggling.

One two three four,
Tell the people what she wore.
She wore an itsy bitsy teeny weeny
Yellow polka dot bikini.

The family talked about 'Australia' for years. I kept in my head a place which was nowhere in particular, but a false start of tropical heat and lost sensations.

In 1988, thirty years later, I saw a photograph in a British newspaper. It was a picture editor's indulgence: a Last Judgment sky glowering over an uneasy sea, brilliant fasces of light streaking downwards. The conjunction of fire, water and air – white light tearing slashes across sky and ocean – stayed in my mind.

I went and found more of the photographs. They were images taken with time-lapse cameras in the middle of the

Pacific. All the naked eye would have seen were tiny fugitive suns snuffed out at their point of impact with the atmosphere. The suns were re-entry vehicles from a Peacekeeper missile, ten in number, independently targetable and each capable of carrying a 330-kiloton charge: twenty-six Hiroshimas. On this occasion they were being tested with ballast in the warheads.

The display happened between eight and twenty times a year, when a missile was fired from Vandenberg Air Base in California and delivered its re-entry vehicles back into the Earth's atmosphere at 16,000 kph to splash down in the lagoon of Kwajalein Atoll in the Marshall Islands.

Like photographs of earthquakes and comets, the pictures bore witness to the camera's love affair with apocalyptic happenings. But this happening was man-made. It was as if God, bored with Darwinism and tired of clever-clever science, had torn up His book of spells. The scraps had fluttered to Earth, first yielding the secret of neutron bombardment and its effect on isotopes of uranium, later the recipe for fusing hydrogen nuclei and replicating the heat of the sun. The strange thing was that, for all its brand-newness, the technology seemed curiously out of date. The Cold War was over. Yet in some ignored backwater, with an air of complete normality, thunderbolts were being hurled across the ocean.

I looked at the photographs again and again. This was the same ocean I had grown up next to, and at this time I was as bored with Creation as God was with Darwin: Creation, that is, as the egotist understands it, contained within the neat borders of my life in London, publishing books in a newly flowering atmosphere of corporate takeovers and well-paid suspicion. I read Alan Moorehead's account of the invasion of the South Pacific, *The Fatal Impact*, fascinated by the dream of the noble savage (the playful version, decked out for love) that became a vacuum for white men to fill. There were few playful Polynesian goddesses left. I found out some facts about the Marshall

Islands. There were slums and a population explosion. There was rumoured to be the highest rate of syphilis in the world. As destinations go, they were about as unromantic as you can get. But I had to get away, and they had the single merit of any fixation. They would not go away.

I wondered, idly, if this was the dream I had had up my sleeve all along: a return to the heliotropic sensations of childhood. I asked a friend, a Freudian analyst, what he thought.

'Probably,' he said. 'You've got a funny way of going about it.'

> *One two three four*
> *Tell the people what she wore.*

Bikini, I found out much later, is not bikini-shaped.

3
Le Capitaine Tasman

Between the sixteenth and eighteenth centuries the Pacific Ocean was the *ultima Thule* of cosmographers and explorers. The lure of the unknown southern continent of Terra Australis, the prospect of riches beyond kingly avarice and the challenge of girdling the globe offered the only risks worth taking for navigators who had already traded and mapped from the Spice Islands to Brazil. (Samuel Johnson was the sole dissenter: he could not understand, he said, how anyone would go to sea who could steal enough money to get himself decently hanged.)

It was a slow business. In 1519 Magellan left Spain behind him and never saw it again; ahead of him lay a rain of javelins on a beach in the Philippines. In his crossing of the Pacific he saw only two uninhabited atolls and his crew was reduced to eating the leather chafing-bands on the masts. For forty years afterwards expedition after expedition came to grief. Without chronometers to ascertain longitude, ships disappeared and were never heard of again. Paradise was discovered and mislaid: having found the Solomon Islands in 1568, Alvaro de Mendana returned twenty-seven years later and died without locating them. His expedition deteriorated into murderous brawls from which the chief distraction was shooting the natives at every landfall. Crazed visionaries like Pedro de Quiros viewed their missions as the equivalent of an ascent into paradise (disregarding the murder and arson required to achieve it). Until the 1760s ship-masters, reduced by illness and with their ships rotting beneath them after the eight-month journey to reach the ocean, followed the same westward course that avoided serious discoveries.

In three voyages, from 1769 to 1779, Captain James Cook changed everything. He demolished the myth of the southern continent that balanced the northern land masses and stopped the earth tipping over; charted New Zealand and the east coast of Australia; probed the northerly limits of Antarctica, charted the Marquesas and rediscovered the lost islands of Mendana and Quiros; discovered New Caledonia and the chain of Hawaii – with fatal consequences.

'The story of his life does not lend itself to exploitation by cheap biographers,' wrote William Plomer. 'He was no "great lover"; he was a great worker; there was nothing scandalous, or equivocal, or cheaply sensational in his career; and nobody ever made fewer mistakes.'

In ten years Cook brought the era of European exploration to an end. A French captain paid him a rival's tribute: he 'left his successors little to do but admire'.

Cook was explorer, cartographer, navigator, scientist, natural leader, medical pioneer (in ten years not one man died on his ships from scurvy) and humanist. Sent to the South Seas first to observe the transit of Venus across the face of the sun on

3 June 1769, he realised that his observations were, as far as the
Tahitians were concerned, from the wrong end of the telescope,
writing after he left: 'It would have been far better for these
people never to have known us.'

The plants collected by his botanist on the *Endeavour*,
Joseph Banks, and his friend Daniel Solander, 3607 specimens
in all, were stored in paper books or bundles. Large quantities of
them found their way into a consignment of unbound pages of
Paradise Lost.

The cannibals and the dog-headed monsters had been
identified. The southern continent had vanished. Ships divided in
purpose but united in efficiency carried men of commerce and
religion and agents of distant states who quarrelled among themselves and eventually agreed the boundaries that, a hundred
years later, covered the ocean with flags of nations three months'
sailing away.

I wanted to come up on the islands slowly, to see the sun rise
and set for days over an empty sea. I had arrived in Sydney
about fifteen years too late. There were only two shipping lines,
the French company Sofrana and Pacific Forum, still working
through island ports. I went back to the Sofrana offices and
asked for the crewing manager. I was shown into a white office
with full-length windows overlooking the docks. A young Indian
with a sorrowful, aquiline face, listened to my request, then
looked at his slender fingers lying on the unmarked blotter in
front of him and said, 'Just a moment.'

He made a phone call and scribbled some notes. With
apologetic courtesy he put my passport in a drawer. The activity
of his elegant hands sketched a ship: the *Capitaine Tasman*,
7000 tons, general cargo, German-designed, built in Durban in
1973; master: Herbert Pape. She was leaving for Fiji via New
Caledonia the following afternoon.

I called Norman at home and told him I had followed his advice and got a ship.

'What did I tell you? I used to have a lot of good friends in the islands, especially in New Caledonia. A bit right-wing some of them, but go and see' – he mentioned two names – 'both cracking good men with dynamite.'

Something had been bothering me. Copra had made modest fortunes in the salad days of the colonies. If you were a schooner skipper and you could stand the sweet, stale smell of the oxidised oils in the coconut meat, the agents of the Victorian soap barons paid a good price. It was mucky work and dangerous. Cargoes got infested by filthy copra-beetles and burst into flames without warning. But until palm oil and soya took over, the discomforts were worth the candle.

The question was: 'Norman, what did the Nobel Explosives Company want with copra?'

He laughed. 'Glycerine, my boy. As in nitro-glycerine. Copra is the best source of glycerine you can find. Up until the second world war Europe couldn't get enough of it. Combine it with nitric acid and – bang!'

That night I was kept awake by the anguished love-talk of a Yugoslav couple in the room next door. I could make out the woman's weeping. By the tone of her voice she was asking: why did we come? I pictured the man stroking her head and heard the deep soothing words of reassurance. They made love, and then there was silence. The next morning I paid my bill at the Occidental and at eleven o'clock presented myself at berth 9, Darling Harbour.

4
Captain Pape

If there were a prize for carelessness in the matter of founding new nations, Cook's botanist would win it hands down. Chic and well-connected, it was Joseph Banks who presented Lord Sydney, the Home Secretary, with the plan of 'effectually disposing of convicts' at Botany Bay. No survey was made, but who could contradict him, even if, according to his journal written on the *Endeavour*, he spent all his time there 'botanizing in the woods as usual'?

When Captain Arthur Phillip brought in the first convict fleet on 17 January 1788 – the height of summer eighteen years later – the place, waterless and killingly hot, appalled him.

In desperation Captain Phillip moved his ships a few miles north to the anchorage at Sydney Cove that Cook had passed by. It was perfectly cast as the place to set down eight hundred criminals you never wanted to see or hear of again. The soldiers and convicts could find no edible vegetables. They had no idea how to make European plants grow. The sun blazed down so hot that bats and parakeets fell dead from the trees. The nets produced few fish. No marine with a musket could get within range of the kangaroos. And far from being able to befriend the local people, the newcomers' presence drove the aborigines into fear and reprisal. The fastest ship from England to the settlement at Port Jackson took four months.

'In Port Jackson,' wrote a marine officer, 'all is quiet and stupid as could be wished.'

Against the odds the colony prospered. By the mid-1830s it had become a place of get-rich-quick colonists. Its position as a staging-post stayed unrivalled until the 1970s.

But Sydney was still a place for criminals. In May 1988, an odd container had turned up on the wharf at Darling Harbour. Marked 'used machinery', it was awaiting shipment to Fiji. The

Pope had recently visited Fiji and described the country as 'a beacon of hope in a troubled world'. In the container were sixteen tons of AK47s, sub-machine guns, grenades and launchers, mortars and anti-tank mines.

In the *Sydney Morning Herald* I had found the report of the trial of the men in Fiji who were supposed to have received the weapons. Having pleaded guilty and apologized to the court, all eighteen of them had, inexplicably, been allowed to go free. The defendants had no records and could have been patsies. The alleged master mind behind the smuggling, Mohammed Rafiq Khan, had not been brought to trial. He was a businessman whose 'investment opportunities' in Fiji were well known. He had a knack of avoiding the attentions of the police and as soon as his container was arrested, he had slipped out of Australia. He surfaced in London, from where the government in Fiji had tried to extradite him. But he was discharged by the British court, probably the only court anywhere that had taken him into custody and then let him go free.

Who the arsenal was intended for remained a mystery. It was as if the Vatican Guard were taking delivery of a dozen T-34 tanks. (Maybe somewhere in the world, after the invasion of Panama, there was a papal nuncio who dreamt of it.) Some said it was for the army; more mysteriously, others talked of a strange resistance movement of conservative but anti-government businessmen. All that was really clear was that the army takeover in Fiji of the previous year, in which a handsome, philandering army colonel called Rabuka had arrested the Coalition government of Prime Minister Timoci Bavadra in the Government Building, installed his own administration and declared a republic, had pretty steeply raised the game.

'There is no chance of her leaving before the weekend.'

The chief engineer, livid-faced and with black curly hair, stood grumbling at the rail of the *Capitaine Tasman* at Darling

Harbour. His thin white legs buckled under the weight of his body. He was German, and I suspected him of suffering from a bowel disorder. Unable to control the flow of his speech, he continued to mutter, pointing in the direction of the mess a deck up and turning back to gaze with suppressed pain at the oily surface of the harbour.

Captain Herbert Pape was sitting in the mess drinking lemon tea from a thick china cup. He signalled to the steward to bring another cup.

'Good morning. Welcome. You will be at home here. Before this became a French ship, she was an English ship. Do you know how you can tell?' – with a sweep of his arm he embraced the tatty panelling and the swirling patterns of the brown carpet – 'because in the officers' mess there is a bar, and' – he jumped up to open a shallow wall-cupboard – 'on the wall there is a dartboard. *No other ships in the world have messes with these two things.*'

Captain Pape was new to the islands. He was Prussian and in his fifties, one of those northerners who go against the accepted grain with their impatience, their volatility and genuine warmth. It was only his appearance, the unmistakable fair colouring, and his emphatic accent that gave away his origins.

He sat drinking his tea with an intent, apostolic expression. His career had been mostly spent on one-stop refrigerated cargoes: bananas to Europe, Falklands squid to Korea and Japan, fish to North America.

'What are you carrying on this trip?'

'Containers. On deck and under hatches. A Woolworths cargo.'

He liked the island ports, places where the jungle rose steeply on either side and where there was no pilot, just a man standing up in a dinghy with a flag as the ship nosed forwards. The previous year the *Tasman* had been rotting away unused, and up for sale. Before a buyer could be found for her, her sister ship *Capitaine Torres*, on her way back from the Cleveland steel mills, was caught in a blizzard in the St Lawrence Gulf. Her engines failed. In nil visibility she and her cargo of steel tubing and billets had gone to the bottom with all hands.

Sofrana had decided to keep the *Tasman*, and a semblance of seaworthiness was being restored to the neglected ship. In the heat haze on the wharf her white hull outlined her sharply against her surroundings. She was slender, her bow flared in an old-fashioned way. She did not look comfortable, but nor did she have the ugly slab-sided lines of the bigger ships in port.

Captain Pape sipped his lemon tea.

'I am sorry about the delay. As usual Sofrana believes everything will be ready on schedule, and I agree because I don't wish an argument. In fact I can tell you now we will not be leaving before Monday.'

Monday was three days away. The chief engineer had wandered into the mess. At the captain's news he covered his face with his hands and emitted a yell of torment. 'Must get out of this port, must get out... anything to get out.'

'What's wrong with the ship?'

'Better to ask what is right with her, my friend. The hull I think is all right. The engine is improving.'

Captain Pape took me to the pilot's cabin, a boxroom with a single bunk on the boat deck.

'It is a place designed for brief residence. All you have to do in it is sleep. You are welcome to borrow my cabin when I am on watch.

'If you want anything, just shout for Kipone, the steward. He is a Tongan but he is usually efficient, and of course he is friendly.'

He looked at his watch.

'Chop chop in half an hour. Then you will see how the Tongans cook.'

An unmuffled howl came from the air-conditioning outlet

in the ceiling. By thrusting my arm into the mouth of the pipe and fiddling with a hinge I was able to shut off the blast. I opened the porthole. Within seconds the cabin was washed by the midday heat.

A midnight blue Jaguar was parked askew on the quay. The light clattered off its wings. The engine idled to keep the air-conditioning going, and behind the wound-up windows a young woman with shining black hair sat as still as a mannequin.

At the captain's table there were two places laid, with a bottle of ketchup between them. A few feet away was another long table set for the Filipino officers with small bottles of soy. Distantly courteous, they nodded and smiled and gestured to the second place at the empty table. They ate their rice at breakneck speed.

The English atmosphere was effortlessly maintained: a lino floor, a large dusty television on the wall, benches upholstered in blotchy brown material. Kipone, the Tongan steward, shimmied to the table, carrying gammon embalmed in gravy and garlanded with tinned vegetables. Like the decor, it had the flavour of something abandoned out of lack of interest.

Kipone came back to ask if I was enjoying my meal. This was a rhetorical question with which to begin the story of the period of his life as a cook at the Cumberland Hotel in Earls Court Road. On his first Christmas Eve he had gone out and seen snow falling and been so shocked that, despite being a Wesleyan, he fled to a nightclub and got insensibly drunk.

London's climate had lightened his skin.

'When I go back to Tonga, I so ashamed my white skin I not go to the market for a month. My aunt she laugh at my white skin. She say snow made it this colour.'

Captain Pape loped into the mess, his mouth set tight. He shook his head and banged the flat of his hand down on the table.

'I *cannot* understand this Mr Ravel. He owns Sofrana, he is a millionaire, a successful businessman. And then he turns up at the wharf asking for all kinds of stupid things. Today he wishes the funnel to be repainted. He wishes the funnel to be repainted, and I have been waiting for maintenance work to be done on the hatches *for four months*.

'There is only one consolation. This Mr Ravel has a very beautiful Polynesian wife. When he makes these requests, she sees my face and behind his back she smiles. I could not think why she married him until I read recently that a Polynesian woman does not mind to marry a much older man – as long as he supports her whole family.'

Pape demolished his lunch in an attack on the memory of Ravel's visit. I thought of the woman behind the smoky glass of the Jaguar.

By the time Kipone served tea, the captain's face had settled back to its apostolic expression. Ravel was a despised abstraction, a man who had allowed himself to become part of the plans of a beautiful wife.

Captain Pape was from Wildeshausen, a small town on the edge of the north German plain. The town was tidy and quiet, surrounded by forests and full of sea widows. He was not from a seafaring family: in the eighty years before the Junker class ceased to own Prussia, his father, grandfather and great-grandfather had all been foresters on the huge estates. If the 1939-45 war had not divided Prussia, he would have made the fourth generation of *Förster*. As it was, among the columns of refugees who preferred the uncertainty of exile to rule by Moscow there was a disproportionate number of woodsmen.

Pape said, 'There was only one problem. They didn't bring the woods with them.'

5
Customs

The officers had had chop chop early and gone to King's Cross to find some girls. As the sun finished its sluggish excursion across the sky, I told the captain the gun-running story. The container had been due to be loaded on a Sofrana ship, the *Capitaine Cook III*, when it was arrested.

He nodded distantly, then sat upright and placed his fingertips on the edge of the table like a sprinter on the blocks. 'This is a *very* interesting story.

'What I want to know is *how* the Australian Customs discovered it. For them this is an exceptionally intelligent achievement.'

'Would the skipper of the *Capitaine Cook III* have known what was in the container?'

'No. His only job would be to match the serial numbers on the manifest with what was being loaded. Captains know less and less these days.'

'Have you ever smuggled anything?'

'No. I have never found myself in that captain's position and for myself I have very boring tastes. However, it is sometimes not the *smugglers* you have to watch out for.'

He had worked the banana route from Turbo, Colombia, to Tampa, Florida, on which a captain faced two problems: stowaways and drugs. The record for a single loading period was thirty-three stowaways. Hidden among the bunches, they had to be winkled out by the watchmen when the bananas were floated out on barges in the Turbo roads for loading.

'The cocaine was more difficult.'

With a good crew and a pump-action shotgun on his

shoulder during the barge inspections, he had succeeded in setting a routine that was too much trouble for the cocaine suppliers to disrupt. But the North American Customs and the Drug Enforcement Agency were not pleased. Their combined strategy worked on a sting that involved captains allowing consignments on board in Colombia and then informing the coastguard so that narcotics agents could trail packages to their distributors.

'It was an efficient method. But it omitted the consequences for the officers and crew when they got back to Turbo and found the senders of the intercepted consignment upset by their actions.

'The Americans accused me of helping the Colombians. They held up my ship, and I found out they were trying to persuade some of my crew to accept packets behind my back. This made me really angry.

'I said, "Listen. I transport Colombian bananas to your country because there is a big market for them. I know there is a big market for cocaine in America too. So if you want me to transport it, you had better make it legal."'

He laughed loudly.

'Did you know that port health officers at American ports used to require the inspection of the crew's penises before they would allow the ship to dock? Why they have this mania for hygiene I cannot understand, and even so they cannot call a toilet a toilet. In Singapore an American asked me where the restroom was, and when I didn't understand, he asked for the comfort station. What the hell is a comfort station? I sent him to Bugis Street. There is no race more inscrutable on the planet, not even the Japanese. I see an American eat, and I cannot eat myself because I am mesmerised by watching him chop up all his food before he starts.

'It takes another nation just as unadaptable, like the French, to beat them. The penis inspections only discontinued when the French began random inspections of American penises at Le Havre.'

He put his hands on the table and laughed again. 'The war of the penises! I like the Americans. Certainly the Germans are not much better, although we speak their language generally better than they do ours. And we would be poorer in spirit without them. I think we all understand instinctively that we have to have their way of life, the hamburgers and guns and drugs, because we know that it is impossible for them to adapt to ours.'

On Sunday the temperature went up to forty degrees and the Tongan cook and an apprentice deserted. At night the temperature fell infinitesimally. Thousands of water droplets suddenly condensed and glittered on the rail.

The captain returned from a barbecue with the ship's agent in an easy temper. His cabin, low-ceilinged and dark, ran the full width of the ship. It was a place to get drunk in. He offered me a beer.

'I knew it,' he said, grinning. 'Those guns were discovered by *mistake*.'

It turned out, from the ship's agent, that Kahan had described the goods differently on two transit manifests. The error would not have been picked up if Kahan had not telephoned repeatedly to make sure the container was where it should be. The exasperated handling clerk had dug out the papers and, seeing the documents didn't match, had made a phone call himself to the Customs office.

Later Captain Pape told me about his first days at sea. He had been a shy, introspective seaman until, at the age of eighteen, he had met Goldzahn.

Goldzahn was an ex-French legionnaire, who had deserted from the Legion on the grounds of boredom. He was a child of the war. He had grown up in the catacombs of Berlin; all his schooling had been in the black market, pimping at fourteen and trading in bread and rags and cigarettes. His superstition about gold stemmed from those days. Whenever he had any money, he had a tooth replaced with it, despite the fact that the minute market value of the metal was far exceeded by the cost of the substitution. He had taken the képi and served in Indochina, and been captured and released – these were the early days – in an exchange of prisoners with the Vietminh. But legionnaires who had been captured were not allowed to go back into the jungle. Goldzahn was posted to Algeria, where he mourned the loss of his beautiful lacquered Vietnamese tea service, the only thing he owned, and became sick with idleness.

It was a simple matter to desert. Once he had crossed the border he went to the German consul in Tunis, who congratulated him and put him on a ship back to Germany. There he decided that the merchant marine offered the most exciting alternative to combat.

'I only ever called him Goldzahn,' the captain said. 'He lost his name with everything else in the war. The one thing I ever saw him attached to was the tea service. He used to describe it over and over again.

'We went to places you have never been to. We went to places I have never been to since that time. In ports he had just arrived at, Goldzahn would find somewhere to smoke opium or to play roulette for girls within ten minutes of going ashore.'

'Why did the cook and his boy desert?' I asked.

Captain Pape picked up an empty beer can with the tips of his fingers and swung it back and forth.

'They think this is paradise.'

In the small hours I was woken up by the sound of a radio and female laughter from the first mate's cabin. I went to get a glass of water. Through the half-open door I saw everything you'd expect to see.

Customs men were inspecting the deserters' cabins. Just after three they finally left, and the mooring lines were let go, stern out first, then the bow.

The bones of the ship rumbled. The *Capitaine Tasman* glided past the old timber-built wool and wheat warehouses and the brown cube of the Palisade Hotel on the rocks; under the wild arc of the Harbour Bridge; past the downtown steel and glass money-silos, and the triple repeating spinnakers of the Opera House.

A mile further on were the dredged channel and Quarantine Head. A coming storm had lowered the sky. The Old Man's Hat, an odd-shaped fissure in the rock, was a slumbering ichthyosaurus. Twenty minutes later the ship pitched easily between the jaws of North and South Head into the Tasman Sea.

6

Passengers

A friend in London had said to me, 'Imagine leaving all this behind.' But you didn't need imagination to leave London behind. You only needed to hate it, which everyone did sometime in the Eighties. It was famously horrible, a third-world city that had the toilet habits of Jakarta and the smugness of Jeddah. Maybe you also had to want what Graham Greene described in *The Lawless Roads*: 'The atmosphere of the border – it is like starting over again...' And beyond the border and getting out of London, beyond sprays of fugitive suns and refractory memories of childhood, there was another agenda, not so much secret as inadmissible. I was skirting it for the moment. The consolation of travel is the control it offers to cowards: you get up and leave; you abandon people; there are fresh winds and fresh places for faulty egos to dilate in; there is a sort of enjoyment to the fear. I had already noticed, in an academic way, that I was scared: I suppose borders have all kinds of fears to go with the thrills.

At dinner Captain Pape said, 'You know something. Even though the cook has gone, there is no change in the food. The second cook is down there, saying to himself: "Standards must not slip." Perhaps there is one slight problem, that the temperature of the food is slightly cool.'

I tasted the pork chop and pygmy roast potatoes, and laughed. They were stone cold.

The drizzle came down like mist. Sooty shearwaters hugged the coal-coloured swells and flew extravagant signatures across the stern. By the schedule it was four days steaming to New Caledonia. Grande Terre, the principal island, was sinking on the edge of the Australian Plate – another fifty million years would see to it – but New Caledonia still lived up to Cook's name for it: a dislocated mountain range climbing out of the sea to 1600 metres.

Captain Pape rarely took passengers. On his last voyage he had carried a husband and wife who were visiting their son at a missionary college in the New Guinea highlands. Politeness forbad him to voice his disapproval of missionaries to them.

'I do not have anything against people believing, but the force behind this teaching is evil. Wherever the missionaries went, people who had been quite happy were made unhappy. They were made to give up their old lives and given nothing in return except guilt.'

I said that the Catholic priests I had met were more humane than their Protestant counterparts.

The captain flew into a rage.

'You are completely wrong! Catholicism is the worst! This religion is baloney. Why should there be no women priests? Why is there never a Latin American pope? Why should this vast church be ruled from Rome? And why, if it is a beneficial religion, was there only one prostitute in Avignon before the popes came, and after, thousands? *Thousands*?' He pronounced it 'sousands'.

The German for pope was *Papst*. I decided not to ask the captain if he knew that the French for pope was *pape*.

The missionaries' first convert in the Pacific was a chief on Tahiti, Pomare II. 'Though a sad debauchee and a drunkard,' as Herman Melville described him, 'and even charged with un- natural crimes, he was a great friend of the missionaries and one of their very first proselytes.'

In place of 'though', Melville might have written 'because'.

Pomare was the son of Tu, whom Captain Cook had met and befriended on his second visit to Tahiti in 1773 in the *Resolution*. By then the island was widely infected with gonor- rhoea and syphilis. (Capts. Wallis and Bougainville – who preceded Cook's first landfall in 1769 by a few months – were still trading accusations as to who started it, Wallis's doctor denying on his honour that any of his seamen were afflicted by 'the French disease', the French doctor repudiating the identical charge about *le mal anglais*.)

The welcome for the sailors of the *Resolution* was no less warm than it had been for the *Endeavour* four years before. With the ship overrun by Tahitian girls, according to her draughtsman George Forster, 'the excesses of the night were incredible'. Forster's father, the ship's naturalist, wrote in pompous contra- diction: 'My spirits were damped by this unexpected scene of immorality.'

The first 'godly mechanics' arrived at Cook's anchorage in Matavai Bay in March 1797, twenty-four years later. They had been selected, all thirty-nine of them, by the newly formed London Missionary Society – only four ordained clergymen, the rest craftsmen, shopkeepers and domestic servants – by whose hand a new suburb of Jerusalem was to be built and the emergency of Polynesian sin set right.

In the meantime further changes had occurred. Whaling ships were calling regularly. Alcohol was a new component in the social equation and Tu's kingdom was disordered. Before retiring to Pitcairn, the *Bounty* mutineers had given him some muskets with which he now kept an appearance of order, surrounded by competing chiefs and Western vices.

But neither he nor his people failed in their hospitality to the strange new colony of evangelists. They provided them with food, servants and land in Matavai Bay, and otherwise for several years ignored them.

Pomare, charming, lazy, self-indulgent and bibulous, was the key. In their own camp, the evangelists eventually discerned the potential for corruption in him which could bring about their godly ends. After more than a decade of mutual incomprehension, he was established in his father's place and realised there was benefit to be got out of a marriage of interests. It was not clear to him, having never been to England, that what the evangelists intended in Tahiti was a recreation of their cramped, guilt-ridden home in which most innocent pleasures – nudity, dancing, spontaneous sex, idleness – were forbidden. But he instinctively saw that by making Christianity his, he would outclass his rivals.

The missionaries saw that they could only change the people by working through the chief. Their success was ensured by covert bribery of Pomare, first by alcohol (most of the brethren, in any case, were distilling spirits for their own consumption) and later by supporting him in a war against the other island chiefs.

By 1815 the plan had been wholly successful. The alcoholic Pomare, once a cheerful and imposing figure, defeated his opponents in a ferocious and bloody battle, built a vast cathedral with a stream running through it, and had non-

Christians murdered.

The Russian navigator Bellingshausen, who came to the island in 1820, described the transformation of its people. The wearing of European clothes; the shaved heads; the disappearance of tattooing, dancing, Tahitian music; the forbidding of flower garlands; the vice squads that watched at night for any sign of illicit coupling; the *marae* – old temples – fallen in ruins; Sundays of compulsory church-going: the hold of the Christians was complete.

Pomare had served his purpose. Once the souls of his subjects were remade in the image of the Lord, the missionaries didn't give a damn whether he reformed or not. While Bellingshausen was there, the stupefied king requested a bottle of rum from the Russian, who felt sorry for him and ordered from the ship 'three bottles of rum and six bottles of Teneriffe wine'. (Trust a Russian.)

A year later, in the throes of alcoholic dementia, and to the pious regrets of the LMS brethren, Pomare took his chances with the afterlife. The pattern was established that within fifty years would have redeemed and reduced the spirit of almost every islander on every archipelago across the ocean.

Every minute or so another shudder went through the hull as the screw came out of the water and tore at the air. The storm had started in the early hours. The only place to be was on my bunk. I tried to read but it was hellish to concentrate against the changing light. On each roll the side of the ship darkened, the portholes turning away from the sky. Later, when the storm got worse – for the crew it was no more than a squall – the relation between gravity and light got completely out of hand and I couldn't move.

I hadn't eaten breakfast or lunch; at dinner there was stiff chicken that I gnawed for ten minutes. The captain raised an eyebrow and said, 'You will be used to this soon.' I went to bed.

The next morning the weather was unchanged. Showing inky borders that made them look carelessly glued in place, the clouds inched apart to show the northerly sun behind, then slammed shut again. The air-conditioning had bust. I couldn't see how I could avoid spending the rest of my life in this changing-room humidity.

At lunchtime I forced myself to move, a form of self-compulsion like some onerous religious rite in which every step performed in strict sequence, the washing, putting soap on the shaving brush, moving the razor over my cheeks, rinsing the scummy relics out of the basin, pulling on first the shirt, then a creased pair of shorts, rather than affirming my status as a human being, made me feel like some unappetising sacrifice. I tried to comfort myself with the thought that only two days ahead lay land, and French food, and failed.

I stood at the stern and watched fields of foam slithering over the cobalt wake. On the starboard boat deck, the trade wind blew with pentecostal force. I retreated to the other side. The chief engineer stood at his post at the rail, glaring at the horizon.

'This is nothing,' he shouted. His hair cavorted around his neck. 'I was in the Pacific for four years before this, four years with no leave. I was divorcing from my wife and it cost me a pile of money. But after four years I finished with 150,000 Mark. I never went ashore, I saved everything.'

He stared wildly out to sea, the pictures of his faithless wife and the pile of money fighting for the upper hand.

'I saw some storms then. Going to Japan we were stuck in a hurricane for twenty-four hours. You cut the engine and drift, but you have to do it early enough so you have some calm water on the windward side of you for the sea to break on. We didn't do this. Twenty-four hours and you couldn't stand for a minute. Everyone was trying to save the ship. Afterwards it felt like a storm two weeks long. There were broken fingers, broken arms, a broken leg.

'But Cyclone Nancy is outside Nouméa, they say on the forecast. We might see it.'

I gestured towards the lifeboat creaking in its cradle further along the rail.

'Completely useless. Unless there is a very slow fire on board and a very calm sea. Completely useless.'

Later, the chief appeared on deck and on the bridge between watches like a bad prophet of Neptune. His reports on our speed, dropping from 12 to 9 knots, had an air of grim satisfaction. The captain avoided him. I was no better, mooching morosely round the ship, sweating on my bunk, wishing for some of Gilbert Pinfold's chloral and bromide, catching the sweet smell of overboiled vegetables round the corner of a companionway, stumbling to the stern for some air. The shearwaters had cleared off.

At dinner the captain, normally ready for talk by the end of the day, was tight-lipped and furious. The storm kept changing the ship's schedule, forcing him to leave the paperwork incomplete. It was worse than having an engine-room full of water.

As I left to go back to my cabin, he looked up and said, 'You shouldn't spend so much time at the stern. It is the favourite place of suicides.'

In bed, when I finally slept, I dreamt of coming back from Australia by ship, aged six. The ocean was a perfect indigo lake, the sky duck-egg blue. I ran up and down the promenade deck of the *Iberia*, shrieking and laughing and knocking over the footrests of people's deckchairs as I went past.

7
Iberia

I stood on deck and tried to picture the lives of the first navigators. The Polynesians, copper-skinned athletes from South Asia
whose triumphs of endurance and discovery were well docu-
mented – the weeks aboard lateen-sailed outriggers, navigating
by watching cloud patterns, birds and the colour of the ocean –
must have sent out twenty craft, maybe even a hundred, for
every one to make a landfall.

They came to settle. Four thousand years later two squab-
bling nations decided you didn't need to settle a place to own it.

On 3 and 4 May 1493 Spain and Portugal, the first super-
powers, invited the Pope to settle their territorial claims to the
world. Alexander VI – Rodrigo Borgia – a man with outstanding
gifts for corrupting men and exciting the passions of women (at
fifty-nine he openly took as his mistress Giulia Farnese, whose
golden hair reached her feet and who was nineteen), signed three
Bulls declaring the world divided by a meridian passing 500
kilometres west of the Azores. Everything to the east of the
meridian, excluding Europe, was to belong to Portugal. Everything to the west of it went to Spain, which meant both the
Americas. A year later the meridian was redrawn roughly along
the longitude of 46 degrees west, to give Portugal a foothold in
Brazil, which she claimed to have discovered.

The Spanish, with characteristic mercantile agility, extend-
ed the division around the other side of the globe and came to
the conclusion that the treasures of some of the Spice Islands,
those east of 134 degrees east – the islands had not all been
accurately located – belonged to them.

When Ferdinand Magellan, Portuguese by birth but cold-
shouldered by Dom Manoel I, offered his services to Charles V,
Spain was ready for him. If Dom Manoel's great-great-uncle,
Prince Henry the Navigator, had been on the throne, the deser-

tion would never have happened, but Dom Manoel was no judge of captains or heroes.

The expedition that left Seville in 1519 would have been laughed at by the Polynesians. The ships were patched and ancient; provisioning was hopeless; their crews were the bottom of the waterfront barrel. Magellan's second-in-command went mad before they sailed. Out of apprehension, Magellan did not tell his crews where they were really going.

Within days of Magellan's murder in the Philippines there was an incident in which many of the officers were treacherously killed, and the expedition fell apart. Magellan's flagship, the *Trinidad,* decided to return the way she had come, beating hopelessly against the trades before giving up; only four of her crew got back, years later. The *Victoria* had better luck, though half her crew were imprisoned by the Portuguese on the return journey. Only eighteen men returned to Seville; the circumnavigation had taken twelve days short of three years.

Half the world was Portugal's, the other half was Spain's. Legally – an interesting word in the circumstances – there was nowhere for the English to go. But Drake went round the world 'to that place', as Queen Elizabeth's geographer John Dee described it, 'being the very ends of the world from us to be reckoned', and made hay with the Spanish treasure ships to the tune of a million pounds in Spanish gold and silver.

Somewhere on the southern half of the sphere, Dee was convinced, there *had* to be land to balance Europe-Asia-Africa and stop it tipping over. A continent stretched in all directions from the south pole, uniting with Tierra del Fuego and reaching north almost to Java in the western Pacific. Ortelius' 1570 map *Typus Orbis Terrarum* set out the position of Terra Australis. In it were located Marco Polo's kingdom of Locach or Beach, his land of Malaiur or Maletur, his island of Pentam or Petan – all overflowing with fabulous wealth – not to mention Solomon's nearby land of Ophir. Mendana had already discovered in 1567 a group of islands he called the Solomons.

At that moment, with the endless rolling of the *Tasman*'s decks, I would have taken on all of Dee's gullibility and reliance on spiritualists and quacks, plus the accusations of sorcery levelled against him, in preference to a day at the command of the *Golden Hind*.

Drake's voyage was officially camouflaged as a visit to Alexandria. The confidential plan makes no mention of furthering Dee's secret investigations into Terra Australis, only the intention in 'the South Sea... to find out places meet to have traffic for the venting of commodities of these her Majesty's realms'. When Drake left England, as unreliable as any opportunist, he had no intention of doing either.

The answer to his first question on his return to Plymouth in 1580 – 'Is the Queen alive and well?' – was important to him. He was the first Englishman to circumnavigate the globe, but if Elizabeth had died in his absence or there was a new alliance with Spain, the Spanish gold he had on board might not be an asset but a fatal liability.

His promoters had been the usual consortium of court, privy council and navy. Walsingham had seen the secret plan and almost certainly handed it to the Queen. Drake had been summoned to a private interview. What was *not* said implied her permission and collaboration, for she imposed no restraints on his actions. What *might* have been said could have committed her to a financial stake in the venture. Either way it was a dangerous game, as Elizabeth knew, commanding Drake that 'of all men, my Lord Treasurer', Lord Burghley – the peacekeeper with Spain – was not to be told.

Drake left England with a large parcel of dainties and perfumed waters on board, delivered by royal messenger, and caught the Spaniards so unawares that 'it was as though a fox had broken into a poultry farm'.

The weather in the Pacific came close to wrecking his fleet.

By the time he was through the Straits of Magellan, Drake was down from his original five ships to one. One had turned back in the straits; the other three were lost. But for exploits like the taking of the *Nuestra Señora de la Concepción* (nicknamed the *Cacafuego* by Drake's crew – the *Shitfire*) with 360,000 pesos of silver on board, Spanish mothers menaced their children for years afterwards with the threat that '*el Draque*' would come and get them.

Even with the knighthood and the admiralship and the fame that struck terror into the hearts of foreign sailors and children, I would not have been Francis Drake.

8
Territoire d'outre-mer

Cyclone Nancy skirted the *Tasman* in the middle of the next night. The aerial disturbances produced an electrical storm; purple spears threw themselves at the sea and invisible buildings collapsed all round.

As usual, the chief failed to put in an appearance at breakfast. I asked Captain Pape: 'Why doesn't he ever stop talking?'

The captain looked at me sharply. 'This I do not know. It is my suspicion that his hearing has been ruined by engines. He cannot talk to anyone in the engine room, and when he comes up he cannot hear what you say. Also he has something wrong with his stomach. Perhaps it is nerves. He finds talking easier than eating. When he talks to me I find the best thing is to say nothing. That way I avoid saying the wrong thing and showing that I have not been listening for twenty minutes.'

Since dawn, an affair of smoking purple cumulus and a lilac sea, the water had changed every half-hour. Long cresting swells dropped to an oily calm.

But the changing-room atmosphere was disappearing at last – you could tell by watching the flying fish flop short into the sea, their fins suddenly dry – and the sky was smooth. Before midday three thin watercolour smudges, hardly darker than the layers of pale clouds behind them, came into view about sixty kilometres away. An hour and a half later they lifted above the horizon and rearranged themselves as the topmost points of a long, uneven smoky-blue slash.

Over the radio Captain Pape was instructed to change course. It turned out to be a symbolic introduction to the French colony. (By a bureaucratic fiction, France has no colonies. In defence of their *territoire* of New Caledonia, they said it had been a part of France for longer than the comté de Nice which was only annexed from the House of Savoy in 1860.)

The straight path through the reef was not convenient, and the pilot preferred to bring us through the south-west approach, which would take two hours longer.

The captain said, 'The ship serves the pilot, you see, in France.'

At three the pilot came on board, a tiny Frenchman in baggy trousers. The first thing he said was: 'May I wash my hands?'

While he was gone Captain Pape said, 'The ship goes aground because the pilot washes his hands.'

The captain said the two lighthouses were in line, and the course good. The pilot altered course by a degree, then told him he could go at sea speed. The captain said, 'Thank you. I prefer to stay at half-speed.'

I went out to the wing to avoid the skirmish. Ahead were the wandering rope of the breakers falling on the reef and the islet of the Amédée lighthouse. By the lily-shaped art nouveau sweep of its white flanks you couldn't have been entering anything other than French territory.

The ship slid between the limits of the white water. To the right dozens of tiny storm-petrels fished on the crests of long, slow rollers that curled onto the coral shoals. The intact hull of an old coaster perched in the spray on top of the reef. The sea changed again to malachite blue, then inside the reef it was jade-green and glassy. Captain Pape came onto the wing wearing his Ray-Ban clip-ons. He grinned and leaned out over the rail.

'In my next life I want to be a pilot.'

'Maybe we came this way so the pilot could show you the beautiful lighthouse.'

'You are right. Did you know they built it in Paris in sections and brought it out here in 1865? It is still the tallest metal lighthouse in the world. Whenever we come through this passage, the pilot always tells me this.'

'It looks like a pretty easy course, if you know what you're doing.'

'You are right again. In some ports and harbours, where you really need a pilot, you don't get him. Not here.

'But you can always guarantee a good pilot service where there is a good living.'

When Admiral Febvrier-Despointes annexed New Caledonia on 24 September 1853, he laid the ground for a successful penal colony. He had no idea of what else the French were sitting on.

Ten years later, Nouméa was a fetid cluster of military barracks, prison, bars and brothels. There was little variety to life: Governor Guillain's ball in 1864 was attended by sixty men who scraped up nine women between them.

The same year a hard-headed mining engineer named Jules Garnier discovered nickel deposits on the banks of the Diahot River in the north of Grande Terre. In 1872 copper was found close by at Balade, where Cook had landed ninety-eight years before, and cobalt in 1875.

Grande Terre was a huge chunk of metal.

There was chromium, iron and manganese in extractable quantities, and for years New Caledonia was the world's biggest producer of cobalt, chromium and nickel. The settlers called the land *le caillou* – the rock. Despite Nouméa's being built on a swamp; despite the difficulties of attracting settlers to a land of heat, fever-bearing mosquitoes and mud; despite the mounting violence needed to squash Melanesian protests at the occupation, the essential function of *le caillou* in providing resources for the distant owner was being richly fulfilled.

In the Pacific the independence movements of France's other territories, French Polynesia and Wallis and Futuna, have been assuaged by the balm of money. They call French Polynesia, the Society Islands, the Marquesas and the Tuamotus, '*la danseuse*' and shrug and say 'You have to pay the dancer if you want her to dance.' In New Caledonia money apparently had not been enough.

Nouméa is a French town in a hot country. There are white villas, spreading scarlet flamboyants, clicking yacht masts and seafront hotels: all the pleasant, mannered, characterless poise of any Côte d'Azur townscape.

The berth was on the far side of the Ile Nou. On this pie-crust of rock, between 1864 and 1897, a prison took in 16,000 deported *droits communs* – ordinary criminals. (Another 4000 *communards* and Moroccan nationalists were transported to the Ile des Pins to the south of Grande Terre.) Watchtowers and bunkers sat on the summit of the island protecting a munitions dump; on its slope was a dazzling satellite antenna. At the inland end of the island the Camp Est prison was still in use.

The brown smoke from the nickel smelter – a collection of Cubist slabs and lines coloured by Braque – washed its sweet acrid fumes down the channel. We berthed between a

Monrovian-registered container ship and another Sofrana freighter, the *Capitaine Wallis*. Three French gendarmes in khaki shorts with revolvers at their hip leant against a wall, watching us. Four Melanesians, stocky and sump-oil brown, ran for the mooring lines.

Marconi, the radio officer, and the third officer were reading out signs to each other:

'Parking du Rond Point.'

'Disco, disco.'

'Locamat.'

'Sofrac.'

'Bar-Restaurant.'

'Casino.'

'Les Tropiques. Les Tropiques.'

9

This was France

I went to the beach to change some money in the Novotel Surf. There was a bar called Le Petit Trianon, the Crédit Lyonnais, the Novotel ('Grill, Piano Bar, Casino') and unending rows of Peugeots and Renaults under fatigued coconut palms. No country except America was so partial to its own manufacturers' automobiles.

In the water a Kanak – with a sly perversity the Melanesians had stolen the Pacific word for 'nigger' from the French; they called their country Kanaky, so the French had to call them '*Mélanésiens*' – was throwing his sons in the air. Japanese girls lay nervously on the beach, uncovering porcelain breasts to the sun, and nailpolish-pink windsurfers shuttled out to a buoy and back.

In the Novotel I asked for a phone and was directed to the

casino. The pit boss, thickset and moustached, was moving about the dark lobby, getting ready for the afternoon session. Lavishly he greeted a short, baggy old woman with a complexion of moth's wings.

'*Ça ne marche pas.*' The old woman attempted to open the coin-return flap on the phone the wrong way. 'Really, this thing doesn't work at all.'

Her motor nerves were not in good condition, and the coin slot was way above her eye level. Expecting to be mugged, she angrily waved away my offer of help. Eventually she scribbled the money into the hole.

'At last a dialling tone.' She rummaged in her handbag for the number. By the time she had found it, the dial tone had been cut off. 'Now it's engaged. I'll try anyway.'

She finally reached her co-phonee. I waited another ten minutes while she described her latest visit to the doctor – a circuitous anecdote involving several metres of colon, new pills and the discomfort of thermometers. She finished, and said:

'All right, darling, now go and find mummy for me.' I went and found another phone.

Monsieur Lemaigre – one of Norman's old associates – wasn't home. When I came back the old woman was still talking. This was France. She pestered her doctor, and had trouble with the phone, and when she had told her daughter every word the doctor said, she had a flutter on the slot machines.

I went and had lunch down the road at a restaurant called La Méditerranée. The waitress looked like Stéphane Audran in *The Discreet Charm of the Bourgeoisie*. Afterwards, on the way to the bus station down rue de Verdun, I had a conversation with a drunk Kanak. Young and tall and watery-eyed, he said in perfect French:

'I'm sorry if I've bothered you.'

'It's all right, you haven't.'

'Are you sure you wouldn't have a couple of thousand francs to help me with my problem?'

He was really very drunk.

'I've only got enough for the bus, I'm afraid, and what I owe the captain.'

'Oh well, thank you anyway. You are very kind. Are you sure I haven't bothered you?'

Passing the Messageries Calédoniennes I saw a message scrawled, in English, on one of the grey shutters. It had the scrupulous syntax of school-learning and said:

'Why should I live like a foreigner in a land that is mine?'

10
Le Saint Hubert

I got back to the *Tasman* to find that another ship had berthed clumsily and stoved in part of her afterdeck. The captain shrugged his shoulders. He had cheered himself up by paying off the Tongan galley crew (except for Kipone) and replacing them with men from Vanuatu. Now he was going to give himself over to French wine and pizza.

Le Saint Hubert was on the northern corner of the place des Cocotiers. It had a terrace lit by strings of coloured bulbs and the sign on the wall saying *'Colons assassins'* had been painted over.

In 1890 Robert Louis Stevenson stepped off the *Janet Nichol* and wrote that Nouméa was 'built from vermouth cases'. A hundred years later the city was a more solid replica: Menton-sur-Pacifique. The details were perfect: the *caisse d'épargne*, the cathedral of Saint Joseph, the rusty Renault 4s, bloomed blue-and-white street signs commemorating military defeats, travel agencies, car showrooms, *tabacs* and lingerie shops; the bespectacled officiousness of the PTT office, sleek youths heeling-and-toeing their Peugeot 205s around corners, thin men in perfectly pressed short-sleeved shirts reading the local paper in cafés, the two beautiful little girls running around the Saint Hubert at ten in the evening.

The bar at the far end of the restaurant was filling up with the simmering haircuts of the Régiment d'Infanterie de Marine du Pacifique. On the place des Cocotiers, a sandy oblong of avenues of flamboyants and coconut palms, Kanaks sat in motionless near-invisible clusters by the pale skeleton of the bandstand, where *le tout Nouméa* had once gathered in linen and shantung for the recital of the convict orchestra. Its twenty-five members, guilty of everything 'from forgery to outrages for which civilised speech has no name', were all accomplished musicians. The *chef d'orchestre* was a conductor of near-professional standard. He had cut out the heart of his wife's lover, got her – telling her it was a sheep's heart – to cook it, dined off it with her, and then told her what she was eating.

The *Caldoches* – the settlers – and the civil servants on fixed contracts went about their business with a purpose that the Kanaks lacked. The amalgam of wealth and impersonality and French-only snobbery was to be expected in a town whose inspiration was purely colonial. But everywhere you went there was the smell – it was like the smell of the frightened steers on the north Queensland freight – of people waiting for something to happen. There was one French soldier to every four adult Kanaks in the territory. Although the Kanaks were liable for military service, there were none in the Saint Hubert.

Captain Pape shouted across the noise of the soldiers drinking Foster's. 'Do you know how much of their food they import here? We bring in many reefer containers, and much more food than anything else. Once we had some asparagus from France, and the refrigeration broke down. You cannot imagine what twenty tons of rotten asparagus smells like on the quayside.'

The police and teachers and administrators came from France, falling over each other for the well-paid three-year contracts with their termination bonus. They called it 'the waltz of the bureaucrats'. The stinking asparagus came from France. I picked up the cold ten-gram square of wrapped butter. *'Fabriqué à Baignes 16360, France.'* I jerked a thumb at the cans the soldiers were drinking.

'Oh no,' the captain said. 'That is not from France, of course. But,' he leaned forward, 'it is not from Australia either. Where do you think it is from?'

I said I had no idea.

'New Caledonia is in the EEC. So they buy their Foster's from Felixstowe.'

Later, having got a departure date out of him, I decided to leave the captain with his hated insurance paperwork and go north for a few days. There was still no answer from Monsieur Lemaigre. I was on the bus for Hienghène at eleven the following morning.

11
The mermaid of Poindimie

Until the express Mercedes had climbed the *niaouli*-covered slopes of the Central Chain and wriggled through Flying-fox Pass past the waterfalls down to the riverland on the other side, nothing distinguished the landscape from a remote part of the Auvergne, except at La Foa where, just up the road from the *pharmacie* and the peach-painted Hôtel Banu offering lunch of *plats de langoustines*, there was an army post with machine-gun emplacements outside.

La Foa, tranquil and dull, had a special place in the topography of French colonialism. After the elections were boycotted by the Kanaks in 1984, Eloi Machoro had been murdered at a farmhouse out of town by French police snipers. Machoro was a strong and violent personality, a Melanesian 'big man' who had been minister for security in the newly declared government of independent Kanaky. His assassination was an important event in the Kanaks' independence struggle, one of the key moments of blood which had produced the Matignon accords, allowing for a referendum on Kanaky's independence after a period of self-government. New Caledonia was quieter now. But if the military felt more relaxed, they weren't showing it.

Over a hundred years before, in 1878, La Foa had seen the beginning, and end, of mass opposition to the settlers by force of arms. By the mid-1870s 80,000 head of French cattle were being grazed on *le caillou*. Atai, chief of La Foa, complained to the governor that cattle were trampling his people's crops. His complaints were answered with the suggestion that he build fences to keep them out; he retorted that 'When my taro plants go eating their cattle, then I'll build fences.' When the policy of concentrating tribes on reservations began, land was taken from them on the basis of their relations with the administration. Atai, for being a mischief-maker, lost most of La Foa's best land. Again he confronted the governor, with a sack in each hand, one of soil and one of stones. 'This is what we had,' he said, 'and this is what you have left us.'

It takes a spark to start a bushfire. In the night of 18 June 1878 a freed convict and his Melanesian wife were murdered by Dogny tribesmen for sheltering a Dogny woman who, they said, didn't want to marry the man chosen for her. Several Dogny and other chiefs, who were certainly innocent, were imprisoned at La Foa for the crime.

Six days later the revolt began. The gendarmerie was stormed and four gendarmes were killed; the next day Atai and Dogny tribesmen attacked the village of La Foa and killed twenty-one people. Another eighty foreigners were killed at Bouloupari to the south.

The administration fanned the flames before it controlled them. Most of the ex-communards turned out to be racists and fought with the French. Colonel Gally-Pasbosc, the French military leader who had sworn he would wipe out the native race as the British had done in Tasmania, was killed. The butchery that followed his killing was hideous. Atai (popular accounts said it was he who killed Gally-Pasbosc) was ambushed in August and himself killed. By October the military clampdown had begun.

Several features distinguish the uprising. There was a remarkable degree of cooperation between the tribes on the west coast, who knew they were going to have to fight a big war one day – the injustice had gone on too long – and they were prepared. For their part, most of the French failed to understand that the revolt had started among Melanesians who, living closest to the capital, were most familiar with French customs and the most civilised. The French fell into the trap of equating anger and frustration with the European notion of black savagery.

Maybe the French had chosen not to see things as they were. All the tribes wanted was the thing they were never going to get from a colonial administration: their land. 'The plan of society is written on the ground,' wrote the missionary-anthropologist Maurice Leenhardt. 'Landscapes, village cultures, the society, the defunct men and mythic beings form a single ensemble, not only indivisible but even practically undifferentiated.' Sold, sequestered, redistributed: along with the land, it was Melanesian society, their ancestors, their spirits which were being confiscated.

As for civilised behaviour, the French authorities paid for severed heads in cash.

On the far side of the mountains the houses turned to shacks and the smooth macadamed road broke up between the bridges that traversed sprawling brown rivers. After six hours the bus reached the north-east coast and sprinted up the beaches and through overgrown coffee plantations.

Kurt was a Danish schoolteacher who dreamed of a Harley-Davidson. In the two seats across the aisle his blonde daughters slept like cats and dreamed of the journey ending. We argued about frontiers and food surpluses and European materialism (he hated all three), and he told me about his daughters' political education.

Kurt's wispy beard gave him away. At forty he was still a utopian idealist. Denmark's liberal education policy gave him the perfect chance to educate his daughters. The Harley-Davidson could wait: he would go round the world with them first.

One was fourteen, the other seventeen. They had begun in Poland, then taken the train to Moscow and the Trans-Siberian express to Beijing. Mille woke up and told me disgustedly about the hyperborean Swedes playing their ghetto-blasters at full volume in the intervals between vodka bouts. They spent six weeks in China and the next four months in Hong Kong, Thailand, India, Nepal, Malaysia and Indonesia; from Darwin they drove across Australia in a 21-year-old Toyota with Mille lying on the back seat with pneumonia.

They had reached the halfway point in their journey. Mille said sarcastically that the maths textbook her father was supposed to be coaching her sister with had stayed in the bottom of one of the rucksacks for three months. Kurt said she should think of all the other calculations, about poverty and wealth, her sister could now do. Mille's retort carried nuances of cruelty: her sister was not getting enough maths tuition.

The rumour was that the hotel in Hienghène had been

closed since the massacre in 1984. I got off the bus at Poindimie, seventy kilometres short, with Kurt and his daughters. In the shadow of the black hills the sun set fast on the straggling esplanade. Soon it was all in darkness but for the PTT, lit up by the floodlights from the two tennis courts between road and sea.

We bought some steak and lit a fire. There was a campsite run by the Dubos brothers, one fat, one thin. In the store the fat Monsieur Dubos said that there was a bungalow – a hut – to rent. Kurt and his daughters whipped up their tent and I spent the night next to them at the edge of the airy bay where the water fell glassily onto the sand.

The mermaid of Poindimie, said the thin Monsieur Dubos, was a
story that everyone knew. Unlike traditional nereids, she was not
half-maiden, half-fish. She had first appeared to a French navy
lieutenant sailing with Captain de la Ferrière on the *Bucéphale*
which had passed this way and stopped to collect water after
letting off the first Marist missionaries further up the coast.
Monsieur Dubos, dark and sixty, had a gift for mimicry that
turned the story from a sailor's yarn into a Chaucerian interlude.

The year was 1844. Away from France for seven and a half
months, the *Bucéphale* had raised the coast of Grande Terre just
before Christmas and stayed to set up a mission station at
Balade. The visitors had been welcomed by Chief Pakili Poumai,
and a month later the ship sailed away, leaving five Catholics
and a French flag behind.

This is the beginning of another story. Dissension, confusion, exploitation followed the missionaries' arrival. Land was
expropriated, and Melanesians found it an arduous business to
understand the new ideas. Baptism and polygamy were incom-
patible, they were told. Reluctantly, the men began killing their
wives. Four years later the chiefs cracked, and attacked the
Marists. They called them sorcerers and exploiters; the Frenchmen picked up their soutanes and ran for their lives. Today the
Marists are among the biggest landowners in the territory.

Captain de la Ferrière dropped anchor briefly in Poindimie
bay and an officer named Delrieu, a man subject to fits of
melancholy, went ashore to request permission to take on water
from the local chief: the same one who later sold land to Dubos'
great-grandfather and provided him with a wife.

By the time Delrieu was ready to return to the ship with the
chief's say-so, the sun had set. Looking back to the beach he
claimed to see a 'lovely golden-haired siren' standing in the
shadow of the she-oaks. Ignoring his escort's entreaties, he
became convinced it was the fiancée he had left on the quayside
in France and dived into the water.

They didn't find him until daybreak, sleeping the sleep of exhaustion on the beach, watched over by two polite Kanaks who handed him back.

Delrieu only woke when the search party had carried him aboard the *Bucéphale*. But he was transformed, exalted. Still maintaining the woman had been his fiancée – she had called herself Béatrice, he said; what other proof did they want? – he painted their reunion to his brother officers in the colours of love. Her sex had smelt like hot wax and frangipani; they had made love like innocent and tireless children; there were 'plenty of other erotic details'. The last he had seen of her was her slim unwrapped form disappearing into the waves.

Dubos hugged himself, swooned in a passable imitation of a man in the throes of amorous exhaustion. 'Delrieu was a changed man,' he said. 'When he got back to France he left the navy, broke off his engagement to his fiancée and came back and married a Melanesian woman. Until a few years ago his great-granddaughter used still to live here.'

I said: mermaid stories are always wish-fulfilment. Dubos was offended by my scepticism. Since the *Bucéphale* episode, at least half a dozen sailors, whalers, a US Marine during the war, travellers, had told of meeting a female figure who looked like their own lover or wife. No one from Poindimie had seen her, of course, he said. This was because they were not transients. They lived here.

Dubos was on his way to his boatyard, a wall-less building with a green Land-Rover parked outside. It contained all the woods and planking for his *charpenterie maritime*, with a bench and a vice in the corner. In the middle of the dirt floor, leaning on the edge of its stubby keel, was a jewel of a dinghy he had recently finished building. Clinker-built and broad-beamed, and drawing no more than a few centimetres, it was painted white with an interior of duck-egg blue and varnished wood: a museum piece last seen around Louveciennes in the 1860s. A nineteenth-century Seine rowing-boat was the perfect thing for negotiating the blades of the reef.

Dubos was a likeable, garrulous man with a worrier's face. His eyes bulged behind the thick lenses of his spectacles and his arms worked all the time from his elbows. During the *événements* of 1984 there had been no trouble at Poindimie apart from a few placards saying *'Mort aux colons'* and *'Blancs à la mer'*. It was because there were no freed convicts here, he said, only pure European settlers.

He really didn't have very much to do these days.

'It's all the influence of the communists just after the war. I have seen what they have done in the tribes. It was them who got all the sawmills closed down. We all used to build boats along the coast. Not any more.

'The French government have betrayed us. They *betrayed* us,' he spat the word out, 'with the Matignon accords. They took everything from us and handed it out to the Kanaks. If their credits stopped now, we would be ruined overnight.'

He was an attractive bigot, talented and vulnerable. His impersonation of a Kanak hoeing a field, turning over two spade-fuls then spotting a friend and stopping to talk for two hours, made me laugh.

'If you want, you can give a Kanak a mechanical job, and he will do it very well. Give him an earthmover and nothing will make him happier. *Vroom!* – he enjoys the big machine, the power underneath him, backwards and forwards, roaring up and down the road' (he mimed double-declutching). '*Vroom!* It's like a big toy to him, he thinks, "Now I am the chief." But give him a job with responsibilities, and he will be talking to his friends all day.'

For him, almost everything was over.

'I haven't got anything against independence but now they are taking back the land. We, *we* made this country.'

Life was a mess, but he had come to ask us if we had

everything we needed. He remembered, and stopped.

'Here I am taking up your time. Forgive me.'

Kurt had decided he was going to catch the big reef fish he had seen in its cave in the coral. He stayed hovering over the spot in his goggles with a fishing line all day. He baited the line with hermit crab, then clam and small fish, but caught only more small fish. I thought: If he had been a *Caldoche* instead of a Danish hippy, he would have been the worst kind, intelligent and determined and about as flexible as an iron bar.

In the evening we cooked a sweet chicken and bought two bottles of Côtes de Roussillon from the store. I slept and woke to the moon shadows coming in under the eaves, silvering the forms of hundreds of mosquitoes at rest on the outside of the mosquito net. Never believe an old man who tells you there's a mermaid around.

12
Sharks' eggs

The bus broke down twice on the corniche road, and the rumour about the hotel was true.

Hienghène lay at the river's mouth in the embrace of a circle of rock. I walked to the bay down a road snaking with crevices from a landslide. The police station on the promontory was behind high locked gates. At the back of the town the steep valley sides were folded and dark and splotched with scrub, and out to sea black limestone spires cast their shadow over the bay, as inviting as the pincer of a giant crab.

A few months after the *Bucéphale* landed them, the Marist priests were starving in the drought. Bouarate, the chief of Hienghène, gave them a field of yams and invited them to live in his territory. Their gratitude was the theft of land, the enlistment of converts as slave labour, profiteering, until Bouarate cried out: 'We don't want these sorcerers any more. The gown of a priest thinly disguises the exploiter under the name of brother-worker, the spy under the name of catechist!'

When the French navy returned, Bouarate was exiled to Tahiti.

Native revolts were a closed loop. Missionaries and administrators used them as an excuse to confiscate more land. In the Hienghène valley in 1914 the *Caldoches broussards*, the rednecks of the Pacific, were expanding their pastures. In desperation the local people fought them and killed sixteen. Two months later 200 Kanaks were dead.

In spite of other moments of blood and dislike, and the ever-latent land struggles, Hienghène got itself established as a busy European town. Until the *événements* it had a hotel, a cultural centre, a gendarmerie planted in a grove of pines, shops, a diving and windsurfing school, a millionaires' resort by the airstrip. People from Nouméa came for the weekend. They said there was nothing to match the hotel anywhere in the South Pacific.

The town was like a mussed jigsaw, with a lot of pieces missing. Half-abandoned, sheltered by the limestone stacks from the fresh traffic of the trade winds and a horizon it might forget itself in, it had no alternative but to simmer in the still air and brood on its past.

At Hienghène post office a man spoke to me through the security screen and suggested I try the lodgings of the school director. He might have a spare room.

A Kanak with a muscular, symmetrical face, drove up to the lodgings as the light dribbled out of the high hills across the valley. He offered me coffee and food and a bed, and a long gentle discussion about independence. He and Dubos should have met each other. Independence was inevitable, he said, but need not be bloody or exclude the *Caldoches*. It was what the independence leader, Tjibaou, had preached before he was shot.

'The villages are hidden in the bush and the mountains. You cannot forget the importance of landscape in the temperament of our people. Tjibaou was able to see things, to talk to people, in a way that others could not. He was a great leader but he almost never stayed in his tribe.'

The road to the village of Jean-Marie Tjibaou lay up the valley of the Hienghène. In November and December the sharks came upriver beyond the bridge to lay their eggs.

The forest greens were filtered through mist. The valley had a silken tranquillity – a preference for mood over realism – that was close to a Chinese painting. The road followed the flat sluggish brushstroke of the river, disclosing smudges of bamboo and stylised coconut palms negligently flicked in. Banks of busy lizzies lined the track of mud.

The finished scene had the unsettling completeness of a dream whose logic eludes you although you can clearly recall the details. It was not difficult to imagine in its peace the possibility of sudden violence along the river.

On the evening of 5 December 1984 a party of Kanaks was driving back from Hienghène to their village at Tiendanite. They were squeezed into a Chevrolet and a Mitsubishi pick-up. That afternoon they had been to a meeting of the pro-independence umbrella organisation, the Front de Libération National Kanak Socialiste led by Jean-Marie Tjibaou. The meeting had been called to announce the lifting of the FLNKS barricades around the territory, in place since the boycotted elections a month before.

Their mood was optimistic on the journey home. The future held out less tension than before. And then there was a felled coconut palm across the road, and as they stopped the shooting started.

Some piled out and ran. Others, including two of Tjibaou's brothers, had no time. Louis Tjibaou was paralysed at the wheel of one of the pick-ups. The river was only twenty metres away, but the gunmen had men on the bank with searchlights and dogs. They shot at one man till he stopped moving in the water. Another was wounded and floated for fourteen hours (he died in hospital). The river ran red. One of the gunmen's sons, a fourteen-year-old, stood and shone his spotlight on it and shouted, 'Hot shit, look at all that blood!'

Six men died during the ambush. Another four died of their wounds. Louis Tjibaou's body was found with more than thirty bullets in it. (The gendarmes from Hienghène did not arrive at the place until midday the following day.)

If no one survived, no one could identify the killers. The attackers dynamited the pick-ups. Periods of silence were broken by the dogs barking, indicating they had found a wounded man. The gunmen finished off everyone they found.

But there had been seventeen men in the two pick-ups, not ten, and seven men had seen Maurice Mitride, Henri Garnier, Rose Garnier, Robert Sineimène, Raoul Lapetite and his five sons, and at least five others, and heard them yelling 'Bastards!' and 'Kill him! *Kill him!*'

The killers were rednecks of mixed blood who lived from nomadic ranching and hunting game. People said they were manipulated by the Right, or that it was a land quarrel. The school director was nearer the truth when he said: 'If you're not thinking straight, you can kill someone because you know they're right and you're wrong. They are *métis*. They don't want to be half-Melanesian. They want to be French. *Pas bien dans leur peau.*'

Five days later, after being sheltered by other settlers, Mitride and Sineimène and most of Lapetite's family gave themselves up. (The fourteen-year-old was found in a Nouméa disco, but released as a minor.)

The story stayed fettered to that strange dream-logic. After two years the examining magistrate, François Semur, ruled there was no case to answer. He cited an old law about highway robbery which, he said, indicated that the men had acted in self-defence. He described the men of Tiendanite as having 'bad characters'.

In historical terms, this judgment on the village was consistent. The French killed fourteen men there in 1914. In the 1917 uprising the village was burnt to the ground. The men were imprisoned in Nouméa, the women sent to work as servants to settlers. Jean-Marie Tjibaou's grandmother was killed as she ran from the soldiers, carrying his father, who was six years old, on her shoulders.

It came as a surprise when an appeal tribunal ruled, at the end of 1986, that the men had to stand trial. After ten days of evidence, much of it in contradiction of inculpating testimony given to Semur, a jury of eight whites and an Indonesian returned a verdict of 'legitimate self-defence'. The courtroom swarmed with well-wishers, who greeted the announcement of the verdict with applause and shouts of *'Vive la France!'* and sang the 'Marseillaise'.

Jean-Marie Tjibaou, mayor of Hienghène and leader of the FLNKS, said, 'The precise rationality of their Cartesian mind gives [the French] no room for dreams, or the imaginary. So they cannot understand the South Pacific.'

In this he was wrong. The French just dreamed things differently.

After the trial Maurice Mitride and the others lived a seedy existence in Nouméa off charity from the National Front. At the roadside where the massacre happened, on ground that was once Mitride's farm, the rusted, stoved-in pick-ups neatly faced the road, strewn with bright rags of mourning cloth and overrun by busy lizzies. The taxi-driver went on past other abandoned pavilions and ornamental cascades. We forded the river four times and passed coffee and banana gardens and miles of flowering banks.

Tiendanite rose up over two alpine meadows, with a communal house of concrete and tin, a small church, family houses with tin roofs. The cemetery included, in a long line, ten identical rough concrete gravestones heaped with plastic flowers.

Jean-Marie Tjibaou's own house stood fifty metres away. It was unfinished. Next to it, dominating the scene from every vantage point, draining all the light from the scene into itself, was Tjibaou's own tomb, massed with flowers more than a metre high.

Tjibaou's death had still less rhyme or reason than the others'. A commando of Kanaks had stupidly stormed a gendarmerie at Ouvéa in the Loyalty Islands off the east coast, killing four police and taking sixteen others hostage in a cave. On 4 May 1988, three days before the French presidential elections, Jacques Chirac ordered three hundred police to attack the cave where the hostages were held. The body-count was: all hostages safe; attacking police, two dead; Kanaks, nineteen. All the wounded Kanaks were finished off.

Exactly a year later a hysterical Kanak pulled a pistol at the memorial service for the nineteen who had died, and shot the FLNKS leader at point-blank range. The gunman, whose brothers were among the dead, believed that Tjibaou had given the go-ahead for the hostage-taking (he hadn't) and then dissociated himself from it.

Tjibaou's leadership had been strong and positive. He had united Kanak clans into a force that seemed to be making political headway. He had signed the Matignon peace accords after the Ouvéa massacre to try to break the loop of violence.

David Couhia – three Couhias had been caught in the Hienghène massacre – was the *porte-parole* of the village. (After Tjibaou had died, there was no chief left.) David had a round face and quick eyes and fatalistic gestures and was suspicious at first. He said he could only spare ten minutes. But he spoke gently and guided me around the village for an hour, more like a curator than someone bereaved.

'In a month's time,' David said, 'we will have the *lever du deuil* for Tjibaou. There will be a feast and some speeches and a presentation to his wife's family, and that will be the end of the story of Jean-Marie.'

I said goodbye. David had picked up his long-handled spade and was leaning on the top of the shank in a curiously formal way. He looked like the soldier-shepherd in Giorgione's *Tempest*, the Renaissance fugitive watching the lightning, listening for the thunder to roll down the narrow valley.

But then New Caledonia had all the abrogated qualities of that period: the judicial murders, the lawless protection of vested interests, the connivance of the Church. Like a principality in which the prince preserved his power by referring his challengers to the mayhem he had already caused, the *territoire* had originated in a readiness for violence among the French to establish their position and gone on in a similarly uninhibited way.

The manner of Tjibaou's death, bitter, random, inevitable, was a measure of how infected the territory had become.

The taxi-driver said: 'Did you enjoy the visit?'

'Yes.'

'Did you like David?'

'I thought he was charming.'

'Did he tell you he was Tjibaou's brother?'

'But that's not his family name.'

'It's a Melanesian tradition. His parents gave him to another family that had no children.'

13
Make me a proposal

Over Flying-fox Pass the clear tonic note of the early sun faded out; at La Foa three trucks convoyed north into the rain, full of chalky boys with rifles and brutal haircuts.

In Nouméa the streets steamed, and the French were still driving around as if they owned the place. You had to hand it to them. They had pulled off a perfect recreation of southern *savoir-vivre*: the elegance, the haircuts, the white villas, cordoned like Nobel's with bougainvillaea; the corniche roads and poodles and perfume and *l'heure de l'apéro*; the dashing down of cognac at breakfast, the streets emptying at twelve-thirty, the tang of caporal cigarettes and women in restaurants dressed to knock their husbands dead, but paying them no attention and watching over their children instead, unconcerned at a small hand pulling a jacket aside to disclose the most expensive underwear.

The third-generation *Caldoches*, the exiles from Algeria and Indochina, and the metropolitan expatriates had got it so right they didn't think twice. Nouméa reassured and deceived them at the same time. Menton-sur-Pacifique.

When I thought of France, I thought of technology and religion, twin peaks, one with a radio mast on its summit, the other with a cross of Lorraine. They were both here, along with the import economy and the replica bureaucracy. But the transcending belief in God and science had become a philosophy of exclusiveness, in which the Kanaks were invisible. From restaurant habits to defence policies there was no compromise. French colonialism was about waiting for the rest of the world to see sense.

In a town like this everything was to be expected, nothing new was to be welcomed or awaited. I was suffering from the boredom of not being able to get round my dislike of a place, and it gave me a thirst for something to take it away.

I walked to the bar of the Hotel Caledonia, a four-storey building decorated in the full ceramic passion of the Forties. The walls were decorated with self-adhesive *tricolores*, and at one end of the counter three young Frenchmen were drinking Suze cassis. One, with a waxed moustache, was rolling his r's in English to a fat man in black shirt and shorts whose temples ran with beer-sweat.

'Make me a proposal.'

On the wall there was a long wooden jigsaw map of Grande Terre with a bigger *tricolore* slapped on top of it. Beneath were the sporting stickers of the French Right:

'Jean-Marie Le Pen – top gun,'

'National Front,'

'Hands off our rock,'

'Association of Indochinese Expatriates,'

'France – *love* her or *leave* her.'

They mingled with the two dozen regimental stickers commemorating the soldiers (6000 at the time of the *événements*) who had passed through the bar, parachute regiments and naval squadrons, units of the air force with mottoes like 'Dead cunning and rock hard.'

I ordered a beer and finally got through to Monsieur Lemaigre. He lived around the corner and was surprised to hear from a friend of Norman's. He said he'd meet me in half an hour.

The man in black – a German – was explaining the absurdly low prices he could offer on Mercedes exports to New Caledonia. The Frenchman repeated: 'Make me a proposal.'

It took a German to make the French speak English, I said to the barman. His face was the colour of mushrooms. Polishing glasses flamboyantly, he asked where I had been.

'Hienghène. It's a pity it's empty now.'

'Oh, the place was completely ransacked by the Mélanésiens.'

The shovel-faced man next to me said, 'The hôtellerie was marvellous.'

'Why don't the French want independence?'

I half-expected to be thrown out for this enquiry, but the result was stranger. Shovel-face gulped his beer, slid off his stool and left. The barman's swagger began to evaporate. He temporised: 'Oh, it's very difficult. You know, the Matignon accords have done nothing except for the Mélanésiens. And they are more or less reasonable people, they just don't know what they want. Some of them want this, some of them want that...' And then he too gave in and retreated down the bar, where the discussion was still about cars and the Frenchman with the moustache was still saying:

'So, come on, make me a proposal.'

Lemaigre had been a mining engineer. He was a square-headed, practical man, his face burnt by the sun. He had no time for politics. I could see him thinking: When there is a job to be done, why discuss it?

'Independence is no problem,' he said. 'The only important thing here is the military base. Independent or not, with a population so francophile, it will always be here. In any case, the Mélanésiens are only forty-five per cent of the population, and twenty per cent of them definitely do not want independence.'

'Why did the French use all that force to deal with a minority protest?'

He tutted and waved his finger at me.

'We used the correct amount of force. The military and the police here are quite impartial. They have to be.'

'Someone made a mistake about the right amount of force to use when they blew up the *Rainbow Warrior*.'

'This was a great *connerie militaire*. They could have done a much better job with half the explosives. But it wasn't a mistake.' Did I think the French intelligence services would do such a thing without telling the British intelligence services? It would never have been such a big story if they hadn't killed a photographer.

'The Mélanésiens will not get independence. You know why? Because they don't want it badly enough. They can't agree because tribal loyalties are too strong; they're not committed people; they aren't hungry enough. They can have as many children as they want and get maximum social security. There's infrastructure here, investment, tremendous mineral wealth, employment, no homelessness. You have to be hungrier than that to want independence. This is a very modern country. The phone system is better than New Zealand's.'

'Does New Caledonia have a constitution?'

'But of course. We have the constitution of France. Everyone here is a French citizen.'

The logic was flawless of course, and as brutal as common sense and not without a kind of wit. The Kanaks could vote; join the army; acquire one of the best educations in the world. In the territory's schools almost all the teachers, like the other professionals, were French. For every Kanak who passed the baccalauréat, thirty white children passed. Before 1951 the Kanaks weren't allowed more than primary education, and until recently Kanak children were taught that their ancestors were the Gauls. The school textbook described New Caledonia thus: 'It is thirty-three times smaller than France. Its structure and dimensions are approximately those of the Pyrenees.'

Lemaigre would have preferred it if I had asked him to help me blow something up, instead of asking all these stupid questions.

14
Ghosts

Shore leave expired at two.

The Camp Est prison on the Ile Nou was a low, sparkling collection of buildings with red tin roofs. Fifty yards away the breeze blew through the ruined chapel next to the first execution-ground. By decree a man slept in the condemned cell, not knowing if it was his last night on earth, and was dead, after Mass and the instruction 'Uncover and kneel!', before dawn.

George Griffith, a Welshman with a morbid but enlightening fascination for prison life, inspected the colony's prisons in 1900. Noting the laxity of some of the conditions the convicts were kept under, he was then taken to the second storey of the prison block, where he concluded that death was far preferable to life.

The cells he saw were the *cachots noirs*. A man could be sentenced here to up to ten years' solitary confinement in the dark, seeing the sun only once every thirty days for an hour's exercise.

Griffith went inside. 'After the first two or three the minutes lengthened out into hours... The blackness seemed to come down on me like some solid thing and drive my straining eyes back into my head. It was literally darkness that could be felt, for I felt it, and the silence was like the silence of upper space.'

In the prison hospital he saw 'pitiful parodies of manhood', and one man in particular: 'His lips were drawn back from his teeth like the lips of an ape in a rage, and his hands were half-clenched like claws. The man was simply the incarnation of madness, savagery, and despair. He had gone mad in the Black Cell, and the form that his madness had taken was the belief that nothing would nourish him but human flesh. Of course he had to be fed by force.'

An Alfa Romeo stopped on the road, and the driver, a Frenchwoman in her late twenties, drove me to the path leading up to the Fort de Tereka that stood guard over the roads.

Left and right you could see for sixty kilometres over the ocean. Fritillaries flopped back and forth on grass stems, and tiny red avadavats twittered in their hundreds in the broom.

At the fort two cannons on iron railroads could be brought to bear against any attack from the sea (the French certainly had the British in mind). Beneath the hill was a Gibraltar of tunnels. Out of the culvert leading into the hillside a Kanak dwelling had been constructed, but the inhabitants had heard my approach and fled into the darkness.

I walked back to the crowded French-only beach for a swim. Nicole, the driver of the Alfa, was sitting with her children. She had slender, unrelaxed shoulders and a mass of dark curls. Once she started talking she didn't stop. Her mother, grandmother and great-grandmother had been Caledonian; her father was a *pied noir*. She resented *la métropole*, she said; it imposed civil servants and police on them. For a *Caldoche* woman it was hard to get a job but if you were the wife of a Customs officer on a new posting you would have a job in forty-eight hours. In a voice that said she wanted to believe it, Nicole explained that the quarrel was not with the *Caldoches*, but with France. (The *Caldoches* called the expatriates *les oreilles*, 'the ears'; the implication was that they came to the territory to spy for France.)

Nicole had been brought up in Nouville, the island's township. She drove me back past the Théâtre de l'Ile, burnt-out in 1985, and suddenly turned off the road to the old jetty where the whaler ferries once tied up.

She hadn't been here for ten years, she said. The weatherboard cafe next to the jetty was falling down. For half an hour she looked for the cottage where she had grown up. Eventually she realised. It had been knocked down. In its place was a row of new government buildings.

Nicole stopped talking as abruptly as she had started. Her day had been changed by seeing that her old house had vanished. We went on down the back road flickering in the shade of trees, past the mental hospital (closed), until it wound up on the new road back into town. At the dock gates she looked closely at the *Capitaine Tasman*.

'That's your ship?'

'Yes.'

A wish flared in the angular dark features. It was the Ile Nou that was to blame, with its prison, its theatre and arms dump, its deserted township and its mental hospital. She had grown up in the setting for an Ibsen play. Now, true to the role, she wanted to up sticks and go.

I got out of the car and thanked her and walked across the tarmac to the ship. I had walked more than a hundred metres before I heard the rasp of the car's exhaust as she pulled away.

15
The Herald and the Seal

The south-east passage led past mine-scarred hillsides and cliffs pencilled with waterfalls. Scores of storm-petrels attacked the surface of the Havannah Channel. Overhead three giant frigate-birds each waited to drop like a stone on a feeding petrel and mug it. It was a lee shore, eerie and predatory. On cue, the dragonfly hulls of a squadron of helicopters – rapid-reaction Super Pumas of the Armée de Terre – poured down the channel and wheeled into the hills.

The look of the place suited its associations. At the end of September 1853 Admiral Febvrier-Despointes had sailed past the channel's mouth on his way to the Ile des Pins for a confrontation with a British naval captain. They were heady days. The admiral had received secret orders at the Peruvian port of Callao, including a personal note from the Emperor, in July. His instructions were to plant the French flag on two prominent parts of the islands of New Caledonia and take possession of them in the name of France.

It was at a ball in Sydney that winter that a Royal Navy officer had let it slip that the commander of a British naval squadron had received orders to annex New Caledonia. But the commander was in no hurry to quit the pleasures of Sydney. The French were the only other contenders, and there wasn't a single French warship between Peru and the Portuguese East Indies.

Louis-Napoléon, however, had decided the game was worth the candle. If British and French guns were turned on each other in the Pacific, their new alliance, and with it the outcome of the Crimean War, might be thrown in jeopardy, so there was to be no shooting; but the Emperor calculated that the British would forgive his need to acquire some imperial ornaments to justify his new title.

Febvrier-Despointes sighted the limestone needles of Hienghène on 23 September. The next day he dropped anchor at Balade and, 'convinced that no foreign flag waved on the island', ordered the *tricolore* hoisted with a salute of twenty-one cannon shots. The missionaries at Balade advised him to fulfil the second part of his instructions on the Ile des Pins, where there was another mission and where the chief – an intelligent man – was well disposed to French interests.

At the island's southern anchorage on 28 September, the admiral's sanguine mood fizzled out. His ship, the *Phoque,* had company: the *Herald,* a British sloop, ten guns, 100 crew, now converted to a yacht for diplomatic and surveying duties.

The British captain, Henry Denham, paid a courtesy visit to his ally. His explanation for his presence was that he was mapping the coast. French accounts say that Febvrier-Despointes found Denham oddly irritable and impatient.

Denham had indulged himself in Sydney. His second error was not to have claimed the Ile des Pins on arrival. He sensed that he was about to be caught out. But with the oppression of things already having gone badly wrong weighing on him, he was unable to act. In the night, under cover of dark and a storm, Febvrier-Despointes got the missionaries to erect a flagpole and square the friendly chief in readiness for a ceremony of annexation the following morning.

At dawn the French flag was flying over the Ile des Pins.

Tricked by the French, Denham let the anger of failure take hold of him. He tried to persuade the chief to give up his support of France and held a dinner in his honour at which he presented him with muskets, rifles and a hundredweight of chocolate. When this was unsuccessful, he turned directly to the local people, telling them correctly (if hypocritically) that their chief had sold their independence for the price of a few axes and that they should revolt. They took no notice.

Unheeded, Denham suddenly went down with a mysterious illness and had to retire to Sydney, to face the consequences of his misjudgment. But there is always another option for someone prepared to turn their anger on themselves, and Denham took it. Reports say his suicide was clean.

French reports, that is, which presented the symmetry and harmony of a drama in which they emerged the victors. *Lean's Royal Navy List*, I discovered, notes Denham's year of death as 1887, at the age of ninety-one. I found the green-bound volumes of the *Herald*'s log, which run on to 1861 for this command and suggest that Denham was a prosaic man, irritated by problems with his topgallant sails and given to comments such as 'lost overboard, paintbrushes one in number'. He probably was under orders to annex the islands under cover of his surveying duties, although I can't be sure. He had already named the harbours on the Ile des Pins Port Victoria and Port Albert.

Maybe, for its brio, the French version is the version worth having. It might have been confusion, and not triumph, which led to the French accounts in any case. Denham's youngest son, Fleetwood James, was a member of the *Herald*'s crew; he died suddenly on board ten months later, on 8 July 1854. And perhaps in a way the French accounts were right. Denham's character *was* unable to cope with moments of tragedy: the ship's log for 8 July is blank, failing to record any events at all, from the death of the captain's son to the loss of a paintbrush.

Within hours of leaving, the *Tasman* was heating up again, but as long as there was no need to take a shower or use one of the steel heads, which both flanked the funnel, the air-conditioning kept most of the quarters in a state of stale frigidity. The ship slipped through the reef under a quattrocento sky and Captain Pape came to my cabin to invite me for a beer.

I was scribbling in my notebook and asked for fifteen minutes' grace.

'It is all baloney but I give you fifteen minutes.'

By the time I got to his cabin he had disappeared. I went out on deck. The black southern sky cast out the diamond-dust of a million stars at the end of an invisible giant arm. It was one of the best places in the world to see the pathway of the galaxy, so bright you could take away the moon and there were still sharp shadows against the white rails and superstructure. From the funnel crimson flakes of soot flew upwards, commingled and died on the wind.

'Very beautiful, no? Perhaps you should come and have a beer. If you stay here, you may become light-headed, and then get a little too close to the stern...'

The officers all said the captain was a little crazy. They laughed about him in the first officer's cabin. He sat in his quarters and read novels at sea. In port, when women came giggling on board with their high heels and visible pantie lines, they were mystified that his behaviour did not alter. How could a sailor on shore not be cock-happy? But at sea they trusted each other, because they trusted him, crazy though he was.

In the dark low room he said: 'So. How did you like New Caledonia?'

I said I thought the French were the most comic and dangerous nation in the Pacific.

'How can you say this?' Captain Pape sat back. 'They are very civilised, they can cook very good pizza. You think you have seen a bureaucracy? In Germany we have the time-wasting system to beat all time-wasting systems. And what about Sofrana? If it weren't for the generous Mr Ravel, you would still be on the docks in Sydney.

'You must have some sympathy for them. They did not have the advantage of having all their colonies taken away from them after the First World War, as we did. And giving them up now means they have to admit that someone else's ideology is better than theirs. For a Frenchman this is not possible.

'Did you know the French navy some time ago had a great deal of difficulty adjusting to the new charts that were issued? Why? They were standard navigational charts, based on the Greenwich meridian. Every other navy had used them for decades. Not the French. Theirs was the only navy in the world that used charts based on the Paris meridian.'

16
First view of Fiji

At seven in the morning Lautoka lay off on the *Tasman*'s starboard side, a dusty rigmarole of low, tin-roofed buildings that boasted a main street of royal palms and exhaled the sluggish tang of molasses. It sat in a cradle of foothills that rose to a high double ridge, each successive layer of rock, ochre and madder, divided by a scarf of mist that gave the hills the appearance of hanging in the air and the scene a delicacy that within half an hour would have vanished, driven off by the mundane heat.

In the way that army takeovers have, the new situation in Fiji had made the army jumpy rather than happier. A recent decree, officially enacted in order to give Fiji journalists a fairer chance of covering national events, meant that no foreign journalists were being allowed in the country. I suggested to the captain he could tell the immigration officer that I was a teacher on holiday.

We said goodbye. I was sorry to do it. Possessed by quirks, but free of the private manias of a sedentary life, the captain had kept the sharp senses of men thirty years younger.

We shook hands.

'Good-bye, admiral.' *Amir al-bahr*: prince of the sea.

He waved the compliment away, saying with his word-by-word emphasis, 'Goodbye, Mr Evans. You know, this will be the first time I have ever smuggled anything.'

Lautoka was Fiji's main sugar port on the main island, Viti Levu; it was where the consignment of guns had been headed for. At Queen's Wharf, manned by soldiers in fatigues, a young soldier held hands with a civilian whose dress sense had been superseded by events. His teeshirt read: 'Fiji. The way the world should be.'

The coast road south was a serpentine affair of changing vistas, its course interlaced with that of the sugar railway that snaked in and out of the fields of cane on either side. At the roadside sacred cows banged bones against skin as they grazed, and now and then a supermarket appeared ('S.J. Prasad. Icy Cold Beer and Coke Sold Here. Licensed for Sale of Spirituous Liquor'). Thirsty mountains hid timber trucks that suddenly appeared and threw up clouds of red dust from piles of earth left by maintenance gangs in the middle of the road, and a conjuror's pair of mongeese vanished across the broken tarmac.

'This Queen's Highway, number one road in Fiji,' said the taxi-driver.

He talked non-stop. His great-grandfather had come from India to work as an indentured labourer on one of the European sugar estates, like 60,000 others. He didn't know which part of India his family came from. He had been born in the rainbelt on Vanua Levu, and come to the western division to get out of the rain and marry a girl. When she died he had stayed on, driving a cab and making about 40 Fiji dollars – 15 pounds – a week.

The quickest way to get to the capital, he said, was to get a running cab from Nadi, an extraordinarily cheap arrangement by which, for 8 dollars, you shared a 200-kilometre journey with the driver and four other people.

Nadi town was a shamelessly dreary place, full of slow-moving tourists and duty-free shops and gimcrack handicrafts. Between the main street and the cab rank were milk bars and beggars, the most professional of whom displayed a deep self-inflicted wound on his calf. In the roadway scores of mynas warbled insincerely at each other.

By a fluke, a running cab was waiting for its last passenger to turn up. I squeezed into the front seat next to a very thin woman clutching what I took to be a catatonic infant but turned out to be a metre-high doll. The driver remonstrated with her, and it eventually went in the boot. In the back were an Indonesian woman, greedily made-up, and two silent moustachioed Fijians. After the coups Lt-Colonel Rabuka had set the style in men's grooming: everywhere in Fiji upper lips had sprouted his Earls Court Road gay's moustache.

The running cab was cheap. But back on the Queen's Highway there hung about the new cab driver, hunched over the wheel, a compromised air. He seemed to be engaged in a struggle he could not communicate; after only a few kilometres it became clear that time was running out for him, as sleep or mechanical failure was likely to take over at any moment. The first sixty kilometres scorched past in a rackety blur of canefields and savannah, the occasional school (a flock of flamingo-pink uniforms, a sign: 'Hard Work Is Key To Success') and a landscape disfigured by pine plantations. Changing down a gear briefly, the car rushed through Sigatoka – a town rubbed as bare by tourism as Nadi – and over the bridge across the cement-coloured Sigatoka river with the suspension bottoming out at the merest undulation in the road's surface.

Despite the immaculate seaside reconstructions of Fijian villages that were the favoured hotel idiom, collections of thatched *bures* with a tennis court, bar or swimming pool grafted on, few tourists were to be seen on the sharp moonscapes of the coral bays. The real Fijian villages, visible on the land side of the road, were exercises in breezeblock and tin decorated with the limited resources of the villagers by lone hibiscus shrubs or a stand of coconut palms. They looked fractionally neater but no less ugly with the addition of ranch-style gantries that carried each village's name and beneath it a large panel advertising Benson & Hedges cigarettes.

Cuttings of blood-red rock led to a range of high alps covered with a tight webbing of jungle, over which goshawks wheeled in watchful lethargy. The road was almost traffic-free; something to be prayerfully grateful for. I glanced around and saw a car full of silent entreaty. Although the car's mechanics, apart from the springs, had been temporarily won over to the driver's cause, he was losing his fight against sleep. He nodded off several times, and was only woken by the subliminal sensation of the car drifting onto the wrong side of the road. To keep awake he began to pick his nails and nose, ignoring the animosity of one of the Fijians behind at the small projectiles of dirt being flicked at him. Even when he was awake his bravado led to several near-misses, as he straightened out corners and stayed in the oncoming lane after overtaking, as if there were long lines of invisible cars to be passed that only he could see.

I became impressed at the driver's ability to twitch the car out of danger at the last moment. But it was entirely fitting that, on arriving in Suva, the first views we came upon were the city's graveyard of beribboned tombs stretching up the hillside, and the crumbly battlements, being whitewashed by a detail of shabby convicts, of Suva gaol.

In 1970 recalled British officials had left behind Suva's solid buildings, botanical gardens and sabbatical lifestyle in one of the most tranquil, and regretted, departures ever brought off by a distant proprietor. Fijians were doggily enthusiastic about the royal family – Queen Elizabeth was still head of state and paramount chief of all Fijian chiefs – and for a Pacific nation the broad fan of volcanic islands was considered prosperous, stable and peaceful.

Seventeen years later there had been two military coups in the space of six months. Lacking the troubled past that provides the usual incubation for military intervention, Fiji's subsequent status as the South Pacific's first military-run republic was a puzzle. Why had the coups happened so suddenly, a month after elections which brought in a new Labour coalition government?

The usual explanation was race-panic. The taxi-driver from Lautoka had explained that he was Fijian. But not according to the Fijian authorities, who gave him a Fiji passport and called him, confusing race with nationality, a Fiji Indian.

The army now said the Indo-Fijian population was outnumbering the indigenous Fijians and threatening to take control. Sitiveni Rabuka (whose rank was as labile as his temperament: he called himself everything from Lt-Colonel to Brigadier) was unmoved by the facts that the new Prime Minister, Dr Bavadra, was a Fijian and that the cabinet was exactly divided between Fijians and Indo-Fijians. Rabuka carried out the coups because – the time-honoured excuse – it was 'a mission that God had given me'.

Rumours implicated various other people in the coups. It was the Americans again, of course. There had been smoothly voiced anxiety in Washington about the Fiji Labour Party and its nuclear-free policy. If America lost its bases in the Philippines, there was a gap of neutrality between Guam and the Antarctic. After the first coup someone in the Pentagon betrayed more satisfaction by his indiscretion than by what he said. What he said was: 'We're kind of delighted.' Some members of Bavadra's government who were arrested by Rabuka's troops in the parliament chamber said that beneath their balaclavas and gloves the soldiers were actually US Marines. The joke went that the military takeover had gone so smoothly the Royal Fiji Military Forces could not have been responsible.

By what criteria the coups were Rabuka's and not some other party's – there was the usual support for them among Fiji's wealthy conservatives – remained one of those things people still talked about. Rabuka (he eventually settled for Major-General) was ambitious, it was agreed. But he wasn't *clever* enough.

The losing Prime Minister in the 1987 elections, Ratu Sir Kamisese Mara, had been reinstated by Rabuka. He was still there at the beginning of 1990, unabashed by allegations of corruption and the lengthening period of unelected rule. No one believed the new constitution which had been promised would do anything other than ratify the creation of a two-tier state in which ethnic Fijians ruled, and the haemorrhage of Indo-Fijian businesses and the professional class to Australia was persisting without respite. Mara's party claimed that the economy was growing at remarkable speed, and that stability was returning. Mara had persuaded the Major-General to relinquish his job as Minister for Home Affairs and return to the Army's headquarters at the Queen Elizabeth Barracks in Suva: this was presumably something to be thankful for. These days, it was said, the

General spent his days half-heartedly attending to business at the barracks, and was bored and restless.

17
Miles Johnson

I put up at the Grand Pacific Hotel, a wedding-cake of a building which had seen better times. The first-floor promenade over the harbour had been filled in. I was shown to a shoebox room that peered between its doric columns and reverberated with the rumble of cheap ventilators. A half-dozen engorged mosquitoes triangulated lazily in the bathroom. Downstairs the dining room and bar had not been redecorated since the Fifties. They presented now a faithful imitation of the dreariest commercial travellers' hotel (British version).

In a copy of the *Fiji Times* in the galleried lobby I read that the General had nominated himself for chairman of the Fiji Rugby Union. The report oozed unctuousness, commenting that 'His experience especially in the military will be an advantage', as if responsibility for two *coups d'état* was a valuable part of any chairman's c.v. – like being fluent in French and a good fourth at bridge.

I phoned Miles Johnson.

Miles was a lawyer of Australian descent and the former president of the Fiji Law Society. He had fallen foul of Rabuka for writing editorials in the *Fiji Sun* that suggested the General had no right to attack the institution of parliament. When the *Fiji Sun* had been closed, Miles had had to go into hiding, along with large numbers of other Europeans, Indo-Fijians – and Fijians – who were protesting. Like the rest of them, Miles had been beaten when he was found.

'Come and have a drink. Take a taxi. Everyone knows

where my house is. Or if you see a soldier, you can ask him. His mates were round here last night throwing bricks through the window.'

I walked down Victoria Parade past Albert Park and Government Building, a likeable pre-war eyesore that was a cross between Blenheim Palace and an Anderson shelter. Screened by foliage bespattered with red hibiscus blooms, it was part of an architectural sequence. Earlier colonial buildings survived with their grace, their spindly arcades and cricket-pavilion proportions intact; afterwards, since the war, everything had been built in prefabricated concrete and painted in pastel colours.

The centre of town was a farrago of these utility buildings. They housed banks, supermarkets, cut-price emporia and duty-free centres offering everything a tourist off a cruise ship might need in the way of opals, black coral or electrogadgets. Despite all the tokens that contradicted the feeling – the Melanesian-Polynesian-Indian population, the fresh greenery, the port, the clear air, the light that bounced off metal and glass – the city reeked of the London suburbs.

I mentioned this to a friend later.

'It's what makes the expatriates feel so at home,' he said. 'What do you think we're developing the South Pacific for? So everyone can go shopping.'

The taxi rank was on the far side of the market. Strings of tiny black crabs, that people carried much as you would carry sandwiches, hissed and bubbled on lengths of sinnet; land crabs with green and blue claws chopped the air; grey clams were sold in plaited palm-leaf baskets along with red, white and green snacks of seaweed and coconut with chili wrapped in a bread-fruit leaf. There was green orange juice, purple sweet potato, muddy brown yams. The bus liveries on the far side mimicked the fruit-salad colours.

The driver didn't know exactly where Miles' house was,

but he knew who he was. 'He's that lawyer that got in trouble? Very good for him.'

Miles' office was on the verandah of his bungalow, a bachelor mess with a desk piled with papers pushed against the end wall. The long lush garden sloped down to the glittering bay.

Miles was a big man in his forties, with a schoolboyish scowl of concentration. His chair was a cushioned recliner draped in towels on which he bounced back and forth, staring out over the hillside and the silver shadows of the harbour.

Cross-examination had become a habit with him. What school had I gone to? What did my father do? In his hand was a bamboo stick with an odd notch cut in the end of it.

The houseboy brought two bottles of Fiji Bitter. 'You don't want a glass do you? No point in pouring cold beer into a warm glass. Go for your life.'

Miles' family had been in Fiji for generations. He was part of the white establishment and had always supported Mara. The new regime could have been expected not to wreak any changes in his comfortable existence. Eventually, he got round to his change of heart. He was a constitutionalist and would not be ruled by tenth-rate opportunists.

He looked at his watch and said, 'Hold on,' and prodded the bamboo stick at the radio, then, using the notch, tuned it to the World Service. When the news was over he turned the radio off again without moving his body by a fraction. 'Can't live without it,' he said.

His concerns now, he said, were with specific events and issues, like the new constitution. He threw a fat copy of the draft constitution at me – 'I'll tell you what's wrong with *that*, to start with' – then the phone rang.

The preamble to the document was full of phrases that hid its true purpose. The authors, whoever they were, were putting up a built-in parliamentary majority for indigenous Fijians and they would not be moved from it. The irony of course was that there was no such thing as an indigenous Fijian. The islands had been settled from several different directions. First the Austronesian-speaking Mongoloid Polynesians, then dark-skinned Sundanoids with frizzy hair – hunter-gatherers from Australia, uninterested in things they couldn't see; the ocean held no enchantment for them. Much later the eastern Fijians had had their gene pool lightened by a back-migration of Polynesians from Tonga. Indigenousness was a veil placed decorously over another word.

Miles was saying: 'Well you tell that fucking policeman that he can come round when he likes but you're not going to answer any questions without your solicitor being present. We can do it in my office tomorrow morning if he wants to.'

Putting the phone down, he said, 'That was two teachers at the university who were beaten up by the police. They want to take the police to court – as they should – and now the police are charging *them* with assault.'

'It sounds as if they're making it up as they go along.'

'Take *that* document,' Miles said. 'What is wrong with that document is something no one has commented on yet. It's nothing to do with the seats in parliament, although that's bad enough: 37 Fijians, 27 Indians, six others, the prime minister always to be a Fijian. The interim government has said again and again that there are rights guaranteed in the constitution for everyone: to life, liberty, freedom of conscience, freedom of expression, security of the person, and so on. But look at section 147. Under section 147 all the government has to do is pull a man in because they don't like his views, and they can put him in prison for life. That section specifically rules out *any* protection by the guaranteed rights listed earlier in the document. Any constitution that says that, from a jurisprudential point of view or a straightforward human point of view, isn't worth two bob.'

Another thought struck him about freedom of expression. 'You know what they said when we wanted to reopen the *Fiji*

Sun? The Minister of Information stated we were perfectly entitled to resume publishing, but he would have to see that "his boys" played a part in ownership and publication.'

The houseboy brought more Fiji Bitter. Miles was tuning the radio to ABC News. He slashed the air with his cane. The thing most repugnant to him in the administration's utterances was their mix of legalese and gangsterese. He listened to the news again, then he said:

'You know what is wrong with those guys in the government? They have got no brains. And they have got no *style*.'

18
Caciques

I could understand what Miles meant: freedom and style, for white emigrants, were inseparable in a hot climate. The adventurers and bullies are always the first. In the Pacific the whalers, traders, deserters looked on native life, Conrad said, as 'a play of shadows the dominant race could walk through unaffected and disregarded'. All the colonies had done was formalise the brisk exploitation and add pocket parliaments and sanitary arrangements. Throughout it all, white men had been more or less obsessed by the mythical dash of wealth and easy sex, space, grandeur, heat.

In a bookstore in Suva, where the shelves were plastered with stickers that said 'No free reading', I had bought three small pamphlets that contained the *Fiji Times'* history of Fiji. Written in the paper's limp style, it nevertheless fascinated me, because it seemed to sum up the mechanics of all transitions of power:

In 1800 the schooner *Argo* was wrecked on one of Fiji's reefs. The same year, Fijians saw a comet with three tails; there was a total eclipse of the sun; and a wasting disease ran through the archipelago, killing thousands. One of the castaways, Oliver Slater, survived the wreck and the cannibals, and wandered through the islands for two years, remarking on the abundance of sandalwood. A single cargo could make a man rich. Selling to the Chinese for 500 times the price they paid the islanders, it took the Slaters of the world ten years to strip the forests.

With bartered muskets, local chiefs became sovereigns of whole island groups in no time flat. But they lacked the expertise to operate and service the temperamental pieces. This was the opportunity of Charles Savage, wrecked on the brig *Eliza* in 1808. The Fijians stripped him and his companions and took them to Bau, where Savage became musket-man to Ratu Naulivou, leading the Bauans on a score of campaigns to annihilate his adversaries over the next five years. Thousands of villagers were slaughtered as they stared at the sky, thinking the gunfire was thunder.

Savage was a natural leader and a brilliant marksman. He did not possess the gift of longevity. On an expedition to the coast of Vanua Levu he was ambushed by some natives who failed to acknowledge the princeling-thug of Bau so far from home. His comrades refused to surrender, so Savage was drowned, quartered and eaten before them in the belief that this would prompt them to the correct course. In the end all but three of his companions went the same way.

Savage was a sexual incontinent. In the *Times*' bland prose he was 'survived by two royal wives and twenty-eight others'. He fathered at least fifty children. But his influence outperformed his guns, and his member. By it a single chief's dominion spread over a large area of the islands. In the 1840s Ratu Naulivou's nephew, Cakobau of Bau, was powerful enough to be addressed by a British official as 'Tui Viti', king of Fiji. Flattered by the title, he kept it. Bau acquired the spurious aura of a place of kings, even though Cakobau was never strong

enough to extend control over the whole country and by the end
of his reign was only holding on with the help of Tongan
mercenaries. In 1874 he invited Queen Victoria to annex the
islands. Rather than see them fall into the hands of the Americans or Germans, the British drew up their Deed of Cession.

Immediately, western Viti Levu rebelled against British
sovereignty. Their chiefs had not signed the Deed and they did
not want to be ruled by an oligarchy of easterners from Bau and
the Lau islands. Their resistance took two years to quell, finish-
ing with attacks on their villages by forces of eastern Fijians led
by British officers.

The most admirable thing about the cession of Fiji, of
course, was that Cakobau had succeeded in giving away something that was not his. More cacique than monarch, he had
conned the British, most Fijians and posterity, and secured all
the benefits sought by the cornered tyrant: protection, preserva-
tion of his material comforts and lasting fame.

Now, according to Miles, the caciques were back. The
'Indian problem' was just a device. What Mara and his cronies
were really up to, as usual, was the consolidation of power. It
was nowhere near as sanguinary as any Central American
republic, nor as uncomfortable as New Caledonia. But like any
junior tyranny it had plenty of freedom to move in the direction
of either.

I returned to the hotel. It was dark and a breath of sweet,
perfumed air swung in the streets. As I walked through the
lobby, a couple collapsed onto one of the sofas. The man, in
shorts and knee socks, had a fever of drink and his blonde
companion could not hold him up. Her eyes were furious; this
was a long way from being the first time. Before I could help, a
waiter – one of the smiling Fijian giants – appeared and slung an
arm around the man's torso and steered him upstairs with the
woman, staring at each tread in front of her, following.

Next morning I was pleased to see that the General had

been unsuccessful in his attempt to become chairman of the Fiji Rugby Union, defeated by sixty-nine votes to nine. I went into town.

Sluttish mynas shrilled in the gardens by the waterfront, having driven out all the other birds. There was a story I wanted to follow, and at the Pattersons office I booked a ticket for Savusavu, a day's steaming across the Koro Sea. The ferry left at midnight in three days' time.

I took a taxi to the forest to get away from Fijians everywhere asking me if I liked Fiji and the mynas that conducted all their business in public. I walked to a waterfall over trees eaten with white mould which fell, consumed but intact, under their own weight. An air force of insects patrolled the air. Mustard-coloured hornets droned past over the heads of giant mosquitoes, and the engines of dragonflies puttered in the leaf canopy. The valley rang along its length with the stereophonic variations of cicadas.

At the Wailoku store I bought a glass of sasparilla for 20 cents. Handwritten signs said 'No credit' and 'No sitting'. The store stocked candies in a jar, Benson & Hedges and tinned mackerel, flour and pulses. There was an empty Wrigleys display unit and an empty shelf labelled 'Horror', 'Action' and 'Karate'.

I sat outside on the step. A small woman on the other side of fifty came and sat next to me, polished and creaseless as teak. I complimented her on the appearance of the village, a string of tidy wooden houses, some with green lawns.

She sniffed. 'We are not Methodist here,' she said. 'We are Anglican.' She paused. 'We are not Fijian, you see. We are from the Solomons. We lease this land from the Fijians.'

She had told the story many times before, but it was a good story. Her great-grandfather and great-grandmother had been kidnapped by blackbirders from Malaita in the Solomon Islands, to work for nothing on the sugar plantations. Some of them had been taken to Queensland, some had ended up in this fertile valley of rich red soil, where flooding regularly made life impossible, neither emancipated in Fiji nor wanted back by the Solomons government.

'In the Solomons they *think*, you see, we have very good lives. Fiji always *say* it is very rich.'

Her name was Vulau. She worked as a cleaner in an apartment block, rooms by the month. The Malaitans couldn't get used to the Fijian temperament, Vulau said. Fijians were used to an easy life. They never really cared to go to work unless they were ordered to by their chief.

'A Fijian is slave to his chief. Even if he is clever, he always do what the chief say. If he do not work, he say he is just waiting for chief's order. And he always get food.' It made her cross to think of all this feudalism and free food. 'In Solomons if you not work you not eat.'

The bus had failed to come. Vulau's nephew turned up in his Toyota pick-up, and we rode in the back to Suva with the fine red dust settling in the creases of our clothes. Vulau saw the problem political commentators, economists, development advisers had been arguing over. The General's Fijians were being encouraged to want it all, to envy the material wealth of the Indo-Fijians, and being told at the same time that what was good about Fiji was the chiefly system that stopped them from doing the same.

Dishevelled and thirsty, I sat in the garden of the Grand Pacific with a beer and watched the sun go down over Suva bay, like a street lamp going on in reverse: white light that congealed to yellow, then opalescent orange and a deepening pink that lingered before abandoning the sky to its steep gradient of darkness.

In the swimming pool a woman in a black swimsuit – I recognised the blonde hair, piled up to keep it dry – swam slowly up and down. The mynas were almost still. Long after it was dark I could still see her moving through the water, a pale sleek head above the black and noiseless ripples.

The course of fate runs strong and straight through most of history. At the beginning of every tragedy, the elements are all in place; they only need time to combine into disaster or chaos or stalemate, or all three. But add good intentions, and fate gets more imaginative.

Everyone agreed, from the *Times* to modern Fijians, that Fiji's first governor, Sir Arthur Gordon, had been the model of a colonial ruler. Gordon had gone out of his way to protect Fijians from brutal white planters. He preserved the chiefly system and, inspired by his success in the West Indies, he brought in the Indian labourers, the 'whores of capitalism', to do the back-breaking work on the cane estates, allowing the Fijians to continue their life of idle subsistence.

All this was no doubt to his credit. But Gordon was an ingenious career diplomat, and knew how to watch his back. The real work fell to his chief adviser, John Bates Thurston. Thurston would have known what Vulau was talking about, although his sympathies lay with the fragile culture:

> No man dreams of making a garden, or building a house, for the simple reason that he does not feel himself to have any individual existence. He is only one of a brotherhood or family and can only think and act with its other members. His wants must be made known to his chief, who discusses the matter with the ... old men of the village, and they decide what shall be done. If a garden is to be made, or a house is to be built the whole village assembles and the work is done. But for a man to attempt doing anything of the sort for himself is from a Fijian point of view either ridiculous or insolent.

Thurston had started out as a cotton planter on the island of Taveuni. He ended up in Suva, after Gordon's departure, as governor. He had a clear brow and a pessimist's mouth that turned down at the corners, but he radiated firmness of purpose. No man was more hated by the white settlers. They hated him for his sympathy with the Fijians and, rough, racist and opportunistic, they hated him for his intelligence and insight too. 'I do not think,' he wrote to a friend, 'that I have a white friend in the country.'

The colony had a bad beginning. Within a year, a measles epidemic killed 40,000 of the 150,000 population. The *Fiji Times* insinuated that Thurston had contrived the outbreak to cut the native population. For ten years he bore the brunt of the white men's complaints about the administration. Most planters came from Australia with all their reflexes intact. They had serious opinions, strongly held, on: property (a nigger had no right to it); work (serfdom was what blackfellows were for); and death (extermination had its place). In 1885, eleven years after annexation, the *Australian Handbook* described Fijians as 'a cowardly, untruthful race, lazy and tricky' with the reservation that 'with a very little management the white man could make them subserviently useful'. Twenty years later the picture hadn't changed. The *Cyclopedia of Fiji* published in 1907 quoted planters and managers who, in the words of one of them, Percy Lyons, had 'not a high opinion of the Fijian as a labourer, considering that he is a lazy, good-for-nothing fellow'.

Thurston had to wait three years to be made colonial secretary. Sir Arthur Gordon, mixing benevolence freely with careerism, was a man of lurking personal uncertainties who hungered for praise and a peerage and mistrusted his adviser's fixity. The architect of modern Fiji was inspired and practical – and two-faced: in 1889, as governor of Ceylon, he was informed that his successor was to be Sir Arthur Havelock, his former

ADC. He wrote in his diary: 'Havelock is an actor, insincere, selfish and a humbug...' To the new governor he wrote: '...it is *such* a relief... to know that a gentleman and lady are coming here...' Gordon could easily have met Conrad, and been the man to provoke him into the explanation of diplomacy that Heyst, the wanderer of the archipelago, gives to the girl he falls in love with: 'A diplomatic statement, Lena, is a statement of which everything is true but the sentiment which seems to prompt it.'

A hundred and twenty years on, fate had thrown a sharp bend in the too well-organised course of things. The Indo-Fijians had become the scapegoat in a power struggle in which the chiefs and caciques of Lau still held the upper hand against the west of the country, and that elite, always susceptible to invitations to vanity, had allowed Fiji's democracy to wither in the name of Fijian racial superiority.

When a Fijian chief was first shown a globe, he looked with pleasure on it until asked to contrast Fiji with Asia or America, when his joy ceased and he acknowledged with a forced smile, 'Our land is not larger than the dung of a fly.'

On rejoining his friends, he told them what the white man had shown him. Scoffing, he pronounced the globe 'a lying ball'.

19

A weekend in Suva

The next morning I went to see a man who had connections in the motor trade.

Krishna Datt, the secretary-general of the Labour-led Coalition, changed his car every two or three weeks. He said he felt safer that way. Three years before, he had had the use of a government car as the Minister of Foreign Affairs in Dr Bavadra's government for a month and a day.

Now Krishna lived on his nerves. He sat in a borrowed office above an upholsterer's outside Suva and said:

'Mara knew all about the coup. The Americans knew all about the coup. Some people thought they actually carried it out. I don't think they did, but I can tell you there were some strange white men hanging around Suva at the time. This fellow William Paupe who worked for USAID used to go around barefoot and hand out licorice jelly beans in his office. He was supposed to be administering rural aid programmes and some military aid. He served in Vietnam for ten years when USAID was collaborating with the CIA. Bavadra had evidence he was financing Taukei opposition to the Coalition.'

The Taukei was a lunatic fringe of Fijian nationalists. One of their leaders (also the secretary-general of Ratu Mara's Alliance party) had boasted that his movement's dedication to the cause of indigenous Fijians was similar to the Nazis' dedication to the German people.

Krishna said: 'The Americans and the French were Fiji's only friends after the coup. The French are showering Mara and the Army with gifts, and the US are steadily pouring money in. They have been looking at the deep-water harbour at Savusavu as a base, and further up the coast at Natewa Bay, even surveying the market-garden potential for provisioning.

'Nobody knows for sure what is going on. For a country whose problems are supposed to be internal, there are an awful lot of spooks around here.'

He drove me to the centre of Suva in a dusty gold Nissan. White Renault trucks with 'France-Fiji Cooperation' on the side and empty apart from a couple of soldiers, kept appearing in the procession of Mitsubishis, Holdens and Fords. They stood out for their note of chic as much as anything else.

Krishna said, 'The French donated fifty-three trucks for rural development. They went straight to the Army. You'll never see them in the country.'

Later I asked a taxi driver what the soldiers were doing in the trucks. He waved his hand angrily. 'They just fucking messing around. They got nothing else to do.'

After the edge had gone off the midday heat I walked down Victoria Parade to the museum and botanical gardens. The flamboyants spread their feathered leaves and red blooms and cast ripples of shade. They came from Madagascar, but everywhere the civil servants went in the Tropics they took the red flamboyants with them.

In the museum, next to a double war canoe, was a yellowing typewritten caption bearing a précis of Polynesian navigation. Land clouds, bird zones, swell patterns were all watched for, along with the mysterious flashes of light in the depths. The best navigator, it was said, would 'sit in the water for a sensitive reading of the land swell, sensing its character through his scrotum'.

Another caption, beneath some stained brown cloth like bookbinder's gauze, informed the visitor that circumcision was widespread. After the operation (I imagined the colonial officer's wife typing briskly on the government Remington), tribes kept the bandages in the temple, and in war used them as a slow match to fire enemy villages. Captured opponents were dragged to the temple with the drum sounding; around them the women danced the death dance and sexually abused the victims' bodies.

Outside a Fijian in a torn green rugby shirt fell into step alongside me.

'Do you like Fiji?' He hugged himself and growled and hit my shoulder with his clenched fist.

'You married?' he said.

'No.'

'You had Fijian girl?'

'No.'

He tapped his breastbone.

'I can fix it for you. In two hours.'

'No thanks.'

'My sister is very nice girl.'

'Oh well, if it's your sister... no thank you.'

The next day was Sunday. The comprehensive decrees enacted after the coups under the influence of the Methodist church had been relaxed, and a few taxis discreetly plied for trade. Suva was otherwise a ghost town.

In the warm afternoon I walked across the playing fields of Albert Park to the service quarter. The leafy streets lined with traveller's palms and frangipani, the verges watered and sprung with lawn, were a grid of diplomatic and consultancy addresses: the supplanters of British colonial officers. Since the coups, Krishna had told me, the capital had swarmed with consultants and advisers. The waiting list for houses in the quarter was long.

I walked past the long frontage, manned by a single sullen sentry, of the President's residence. Anglo-Indian in design, it sat behind a line of royal palms and a brake of dark evergreens. It had originally been the Governor-General's house; now the same man was named President and a new chainlink fence ran the length of the perimeter. Inside, it was said to be an unholy mess.

The brick and clapboard bungalows with their cracked concrete drives, a strip of lawn running down the middle; the royal palms and Queensland umbrella trees; the men in knee socks; the silence of Albert Park, the chipped cream paint of the spectators' stand, the smell of hot grass: it was as complete a montage of the Sundays of my Australian childhood as it could be.

I sat on the grass. When it showed 4.30, the clock on Government Building struck the quarter. I heard the half and the three-quarters, and at 5.15 it finally struck the hour's chimes.

20
Good Earning!

The enterprising firm of Lever Bros., manufacturers of
Sunlight Soap, own the island of Rabi... Its shores are
studded with cocoanut palms and the richest tropical
vegetation, while the hills are clothed with ferns, forest
trees, shrubs and flowers, in the wildest luxuriance and
beauty. Attention is devoted almost exclusively to the
production of the cocoanut, and the output of copra ex-
ceeds 400 tons per annum. The manager for Messrs. Lever
Bros. is Mr Percy Lyons.

Cyclopedia of Fiji, 1907

Suva had begun to feel like Nouméa. Its suburban lawns bored
me. The smiling politeness of the Fijians and their unwillingness
to think about the future were giving me the willies. The papers
said little, the politicians nothing, the people always asked the
same questions and would not answer any new ones: I had found
exactly the same tedium I had been unable to dispel at home.
Was this the way you always ended up? To be on the move was
a necessity as well as a relief. At least you smelt different air,
your mind went off on its own excursions, the new evenings
lengthened or shortened like the odds at a poker game.

Pattersons' MV *Ovalau* lurched against the wharf outside
Suva, a greasy packet with rusting, filthy decks and toilets you
couldn't get within five metres of without gagging. Cardboard
boxes, pandanus mats, suitcases, sportsbags, laundry bags and
string packages were piled to the ceiling, walling out the scant
late-evening breeze. I found a tiny section of unoccupied bench.
From the deserted bridge wafted the strains of 'The Blue

Danube'.

Rabi was at the other end of the islands. The ferry took twenty-four hours to Savusavu on Vanua Levu. Then it was a matter of a bus and taking my chances. It was just another remote knob of forest and hills, but there was a strange history to the place – a peculiar story of a fortune made and an island lost – that I wanted to follow. If Fiji was the paradigm of a humanely run colony, this was its mirror. Sir Arthur Gordon, being the man he was, was involved in both.

The island had been bought and sold several times over. Flirting with island plantations, Lord Lever picked it up with several others and then, in the Depression, when the Belgian Congo offered better returns and more corruptible supervision, he tired of it. In 1941 Rabi was sold for 25,000 pounds to the people of Ocean Island, 2200 kilometres north-west of Fiji. They needed an island because the war had given Britain, in the form of the British Phosphate Commissioners, the perfect opportunity to deny them their own.

The story started with Albert Ellis. In the 1890s Ellis was supercargo of a guano steamer when, on Ocean Island, he discovered the purest phosphate of lime ever found in a natural state. On the recommendation of Lord Stanmore (Arthur Gordon had got his peerage) the island was swiftly annexed in 1901. Two strange circumstances surrounded this. Lord Stanmore was also chairman of the Pacific Phosphate Company, and later helped push through legislation ignoring his own law against the sale of native land. And the island lease, like Fiji's Deed of Cession, was a fake, this time tricked out of eager and coopera-tive, but illiterate, chiefs. Gentle and obliging, the islanders put their signatures to further pieces of legalese incomprehensible to them. They had no idea that the mining of the fossilised fertiliser was going to quarry their island into dust.

In *A Pattern of Islands* Arthur Grimble told the story of the fabulous mineral of Ocean Island (the islanders called their

home Banaba). The phrase he used was 'the romance of the Company'. What he did not say in his creation of a Pacific arcadia was that, as resident commissioner in 1928, when the land the company had already bought was mined out, he had been asked to persuade the islanders to sell more land. He carried out the sleazy task with his usual zeal, writing to the people of the village of Buakonikai that if they did not sign the new agreement, their land would be compulsorily purchased, and in a postscript threatening the destruction of their village.

In 1928 the company wanted only 150 acres. Eventually of course they wanted the lot. Rabi was bought, with the Banabans' own money, and the islanders arrived from the Equator in the middle of the cyclone season and slept, and died, in makeshift tents. They came because the British Phosphate Commissioners had made them a promise that they could return home in two years. The BPC had no intention of keeping their promise.

The *Ovalau* sailed at one o'clock. It was like a slow boat to hell. The ferry bucketed through a downpour and absolute blackness, while from the bridge came snatches of endless Viennese waltzes, as if to lull us into acceptance of whatever ghastliness awaited us. Fijians slept on every available centimetre of floor. All night my head banged against the rusty bulkhead.

Just after dawn we came in stern-to under sinking clouds at an island where the fan of palms stretched across the hillside like chased aluminium. A Fijian I hadn't noticed asleep beneath my bench sat up and offered me some fried fish in a banana leaf. I couldn't cope with the gamy taste and I went on deck to watch the leeward sides of the islands slip by in sunshine, while their windward sides were erased by a fine mesh of rain.

A woman from Nadi said, 'I wanted to see what the ferry was like. Never again.' She was an old-style Fijian beauty – shining thick hair and high cheekbones – with a small daughter whose hair was silky and wafted around her. The girl's skin was the colour of hazelnut and her name was Mariana. I wondered if she had any Scottish ancestors.

'Her great-great-grandfather was John Ferguson,' said her mother proudly.

In the wild islands women were always more or less at a discount. John Ferguson, a trader from Wallis with an unkind hand, had run down to the Koro Sea in his pygmy schooner and bought Mariana's great-great-grandmother for a shotgun. Two daughters were born before the mother worked up the courage and the means to get away.

Back on her island there was trouble. The daughters grew up with the good looks of mixed blood, exciting the jealousy of their pure-blooded rivals. They were *luve ni masimasi*, 'children of a rusty gun'. It meant as good as nothing. But in the end beauty could not be resisted. Married to chiefs' sons and with dispositions as kind as their father's had been unkind, the daughters gave no opportunity for fault to be found. Mariana was 1/16th Scottish. She was going to an Indian school.

'With Indian children there they work hard,' her mother said. At eight her daughter could speak Fijian, Hindustani and English.

There was island after island. At one the wharf was daubed in bazaar colours: a hundred islanders waiting for their kerosene supplies and their relatives, sandwiched between the haphazard forest and the water that shifted from aquamarine to chrysoprase. On deck I noticed a well-dressed Polynesian, his skin as smooth as malt extract, paying no attention to the coming and going around him. He lay full-length on a bench and played 'The Happy Wanderer' on his harmonica ten times without stopping.

The last conversation I had on the ferry was with another Fijian, tall and polite. He was an army corporal on his way to Drekeniwai, the General's home village, with a Renault truck full of cassava, flour and biscuits. The truckload of food, he confirmed proudly, came from army stores. It was a great privilege to be delivering this free food for the army commander.

Savusavu bay finally appeared at dusk, then vanished again in squalls and darkness. Half a mile from the wharf I found a room at a Seventh Day Adventist guesthouse. The owner was a pleasant Indo-Fijian who directed me to the rules of the house. They concluded: 'Good Luck! if you are working, and Good Earning! if you are on a business trip.'

After twenty-four hours without a bed or a wash, I fell asleep at the table on the verandah, watching the big dusty moths blunder into the light and the geckos ripple across the ceiling and the toads come in out of the rain.

The Adventists' motto was over the breakfast table as I bolted cold fried eggs and onions. 'Christ is the head of this house, the Unseen Guest at every meal, the Silent Listener to every conversation.' The influence of the invisible patriarch-spy was the unifying factor to the room. Several portraits of Him decorated walls covered in a green gloss frieze of hand-painted tropical blooms. Illustrated medical charts obliterated other areas of this jungle, some, on the subject of feeding your baby correctly, that conjured the unprecedented spectacle of a working Fijian mother on a business trip into the bush with her unweaned child. Others revolved inevitably around the perils of drink. The table was strewn with hibiscus blooms and art-deco table mats advertising French bicycles. The delicious cocoa served with breakfast (tea and coffee, for their stimulant qualities, were also on the Adventists' Index) was served in a Barbie-doll mug.

Savusavu was a town built to the specification of someone who had misremembered the concept, with more churches than shops and acres of empty lots in between. It was a town of a thousand people and from the wharf to the post office was over six kilometres.

On the opposite side of the street the bus, dusty and windowless, sat at the edge of a perfect calm bay, the peanut boys circling it lazily. A man in spectacles read a book with a green spine entitled *Is This Life Really All There Is?* and behind him was the malt-skinned man with the harmonica. The driver, gaunt and with trembling fingers, snapped off a yellow ticket from a perspex board that held forty different categories of fare. To judge by some of the books of tickets, curled up and darkened by dust, at least a dozen categories of passenger were expected but never appeared.

The hundred-kilometre journey, taken at bone-shattering speed over the rocks of the coral road, took four hours. The bus travelled this stretch twice a day and had the characteristics of every Pacific bus I travelled on. Serviced only when it broke down, driven by a master of improvisation, it would go on beyond any reasonable estimate of its endurance until, one day, with exhausted springs, burned-out valves, paper-thin pistons, wrecked transmission and sagging chassis, not another kilometre could be forced out of it. It set out in a rickety sunlit cathedral of palm plantations; it rattled to a halt on a road no wider than itself between black cliffs and the sea. Occasionally a villa was glimpsed behind a screen of dracaenas and frangipani: a drive, a planter's prospect over the sea, a single-storey clapboard house with rooms twenty foot square. Halfway through the journey it had been forced off the road to let an empty white Renault truck past.

Tebabati and his family waited in the shade. 'The boat will come soon,' he said, and took out his harmonica. 'You will stay with me tonight and tomorrow I will take you to see the last old man of Ocean Island.'

The four villages of Ocean Island had been resurrected on Rabi, and it was a forty-minute crossing in a plywood boat to the new Buakonikai. At a distance it looked more pleasant than I expected: in the fresh breeze I watched the steep bottle-green hills approach and the antic conduct of outriggers on the blobby sea.

Mildewed by forty years of winter storms, Tebabati's house stood among trees he had planted himself: breadfruit, banana and pungent falling blooms of ylang-ylang. From the fire on the beach drifted the smell of burning sandalwood.

Tebabati split a coconut and sectioned out the white meat. It was satisfying, cool and sweet. The income from copra was all they had here, but what fell or was cut from the remnants of Lord Lever's plantation seemed bereft of any economic power. The economics, in fact, worked in reverse, as copra was a nega-tively price-sensitive commodity. If you wanted more, you lowered the price. The islanders, seeing their incomes reduced, cut more. And the economic circle was bizarre. The tree of life gave the islanders almost everything they needed – water, sugar, carbohydrate, wood, rope, thatch, matting (and booze: Tebabati offered me a mug of fermented toddy – palm-flower sap – that tasted like glue and sulphur). But they sold what they cut for near to nothing, and somewhere along the line, after the trade-up and the makers of cheap oil and soap, the cosmetic and food companies, up popped governments and explosives manufacturers on another planet of values. The tree of life and death: it had a sort of wacky neatness. If you want to get on, see a man in a boater with a purple hydrangea.

I felt suddenly relaxed and stupid with tiredness. Life was makeshift and the people had less to offer than I anticipated, but Tebabati offered what he had immediately without hint of payment. It was something like a natural state, generous, simple and unhurried. You couldn't really care a damn about Suva here.

Rabi had its advantages, but Tebabati still wanted to go back to Ocean Island. 'When the breadfruit tree didn't fruit, we threw gravel into the branches at the full moon. I would like to throw gravel into the holes in Ocean Island and make the trees grow again. But that is all that is left. Gravel and holes.'

A thousand and three people were dumped on Rabi in the winter of 1945. Now there were around 5000 on the island. After school, children appeared everywhere like the black crabs that sidled in their thousands onto the rocks at low tide. We went for a walk at sunset to exhibit the visitor. At the far end of the golden track was a massive Methodist church with a green tin roof and a central tower, the size of a small Spanish cathedral. But Tebabati was another Seventh Day Adventist and took me instead to see a young woman in a house across the street.

Tall as a candle and high-cheekboned, no more than twenty, she stood framed in the doorway, dressed in a blue *lava lava* and white singlet. On the wall behind her head I could see the framed Adventists' motto. She smiled as they talked about the building of the new Seventh Day church and Tebabati's trip to Suva and other things.

Unlike Gauguin's Polynesians, 'having nothing, nothing at all to do, thinking of one thing only, drinking', she breathed the health that was the result of avoiding all intoxicants. She was stunningly beautiful. I wanted to run my fingers down the sense-heaven of her cheek and long neck. At the same time she was disappointingly unreal, as if she had undergone a spiritual leuco-tomy to excise all the outlawed passions.

'The eyes of the women especially are full of expression and fire,' Joseph Banks wrote about the Polynesians he met. This woman's eyes were black and limpid, lovely – and quenched. I cursed the Silent Listener all the way back to the village, and again later that evening when she came to Tebabati's house to sing the evening hymns, serene and glorious and pasteurised.

The room smelt of coconut oil and mildew.

The general offices were at the other end of Rabi between the police station and the wharf, where a stone commemorated the arrival of Sir Albert Ellis in 1948 to greet the Banabans in their new home.

On his first visit to Ocean Island in 1900 Ellis wrote of 'a scene of impressive pristine beauty... All the vegetation was growing in the phosphate.' After the second world war sentiment provoked this tribute to the outstanding loyalty of the islanders: 'We have a responsibility towards these fine native people [they were left behind when the Japanese invaded, and 463 died]... In this respect more frequent visits of HM Warships, always an eventful occasion, would be deeply appreciated and serve as an evidence of the ties that bind the Empire together.' The primitive conditions on Rabi 'would doubtless stimulate their spirit of adventure... wild cattle and wild pigs are said to be numerous...

When the natives learn to shoot these or catch them with dogs, their food supplies will be greatly improved, apart from the excitement of the chase.'

By 1950 the BPC had exported tens of millions of tons of phosphate from Ocean Island. Beneath the memorial stone where Albert Ellis had first stepped onto Rabi was the footprint of a spiv.

The hot air lapped sluggishly through the louvres of Mr Kaiekieki Sigrah's office. He sat with its entire contents on his desk, thick quarter-bound ledgers whose pages were covered with double-columned, handwritten figures, the last of them heavily altered and crossed out.

I apologised for disturbing him without an appointment. In 1976 the Banabans had won a High Court action in London for compensation for the devastation of their land, and secured 5 million pounds. At the same time they lost a case for breach of trust against the British Government, which had paid eighty-five per cent of their royalties to the Gilbert and Ellice Islands government and sold the phosphate at less than the world price.

Mr Sigrah, the last old man of Ocean Island, smiling shyly and wearing Toyota spectacles, knew there was worse than that.

'We had an agreement from 1946 onwards for an extra royalty of twopence per ton which went up by three and a half per cent every three months. It was written in the deeds that I kept in my office. One day the BPC assistant manager walked in and took them.'

He gestured at the spidery ruled lines of figures, the magic repeating figure of three and a half per cent. A pocket calculator lay next to his trembling, branchy hand.

'I am working through year by year. I am up to 1957. I don't know exactly, I think by now they owe us about 50 million pounds. We really just want Ocean Island back, but this is all I can do.'

'Did you ever meet Grimble and Ellis?'

'One day in 1932 I saw Grimble in the street and caught his sleeve. He said, "Yes what is it?" "We want to know, sir, if we can go overseas for further education." Grimble said he must call the old men. A few days later he made a speech to them in the *maneaba*. "You old men," he said, "perhaps you have a son or a nephew here," and he waved his finger at the young men with me. "Now they come to say they want to go overseas to further their education, and they ask for your permission. But when they come back, they will only work for themselves, not for you. What do you say to them?" Of course we did not go.

'It is good to have a visitor from England. You are not a lawyer by any chance? No? That is a shame, but never mind. Perhaps you know a lawyer?'

It had taken the Banabans years to mount their earlier High Court actions, and involved the scrutiny of 10,000 documents. The council members were now uninterested in pursuing new compensation claims. Mr Sigrah scorned their apathy and said he would stand in the new council elections.

It did not trouble him that it would be impossible to reopen litigation with an old man's memory as the only evidence. His obsession sprang from the synaptic tumult of many obsessions, from the encoded memory of injustice undreamt-of. I promised to write the story down.

I thought: Either he is a champion fighting for the dignity and rights of his people, or he is a half-crazed old man drawing up lists of meaningless figures in an airless, mildewed room. Or both.

The Adventist diet was a special test of tolerance. I failed it and, after picking at dried fish and plantain, went to my room and washed down half a packet of biscuits with whisky.

We sat on pandanus mats in the bare main room, in which the only furniture was a 1930s sideboard with a foxed mirror, while the children piped 'My God loves me' before toppling gently sideways with fatigue and sleeping where they fell.

Churches were being built everywhere on the island. Tebabati's wife and sister-in-law had been at a prayer meeting that afternoon and returned with a tale that confirmed their faith. A Baha'i man, enraged at the envangelising of his neighbours, had been invited to preach himself that day. Jesus, he said, was among them and needed no special treatment. 'You can jump on Him, spit on Him,' he urged. Soon after the SDA preacher had stood to deliver his counter-sermon, the Baha'i's breathing became stertorous. Two minutes later, he was dead. Tebabati roared with laughter. He had converted a few years ago, and then his brother, and now all the people they knew were Adventists. Religion was a way of finding out who your friends were.

Tebabati wouldn't admit it, but he still fermented his toddy, and he liked playing cards. I taught him *vingt et un* and then relented and showed him and the two women the principle of pelmanism. It delighted them but there was no suspense. Once a card had been turned up, that was it. I had never seen memories like it.

Raymond Burr, one of the directors of the banned *Fiji Sun*, bought a lease on a near-uninhabited island in the east Koro Sea. His habit was to get away for a Pacific villeggiatura once a year before plunging back into another series of *Ironside*. Often when he returned to Hollywood he took a young Fijian with him. On one occasion he drove the boy for twenty minutes to meet some friends who were taking him sightseeing for the day. When the sightseeing was done, it was arranged, they would leave him to meet the actor on his way home. At the end of the afternoon, however, the boy failed to turn up at the pick-up point Burr had arranged.

He waited. At home he waited and worried. It became dark

and he thought of calling the police. At ten o'clock there was a tap on the door. The Fijian boy stood on the step. How had he got back? 'By walking.' How, in the mindless grid of the city, had he known which way to walk?

'By the shape of the hills.'

21
The Planters' Club

I looked out from the terrace of the Planters' Club at Savusavu bay and thought how much the Americans would like it as a base. Locked in by hills, its broad placid surface was broached by an archipelago of wooded islands and at its edge a belt of flatland as much as five miles wide lay between sea and mountain. It was concealed and unpopulated, a place of voluptuous, Conradian secrecy where among the luxuriance you could forget your motives as easily as all your ships and weapons.

At the bar the Lepper brothers were making a profession of forgetting. Robbie had hawkish eyebrows, and stared quizzically at the beer in front of him. He was third-generation planting stock from a Yorkshire family; he couldn't recognise an English accent.

I introduced myself as a tourist from London. Robbie said:

'Ah. You're from Churchill's mob are you?'

Keith was as fat and brown as Robbie was pale and spare. They called themselves 'nutty buggers'. Neither of them had ever been to England. Keith said:

'When that duke came over after the coronation, I said to him, "One of these days I'm going to come and visit you." And he gave me a card. So I may still go.' He lived in his grandfather's house. 'He built it a hundred years ago and it's still standing. At Buca bay, the big white house on the hill.'

The club had been built thirty years before, for the wives to have somewhere to wait for the boat bringing the children back from school. It was a bungalow on stilts, roughly the size of a small plantation, and its long bar stuck out into the middle of the clubroom like a tongue. The Fiji Bitter that everyone drank came from a walk-in butcher's fridge at one end. Milly, a small brown woman with wavy hair and sparkling eyes, said, 'We haven't run out once in seven years.'

The conversation revolved around drink and escape. Copra had been falling on world markets since the end of the Thirties, when the supply routes were disrupted by the war and substitutes had to be found for the soap and nitro-glycerine markets. Whenever the planters thought it had reached rock bottom, it fell again. Now there was nowhere for the Leppers and the Simpsons, the other original family, to go. Robbie's and Keith's plantations were not large – two hundred acres – and they were just surviving. Robbie sometimes got away to Suva.

'You wouldn't know who I was with there,' he said confidentially. 'I live up, live down, depending. Trouble is, wife won't let me go too often.' By five o'clock his face sagged from drink.

In the dark I went back to the Planters' Club. The gate was locked against drunks. Robbie was still on his stool, just. The noises of the clubroom were of snooker balls colliding and the disapproving *'tut...tut...tut'* of geckos. Vaguely, deeper and fainter, the motor to the butcher's fridge hummed. Passing club members removed boxes of cold Fiji Bitter from the fridge and loaded them into Mitsubishi pick-ups.

Then Mrs Lepper arrived. She differed in her physique so wildly from Robbie that my first thought was of them in bed together. If size is a reaction to the world, they had signalled their estrangement from each other as much by their metabolism as by sitting at opposite ends of the bar, where they now were. She was dressed in huge maroon trousers and a huge floral shirt and a broad-brimmed straw hat with a flowing ribbon. Her skin was smooth from giving orders and her water retention was magnificent. She ran a small tourist resort on the plantation. One drink, and she was away down the drive saying:

'Come out and see us. We've got *bures* and miles of beach.'

'And plenty of girls,' glowered Robbie.

'And don't forget to bring a small bottle of rum for the punch at the barbecue, Robbie.'

Mrs Lepper and Milly shared the same great-grandfather, the first Mr Simpson. Milly worked three thirteen-hour shifts a week. From nine in the morning till ten at night she served beer from the fridge, listened to the same stories again and again, and kept the place shipshape. I told her I was staying at David's guesthouse and she said, 'Oh yes. David was always in here. He drank all day, every day.'

She showed me her pay packet. For thirty-nine hours a week she was paid the net equivalent of ten pounds. 'Do you think it's enough?' she whispered.

At the age of forty, unmarried, Milly had never taken the bus along the coast; had never seen the house on the hill at Buca bay; had discovered that, for all her being a cousin or niece to most of the planters, she would never be a guest.

Robbie Lepper didn't like my hugger-mugger with Milly or my addressing him as 'Robbie'. His hangover was making him angry and he sat and scowled and refused to talk. So I called him Robbie twice more and left him to his beer. I was sorry to leave. As soon as I was out of earshot I knew he would be shouting at Milly for talking about club business to a stranger.

22
Wet season

Back in Suva the General had staged a mock coup while I had been away. It had been, by all accounts, the usual stone-faced frivolities – roadblocks, razor wire, soldiers with M16s surrounding Parliament – to remind the Fijians, and maybe Ratu Mara who had manoeuvred his army commander back to barracks, that the force that mounted the first two coups was capable of carrying off a third.

In the same period the *Fiji Times* and the *Daily Post* reported: a live-firing exercise in the west of Fiji; the Army's intention to spend F$5 million on a ten-seater helicopter from France; and the General's anouncement of his intention to create a rapid deployment force on the lines of the Special Air Service. In the fortnight I had been in Fiji, he had made speeches on tourism, the constitution, the Fijian character and the role of the chiefs ('appointed by God'); he had presented annuity cheques and vowed to prevent Fijian squatters from being evicted from land owned by the university. He had turned the army commander's job into one of pundit with the intention, it seemed, of elevating it to prime minister-in-waiting. It was becoming hard to know which of his two aspects was worse, the thug or the bore.

In the British Embassy the spirit of Sir Arthur Gordon didn't care either way. The British ambassador had recently been on a New Year courtesy visit to the General's village. Afterwards, in a relatively costless piece of goodwill, he had promised the General's village F$10,000 of aid in the form of electricity, piped water and other improvements.

Fiji was under several feet of water, and the rain went on pouring: the kind of weather for running over dogs and cursing humanity. Obeying an instinct to find higher ground, I collected my bags from the Grand Pacific – with an envelope that had been hand-delivered while I was away – and took a bus to Samabula.

Lala, who ran the hotel, was a huge odalisque in a *lava lava* that kept slipping from her breasts. We did a deal on the room while her consort Brian, at least forty years older than her, sat morosely up at his bar, listening to the World Service crash out of his radio and drinking two dry martinis in quick succession. The third he poured more carefully, and sipped.

Brian had lived most of his life in the Gilberts, a place that had ravished Robert Louis Stevenson with its 'superb ocean climate, days of blinding sun and bracing wind, nights of heavenly brightness'. I knew he was an old Gilberts hand because others, not Brian, had told me. Brian's talent for silence was remarkable.

The hotel was an old colonial residence on a prospect over the bay, now a warren of corridors joined together by non-matching lino. The rooms were shiny blue or pink and the wet season had set off the dormant mildew. In the front room of white-panelled wood, students sat in overstuffed armchairs and smoked. The walls were covered with engravings, whales' teeth and Gilbertese shark's-teeth spears, and on a table stood a grog bowl that you saw everywhere, for serving the *yaqona* – powdered and suspended root of *Piper methysticum* – that everyone got high on. (When the French explorer Dumont d'Urville landed on Bau in 1832 and met the high chief Tanoa, Cakobau's father, he and his officers drank their own wine, refusing the offered *yaqona*, a diplomatic snub on a par with peering up the skirts of the chief's favourite wife.)

Lala was at her weaving. She sat in the middle of the floor on top of a ceremonial pandanus mat that spread in all directions, to which she was slowly applying a fringe of brightly coloured wools. I asked what the coming occasion was.

In a voice from the Lords commentary box, Brian said, 'My funeral.'

The Marshall Islands were to the north of Fiji, across 3000 kilometres of ocean. In the afternoon I called on all the shipping offices in Suva. The traffic was fitful and there was nothing going north. A ship for Western Samoa, due east, was coming in on the 22nd, in four weeks' time. (Another had left a few hours before.) For Vanuatu, the island group to the west that was my other flanking option, there was nothing on the schedules at all. Depressed and in a fog of indecision, I went back up the hill to Samabula and opened the envelope that had been left for me at the Grand Pacific.

It was from Miles, an expert in assembling the elements of the overstretched farce of political life in the country. This one was forty-five pages long; its opening page was stamped twice with the word 'SECRET' and five times 'CONFIDENTIAL'.

Dated 23 May 1989, it was a presentation by senior officers of the Fiji Military Forces to the President of the Republic and Prime Minister Mara, one of those pieces of sinister twaddle replicated everywhere army officers are allowed to think that a country can be run like a battalion. Solutions to problems under such circumstances are always simple. So it ran in this document. If the Coalition could not accept 'the reality and the objectives of the coup... they should be neutralised'. The judiciary was full of preconceived ideas about 'the legality of our actions... and as a result their Court rulings were in most cases biased and unfair'. The present trend, the officers said, 'will have to be stopped immediately in the interest of proper justice and fair play'. Trade unions would have to be abolished and censorship and a 'very *dynamic* government information service' imposed.

The document spoke of the external threat to Fiji from

Australia, New Zealand and India, as if one of those nations might contemplate an invasion. (It was the 'lying ball' all over again.) The Indian Embassy was to be downgraded to a consulate and the Indian Cultural Centre closed 'because it is staffed by spies'. Enemies of the state should be stripped of their citizenship; there must be a state religion; rule by decree should continue and the return to constitutional government should be delayed for fifteen years; and the military, of course, should have more executive authority.

Perhaps the most interesting provision in the programme lay in the final pages. This suggested the opening-up of immigration to Chinese farmers, to replace the Indo-Fijians (referred to as 'foreign farmers') whom the new laws and policies would have encouraged to quit the country. The prospect of Confucian peasants, or men and women forged in the economic furnace of Hong Kong, proving any less driven by industry and ambition than their predecessors added the essential flourish of comedy to this blueprint for a coconut republic.

By the morning the hotel had assumed the atmosphere of a private school that should have been closed down years ago. The showers were waterlogged and the place had sprung leaks everywhere. The drunken students from the Technical College had been up until four and Lala was in a rage of sleeplessness. Her demeanour was oddly lightened by her choice of a red sun dress with thin shoulder straps which she had failed to tie up, with the same gravitational effects as before. She lay full length on the sofa, semi-covered, muttering:

'The bastards. The bastards.'

There was thick tepid porridge for breakfast. Afterwards Lala sat up and did her hair. She tied it like a stook of black corn and lay prone on the sofa again. I asked if she could call a taxi for me.

'Yes of course. Maria,' she shouted to the kitchen. '*Maria.* Call a taxi please.'

I wanted to get back to the west to check the port at Lautoka, and then fly out if I had to. I decided to take the King's Highway north from Suva, completing the circuit of Viti Levu. In this expedition the words 'King's Highway luxury express', as the service advertised itself at the bus station by the market, typified a local preference for publicity over fact. Running every variant that could be called a road surface, the driver scorched over loose gravel and ruts and churned through mud, floods and deep subsidence for hours, at a constant speed of 80 kph. The bridges were so narrow you couldn't see their edges as the bus passed over them, and so flimsy you could feel them sway. You felt you were suspended, caught between savannah and a precipitous river valley, between dense forest and plunging ridges, in a world with no foundations.

Two breakdowns delayed us only by fifteen minutes. After the second the driver was transfigured, a being that had laboured up, with white staring eyes in an oil-smeared face, like an exorcism from the crankcase's depths.

Rakiraki on the north coast was four short streets at right angles to each other, muddy and forlorn. There was a tired market laid out beneath a giant Moreton Bay fig; a petrol station; a sugar mill; a paint store; and two miles out of town, the Rakiraki Hotel.

The sugar men were in town: a Dutch chemical engineer, an Australian turbine engineer and a valuer from Worcester. Peter, the Queenslander, had a face aged by cigarettes and a scorn for the size of Europe. 'You'd be off the end of Holland,' he said, 'before you'd got into third gear.'

After dinner we sat in the dining room alone while flying cockroaches impacted on the panelling. Peter produced a bottle of Bundaberg overproof, and told the story of how he had been pulled out of Fiji the day before the first coup by the technical manager of the Fiji Sugar Corporation. Even though he had two weeks left to go, his schedule of works was scrapped and he found himself on a plane. Waking up in Sydney the next morning, he had heard about the coup on the radio. 'The General always said he carried it out entirely on his own. He must have forgotten telling the FSC.'

The conversation strayed to Britain. By the time the rum was below the label, Peter and the Dutchman wanted to know what Mrs Thatcher was really like. Colin, the valuer, as pale as his cream shirt, stabbed his finger at the table. Her priorities were absolutely right. She knew how to save money, and she knew how to motivate the country to make money. Her councils didn't squander money, he said, on unnecessary causes.

'Like what?' asked the Dutchman.

'Like gay rights groups, for one thing.'

'Is she truly so wonderful?'

Flushed suddenly, with a devotion that was more than political, Colin nodded. 'She is the *only* man in our parliament.'

23
Five funerals

Still no sign of any ships: I rented a truck and wandered into the hills between Nadi and Lautoka, a region of feathered rows of cane and rivers and a dam high up on the torn volcanic skyline they called the Sleeping Giant.

Maloni should have been collecting firewood, but he was born under a truant sign and preferred to wave to his friends from the window of a white man's car. The firewood was for the funeral feast of his small mother – the wife of his father's brother – who had died two days earlier.

The road to the dam was impassable. When we reached the greasy Nadale river and could go no further, his small uncle, the dead woman's husband, was waiting for him. He jumped down from the cab of an old flatbed truck and cursed Maloni, waving his arms and kicking him towards the bank, where the wood had been carried by the floods. Maloni slouched off while his uncle turned to me. He would be honoured, he said, if I would come to the funeral.

In the village – two collections of cinderblock huts gathered round grass squares, the gaps between filled in by breadfruit trees, palms, and small garden borders – a cow had been slaughtered. Collops of bloody flesh hung on wires, visited by squadrons of flies, but when it was served, on the ground where the village sat waiting, men at one end of the square, women at the other, it was accompanied by chilli and lemon and cassava and braised to perfection. There was a brief disturbance as the kitchen roof collapsed; otherwise the *fête champêtre* was flawless.

After lunch and the *sevu sevu* ceremony – a moment of meditation, drinking *yaqona* that tasted like snot with cement in it, in a room with the slaughtered cow's rump and tail hanging in one corner and Holy Families and news cuttings of local boys who had made the national rugby side taped to the wall – Maloni came to say that more cassava was needed.

We took a different road. The traffic changed from tractors to horses to nothing. Five men disappeared into the canefields and I sat for three hours under a mango tree while the thunderheads gathered over the Sleeping Giant. Maloni's hands were clean when he came back, and he took no part in the loading or unloading when we returned.

Josaia, a fat boy with an apologetic expression who worked as a night porter at the Nadi Sheraton, said, 'Sorry for being so long' and, 'Sorry for speaking in our language.'

The church service was already over and the committal was about to begin, on a mound already covered with rough concrete tombs. Maloni's small mother was in her forties and had died of a heart attack. Through the glass pane in the top of the plywood coffin, her face was shockingly grey. The ceremony was simple, the sort of thing you would find in an English village churchyard on an overcast afternoon, with a few variations: the choirmaster passed round the Benson & Hedges between hymns, and at every stage I found myself pushed forward, almost on top of the coffin, to take photographs. Weighed down by mats and mulberry-bark cloth, the coffin was handed to four pallbearers – one had the word 'Luv' tattooed on his shoulder – wearing blue *sulus* and grass armlets and necklaces. They filled in the earth and planted a bough of frangipani at each corner of the grave, and it was over.

Fifty metres away, while the burial was going on, the village boys had slaughtered another cow. They wanted my truck to carry it to the village square. So another body was manhandled into position. Maloni was the butcher-boy, Josaia said; inevitably it was all the others who were red to the elbows.

Leaving the guts in the bush, I drove back up the main path. The square was a curious scene. The lawn was strewn with piles of funeral gifts from the dead woman's parents on the chief's side of the village, each heap including a five-gallon drum of kerosene, several mats and a length of decorated *tapa* cloth. In front of these lay the corpses of another cow and calf, both headless, as if they were surreally tired and unable to go a step further.

That day nobody, save Maloni, had done anything for themselves which was not also for the village. I tried to imagine what John Thurston would have made of it. A realist, he would probably have been surprised that the communal ideal had survived so long against outside influences, and depressed at the quality of the influences that were slowly altering it. They were easily guessed: videos; beer; cigarettes; eager thoughts of other consumer desires to be fulfilled.

But if the appeal of traditional communities comes from their means of expression, what was missing was more reveal-

ing. When I asked Josaia on what occasions the village performed their *mekes* – the dancing for which Fijians were once famous
– he answered that the bus came every Saturday and took them
to the Mocambo Hotel where they performed for three dollars
each.

If you wanted to see Fijian culture without self-conscious-
ness, I thought, it was much the same as at home. Funerals were
more enjoyable than weddings by a long way.

Except for the bereaved.

Adi Kuini Bavadra, Dr Timoci's widow, said 'Come' when I
phoned her the next day.

Beneath the steep thatched roof of her *bure* at Viseisei,
between the coast road and the sea, was an ecclesiastical calm.
Furnished with a mixture of Fijian artifacts and late Victorian
woodwork, the long room was a continuous excursion between
two styles and practices into which stray sunbeams bounced and
gleamed.

Tea and muffins were served on the mahogany desk
between us by an aproned helper who stooped as she left. Since
her husband's death four months earlier from precocious cancer,
Adi Kuini had taken over the leadership of the Coalition Party.
She was a chief's daughter and cousin to Mara and the President.
The blood line was supposed to help heal the rift between east
and west Fiji, but the men were not playing. In the framed
photographs behind her – in all his pictures – Dr Bavadra looked
too honest for politics.

Mrs Bavadra was the first Fijian I had met who had
preserved herself from unswerving acceptance of her people's
faults. She was tall and straight, with the solemn poise that was
the outward Fijian mark of power – in the old photographs of the
chiefs it was a reminder of their enthusiasm for war – and she
had come out of mourning a fortnight before.

'Very soon Rabuka and Ratu Mara will have to explain to the people. The majority of the chiefs still want to retain their link with the Crown. You notice that even now, in a republic, we still observe Prince Charles' birthday? Can you believe that?'

She was sure that most people in Fiji were sincere about democratic principles. Sixty thousand people had come to her husband's funeral. But they needed guidance and were not getting it.

'It's sad to say this, but the Fijian people are incapable of sticking to their word. You will come across a minority of Fijians who are steady, but the majority are very fickle.

'We seem to be finding a great difficulty for some of our chiefs to adjust to the money economy. The Tui Viti, Ratu Sukuna, died penniless without even a house for his widow to live in because he distributed to his people everything he was given. Now Ratu Mara is the richest man in Fiji. A few of our chiefs who get lease money and royalties spend hundreds and hundreds of dollars at the bar. I have to explain to our supporters that the chiefs don't know how to get Fiji out of this mess, so what they do is go and drink in order to forget.'

She gave me the vistor's book to sign. I scribbled a signature beneath that of the British ambassador and his wife.

Mrs Bavadra frowned at the memory of the ambassador's visit. Her voice slipped into a harsher register. She urged me, if I had any friends in the government in London, to get rid of him.

'He goes to Rabuka's village,' she said angrily, 'he comes here to my house and sits and tells me that "these Indians" have to understand. He invites Rabuka to dinner.

'But you only have to look at his c.v. Grammar school, then straight into the army, then Foreign Office. What can you expect? They send us this kind of man as ambassador, because *that* is what they think of us.'

I was getting used to waiting. You had to remember that it wasn't something you did between activities, but an activity in itself.

I admitted defeat and booked a flight to Vanuatu, the old Anglo-French diarchy of the New Hebrides. It was a circuitous escape route, but I had two reasons for heading west: I wanted to see the colony that had been messily abandoned a decade before; and it was just possible that there would be cargo heading north from its capital, Port Vila.

There were three days to kill. In the mornings I swam in the murky water of Nadi bay; I tried all the Chinese restaurants in town; at nights I drank too much Fiji Bitter. These seemed to be the things everyone did: they were most people's idea of a holiday.

One afternoon I rented the taxi of an old man whose knuckles shook on the steering wheel, and asked him if he could take me to a cane farmer's house. The house we arrived at overflowed with commercial impulses: it was also a small hotel and a supermarket and a video rental shop. I was placed like an ornament on a chair in the middle of the shop. Sporting the moustaches of Bombay movie corsairs, the man's sons stood behind a counter of teetering, dusty jars and plastic jewellery.

We grinned foolishly at each other for twenty minutes. Then their father arrived, a man in his sixties with an air of distracted deference. He took me into a back room hung with pink and green gauzes to give me sweet tea and *golubjamon*. He was happy to talk as long as I didn't use his name.

'Very hot, very very hard work,' he said. 'I cut. I plant, add sulphate of ammonia, phosphate, I harrow, weed, cut the grass and spray as well. We all help each other, though sometimes there are vendettas between the farmers and the cane is set on fire.

'At the end of the season the last stands are so full of hornets and dust the farmers fire their own cane to get it over with. A farmer cannot get rich on cane. He cannot depend on cane unless he farms other things like rice and beans.'

He apologised for being out when I arrived. He too had been at a funeral.

'Indian people worry very much for their rights. It is a sickness. Since the last coup too many Indians are dying from worry.

'Today I cremated a friend, forty years old. Yesterday I cremated a man of the same age. The day before I cremated another friend, also young. Three people in the last three days.'

That evening at the hotel, I talked to a lanky blue-eyed Australian who sold diving holidays.

'What are you doing here?'

'I'm wandering around.'

We both looked at my notebook open on the table.

Later the hotel-owner came to my room and suggested politely that I didn't speak to the Australian again. He, the owner, had no objection to my reason for being there, but the diving operator had been going around the lounge warning people that I was a troublemaker.

This was what was wrong with life for the Indo-Fijians. You were all right if you didn't like or dislike things too much. If you dissented, things could quickly turn ugly. (Even book-reviewing was a dangerous game. The academic who had given a bad review to the General's autobiography, *No Other Way*, had been beaten up and set loose, blindfolded, on the Suva golf course at night to be chased by soldiers with loaded rifles.)

The surface of life was as bland as a commercial, and if you were happy when the sun shone, and when there was a grog bowl or a drinks waiter nearby, then Fiji was the place for you. I hated it. The world was full of torture for fun, conspiracies of silence, cruelty much worse than this dullness. But people -- tourists and Fijians -- wandered around in teeshirts that said 'Don't worry -- Be happy' and I wanted to shoot them.

24
Once a condominium

The iron was still moving at the bottom of the sea. I had just left
a message at the prime minister's office in Port Vila when the
ground began to shake, and Rossi's Hotel, a low white building
on the lip of the bay that needed less paint than most buildings in
the town, sat up for several seconds and then shrugged itself
back into position.

I asked the Rossi's barman if the tremors were common.
He had a dancer's fluttering fingers and tiny hips, and the raw
eyes of a man who enjoyed his grog.

'Raon bout once a month,' he said, rolling his eyes and
laughing. 'Sometimes they come ten in one hour, with noise like
tam-tams. But cyclone is worst,' he added, his shot eyes widen-
ing until I had to look away, 'like one in 1987 that took off every
roof in Vila.'

It was five past six. The prime minister's special secretary,
a woman with the distant courtesy of the political associate who
had too many calls on her time, had told me to phone again the
following week if I wished to speak with Father Lini. This suited
my plans. Scrawled on a pink ticket in my hand was the departure time – seven p.m. – of a coaster which was heading south
that night from the capital.

Port Vila's recent history was written in its commerces and
street names: Churchill Avenue, Bougainville Street, La Pérouse
Street; Pâtisserie La Plantation, La Cave des Gourmets, Ma
Barker's Restaurant, the obligatory shop, wherever the French
went, selling Parisian lingerie, the Burns Philp supermarket. The
Australians had come as planters and cattlemen, followed by
time-served convicts from New Caledonia. The islands had been

ruled from 1906 to 1980 under a priggish alliance of joint French and British interests that more often resembled the last skirmish of the Hundred Years' War than a serious attempt to govern a colony.

Ten years after independence, Vila had a macaronic air of gentle chaos and disrepair that made it an exotic among far-blooming cities. The town was half-empty. Buildings fell down on the waterfront. The French had left behind a taste for burgundy and good coffee, and the ni-Vanuatu, conscious that white men squabbled among themselves, smiled. The sluggish, pot-holed streets were laid out to the west and recalled the European taste for sunsets.

As the light bled into gold over the waterfront Albert poured me another beer. Behind him the sign in *bislama* read, 'No gat shirt. No gat shoes. No gat service.' I was enjoying its concision when, in one of those moments in which panic is mixed with the knowledge that your education has taken a step forward, I happened to look out over the terrace. The listing, rusty hull of a coaster was bobbing slowly across the bay.

Calmly, I asked Albert, 'Does the *Adela* always leave early?'

The red eyes widened once more.

'You suppose to go on *Adela*?' He leapt out from behind the bar and bore me into the street, yelling at the traffic for a cab.

'She stop at Ifira. You get on there.' He said something in *bislama* to a cab driver and I was driven at high speed through the potholes to the docks. The driver in turn entered into rapid negotiation with a fisherman before hustling me into the man's boat. We set off across the bay. It seemed to be a fool's errand: in the shallows of Ifira island a thousand metres away the bow door was being winched up.

The fisherman shrugged and said that the captain – the voluptuary in a pink shirt who had sold me the ticket that afternoon – loaded the cargo of kerosene, food and construction materials, had several beers and, encouraged by his achievement, set off when it pleased him.

We caught up with the ship, its hull swept by an epidemic of rust, at the last minute and I was hauled on board as she manoeuvred out of the shallows and the last parcels flew over the bow door.

The ship was heading for Tanna, twenty hours' steaming away. The *Adela* was the worst rustbucket I had ever seen still afloat. Her cables were broken and her winches had jammed. Her rails were held on by rope. She had no navigation lights and an out-of-true propeller that shook her from bow to stern. She was less than ten years old and rolled like a dowager. The school of porpoises that played at the bow, as the sun dropped like a coin through a slot in the clouds, didn't seem like a good omen, just a sailor's superstition.

The chief engineer took me gently by the arm. 'You must sleep in my cabin.'

I unrolled my pandanus mat and lay all night on his bunk, nervously watching the cockroaches glinting in the bulkheads. At sunrise, as we anchored briefly at a rocky mist-laden bay, the chief came in and smiled:

'We made it. We are not good navigators.'

One morning he had woken up on his way here and been unable to see the island. He looked on the other side of the ship and there it was, vaguely, in the distance. The ship was 100 kilometres the wrong side. On another occasion the skipper of the *Adela*'s sister ship, the *Fatukai*, woke up between Vila and Tanna and discovered his helmsman had turned the ship through 180 degrees without realising it and was heading back towards Vila. (In 1987, as the big cyclone approached, the crew of the *Fatukai* had had so little faith in their ship that they transferred to another coaster which promptly sank, drowning everyone on board. The *Fatukai* herself was discovered drifting round the coast from Port Vila days later. Having walked her deck in Vila

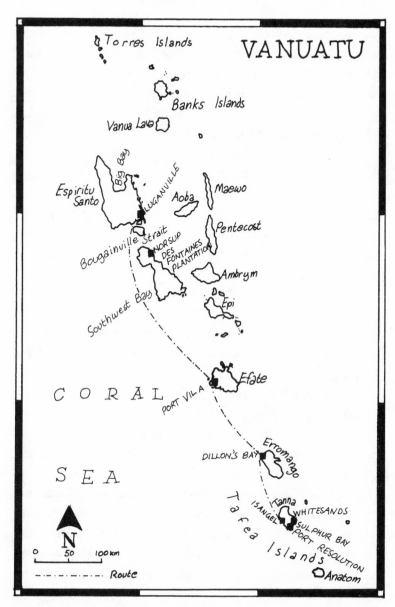

and stared down at rust-holes the size of tennis balls, I couldn't fault their lack of confidence.)

Tanna was rumoured to be a cruel and dark and jealous place, rich in private ceremonies. New polarities were welcomed because they added to the possibilities of rivalry and conflict. East feuded with west; Protestants with each other and the Catholics; in the deep bush, village against village. People did not travel paths controlled by other villages unless there was 'good speech', and middle-speakers in between were essential to the maintenance of these volatile relations.

Conversationally, Captain Cook was asked when he anchored at Port Resolution next to Tanna's volcano in 1774 if he ate human flesh. Shocked, he wrote: 'They began the subject of eating human flesh of their own accord, by asking us if we did; otherwise I should never have thought of asking them such a question.'

I liked the sound of the Tannese. They had not all taken to Christianity. Villages had accepted conversion then at some stage got bored or fed up with the gospels and wearing clothes and reverted to their old *kastom*. They prized any opportunity for a controversy.

If they had been more aware of it – mostly the protagonist-adversaries fought among themselves – they would have enjoyed the Anglo-French Condominium. The dual rule was born out of confrontation and stubbornness; thrived on rivalry, divisions and political manoeuvring; and ended with the souls of most of its subject people intact. The most bizarre colonial administration ever to flourish in the imperial imagination suited the ni-Vanuatu, if they had to be colonised at all, very well. They paid little attention to the masters. The masters, with nine hundred years of dislike and contempt to express to each other, paid no attention to them.

Add to this: the distances between the islands; the islanders' terrible navigation skills; their disinclination to be influenced – the bay *Adela* had stopped at was a missionary execution-ground; their linguistic privacy (on eighty islands with 150,000 people 115 languages were spoken, something like having half the tribes of Africa living in the Home Counties); and the obscure charm of the country that still attracted actors impatient to overplay their part. Whatever else it was, this country could not be as insipid and dull as Fiji.

Quiros was the first European in the islands, and the first of the ham visionaries. Sailing into the broad embrace of Espiritu Santo's north coast on 3 May 1606, he was convinced that he had found the cosmographers' southern continent. He dropped anchor and called his settlement New Jerusalem, after which he shot two islanders to encourage the others and kidnapped a collection of boys to convert them to Catholicism. 'Greater good awaits you,' he told them, 'than the sight and communion of heathen parents.'

Friendless, manic depressive, and with no convictions but his piety and unshakeable self-righteousness, he appointed a cabinet and an order of Knights of the Holy Ghost. He set up a ministry of war and celebrated Whit Sunday by ordering his crew to dance in fancy dress on the shores of the new Jordan River. A few days later his euphoria gave way, and without warning he abandoned the three-week-old settlement and sailed for Spain.

John Higginson came next, as much hothead as ham, but with the same taste for power. An Irishman who loathed the English, he arrived in the islands in the 1880s with French citizenship and built an empire on fraudulent purchases of land from local people – the Melanesians as usual had no conception of Higginson's 'freeholds' – and on buyouts of British settlers whose morale had been extinguished by poor harvests and back-to-back bouts of malaria.

Strange as it may seem, by the time the New Hebrides – Cook's name – began to appear regularly on Colonial Office minutes, Britain was weary of claiming dominion over straggling South Sea island groups. Goaded however by the scale of Higginson's depredations and the arrival of French soldiers, the

British were forced to take an interest.

Predictably, almost all the settlers were land-sharks, and violent attacks by local people persuaded the two European powers into a naval alliance to defend them. A visitor to one island, however, saw the authentic preoccupation of the settlers: 'We have just celebrated Christmas and Christmas in the New Hebrides is a fearful and wonderful sight. Thank God it only comes once a year. The French and the English had a pitched battle but luckily they were all too drunk to shoot straight.'

Under the Condominium of the New Hebrides, formalised in 1914, every aspect of public life – schools, police, hospitals, public works – was duplicated. The tone of the Condominium was set by its first institution, the Joint Court convened to hear land disputes. President of the Court, for the sake of fairness, was a nominee of the King of Spain. The sole drawback to the arrangement was that neither the French nor the British judge spoke Spanish. This mattered little, as the President was almost completely deaf, but proceedings were often further delayed by the non-appearance of the Presidential donkey which, on the grounds of his rider's obesity and the weight of the judicial robes, refused to go any further in the heat.

The British and French were polarised in attitude and in different parts of the country. (Even where they coexisted on the same island their settlements were leagues apart and no communication flowed between them.) Concentrated on the large, fertile northern islands of Espiritu Santo and Malekula, the French outnumbered the British three to one and owned most of the plantations.

It was the British who, during the 1970s, decided that the country was more trouble than it was worth. The French, deaf to world opinion, once again showed the lengths they were prepared to go to to obey de Gaulle's declaration: *'on reste'*.

Tanna was said to be equally francophone and anglophone. It was here and on Espiritu Santo that there had been most trouble at independence. The British district agent had upped and left. Left to his own devices, the French gendarme had at once supplied the Tannese with guns, telling them that independence would be very bad for them. (He would probably only have had to tell them that there were other Tannese who thought independence was a good thing.) A gun battle ensued on the lawn in front of the residency, but the Tannese could not shoot straight either. One man was killed, before they ran out of ammunition.

At two in the afternoon the *Adela* finally bumped alongside a new quay built by the Japanese that looked like a walkway from a Japanese shopping mall – all globe lamps and fresh concrete. I climbed out and walked through the shade of a huge banyan tree to the head of an empty road of bleached coral.

25
Middle bush

Only fools walked in the middle of the day. By the time I reached the top of the hill I was purblind, the landscape reduced to newsreel monotones. At the end of the familiar avenue of flamboyants – the scarlet flowers gone black – that led to the former residencies at Isangel, I dropped into the long grass and lay for an hour under a she-oak. The shade fell like a cool shower through its blue filament-leaves.

Philip Shing, the secretary to the local council, sat in an office under a fan at one end of the low government building. He was a man in charge of an illusion, and his eyes and shoulders sloped downwards in an attitude of refined melancholy. But he had not altogether allowed the island's natural tendency to separatism and chaos to engulf him – mostly a matter of a martyred reticence that came easily to him, and an indulgent attitude to all factions – and I later realised that he had succeeded in creating a helpful mirage of order.

Towards the end of our conversation something like passion crossed his features. He had started life as a French-speaker. 'But after the French disrupted independence,' he said, 'I found I had forgotten every word of it. Every word. I had to sit down at the age of forty and learn English from the beginning.'

I wanted to go to the middle bush in the island's interior where *kastom* had begun to flourish again. Mr Shing said he would send me Jack. Jack was the son of a chief and knew the paths well. Mr Shing did not want me to write stories about funny foreigners: he had had enough of that. 'But you must say what you see.'

The rest-house was the old British residency, a ready-built bungalow with floor-length windows filmed with mould. There was a United Nations statistician staying there.

'Good afternoon. My name is Khan,' he said.

Khan was from Bangladesh and, though pessimistic about everyone else's future, believed fervently in his own. He urged me to guess how old he was. When I was almost twenty years out – he looked about thirty-two and was nearly fifty – he cried, 'Ah you see: it is all a matter of fresh food and healthy living. Do I not look young? Am I not in good physical shape?'

The British resident had gone, but the Parker-Knoll furniture and the cheap chandeliers had stayed behind, along with a full-length framed print of Queen Elizabeth. The Royal Engineers had stayed here six months before, to repair the cross-island road.

Khan shared his fish and rice with me, sweet and delicately cooked. The rhetorical questions poured out. 'Is this not fresh food? Am I not a good cook? Does this not keep my body in the best condition?'

But when I asked him about Tanna's future, he muttered angrily about the uncertainties of data and the people's unhelpfulness. 'Five years before they find the right coffee variety for the island,' he said, 'and they cannot tell me why.'

The Commonwealth Development Corporation and the Vanuatu government had initiated a coffee cultivation programme on Tanna. They had leased hundreds of hectares on top of the island and planted them, only to find that, being on the most exposed slopes on the island, the crop failed almost immediately. Several hundred thousand dollars had been lost; now the research station had withdrawn all seedlings until it found the right strain.

Khan had had a difficult day. Tomorrow he was going to north Tanna on a long walk into the bush to find some cattlemen.

'I may walk thirty kilometres. But tomorrow,' he said, 'work will be done. Feel how strong my legs are,' and he thrust out one of them, thick and glossy, from beneath the table.

In the bedrooms the Royal Engineers had left cans of deodorant behind and centre-spreads from *Men Only* pinned to the wall. I slept well, interrupted by a chimerical and alarming vision of the Queen, looking surprisingly young, reclining in fancy underthings on a broad lace-covered bed.

The beauty of the ni-Vanuatu was strange and striking. They were not conventionally attractive; their faces were too round and open. But they possessed an unblinking solemn gravity, the liquid gravity of the child before it has learned to reflect itself back in the eyes of others, that was a world away from the snobbish manners of the Fijians.

Jack was short, broad-shouldered and strong. He had a tropical sore on his shin, and an intense desire to control events. We waited outside Philip Shing's office for a truck that would take us to the end of the road and he looked at me with a mixture of awe and aspiration. Above his head was a government poster. The initials 'AIDS' were shaped into a shark; underneath was the caption: 'No gat meresin, i kilim man'.

Reversions to *kastom* had taken place all over the bush in Vanuatu: the old agricultural way of life associated with the pre-Christian past in which self-sufficiency, the ownership of pigs, the drinking of *kava* – a stronger variant of the grog they drank in Fiji – and suspicion of your neighbours were the predominating features. And Tanna had always been a difficult country for the civilisers. Missionaries died of malaria or exhaustion, or were murdered. In the thick bush, *kastom* grew back as soon as they retreated, or years later the people abruptly burned their clothes, woke up their spirits and revived the *kava*-drinking and the dances and the elegant penis wrappers.

Jack waved away the first truck, saying it was too expensive, and sent for another (which cost two dollars more). We drove south out of Isangel. Cluttered with brush, the road was hardly a road and the four-by-four slithered round fallen trees and bubbling ditches. A dozen kilometres into the forest there was a clearing where the track finished, an abandoned village *nakamal* skirted with the dream-shapes of banyans. When Jack told him to come back for us at three, the driver nodded vaguely. I was sure he wouldn't come.

We walked on. From any vantage point the forest lost definition; close up, the individual features could only be described in isolation and with details that missed the effect. Here it was coconut groves, then a sudden outbreak of ivies and creepers that smothered the other plants and produced a kind of spontaneous topiary. Sapphire-backed skinks squirmed through the dirt. Jack's bow brought down a tiny yellow bird and he plucked it, the soft yellow down snagging in his hair, and grilled it on a burning stick as we walked past fences of cotton-tree branches that were already sprouting leaves. Unfiltered, the sun was as shocking as ever. In the shade the bush was as dewy and cool as a wood in the Chilterns in spring.

Jack's story was an interesting case of Tannese conduct.

He was a self-made orphan. He had disowned his father, not for personal reasons, but political ones.

The trouble had started when his father defected from Vanua'aku – the ruling party since independence – to the Melanesian Progressive Party. By serious Tannese the MPP was thought to be little more than a cargo cult. Its leader, Barak Sope, had been convicted of incitement to mutiny and seditious conspiracy in Port Vila the year before. Shining and corpulent, Sope was an enigma, a mysteriously wealthy businessman whose party had come from nowhere to present the main challenge to the government of Father Walter Lini. His recent conference on Ifira – the island in Vila Bay which was his stronghold – had cost him personally, it was said, 150,000 dollars. (This was ten times what Prime Minister Lini earned in a year.)

After his defection Jack's father, the chief of a village back down the track, had been deserted by many of his people and his status was leaking away. With his own aspirations, Jack could not afford to be associated with the old man any more. But he kept returning to the one vestige of status his father still possessed, a signed photograph of the Duke of Edinburgh presented after a royal visit to the Condominium. There was a widespread belief that Prince Philip came from Tanna. A logical assumption: every man on the island believed himself kith to the king. If the Prince had not fallen into unspecified temptation – Jack said it was women trouble – he would still be the great chief; as it was, the Queen had been able to demote him and rule over him.

Jack scoffed at the Prince Philip cult – it was rubbish, another of his father's self-aggrandising lies, to claim that the Prince would return to Tanna and redistribute his wealth among the people. But when I told him that I lived only half an hour from Buckingham Palace, he danced down the path with excitement, his arms spread wide, whooping with laughter.

Chief Kawia, his father's rival to whom Jack had now

attached himself, was a tiny, cheerful man smoking a pipe on the earth floor of the village *nakamal* we came to an hour later, a vast empty theatre skirted by giant banyans where the *kava* spirits played and the only sound was the booming of the locusts.

The men were preparing to go to work in their gardens but they lay casually watching the visitor, their small woven penis wrappers lying along their thighs, the limbs of some of them disfigured by tropical sores. The chief was at least sixty-five; his clay pipe looked older, its bowl adorned with a tiny nineteenth-century bust. A boy appeared at his shoulder and, at an order from him, ran to a hut. I dashed the chief a bag of rice and stick tobacco and squatted in front of him. I could see the boy standing in the hut's doorway, chewing hard.

There was going to be a *kava* ceremony. On most islands the root was pounded in a mortar. The bushmen preferred it chewed to a pulp, for ritualistic and maybe gastronomic reasons, by a virgin boy or girl.

The boy came back and spat the contents of his mouth onto a square of coconut fibre through which it was squeezed, like apple pulp through muslin, into half a coconut shell. A little water was added.

The mixture was off-white, with the viscosity of gloss paint. In a spirit of investigation I had drunk *yaqona* or *kava* everywhere I had been offered it. The taste was always disgusting – that tang of snot and cement – and I had decided that either the business was overrated or I was immune to the effect, beyond a cocaine-like numbness of the gums and mucous membranes. Chief Kawia handed me the shell and I held it out with both hands to thank him and took a first mouthful.

Nothing happened. Usually the effect, though feeble, was instant. The taste was unvaried, maybe sweeter this time with a stronger hint of pepper. Twenty faces smiled at me to continue.

I was about halfway through the shell when my eyes

thudded back in their sockets. At the same time scattered fires ignited spontaneously on the roof of my mouth. This was the prelude. I began to sink up to my eyes in some cool but inescapable liquid. If I tried to look down, I was going to drown in a well with no bottom. My throat reached back hopelessly to an earlier era of non-violence. Everything went numb, as someone threw the switches on my sense-receptors. My stomach was a cold dead weight that had slipped to somewhere deep in my abdomen, and lips, mouth, tongue, gums, larynx, throat were a dead region laid waste by *Piper methysticum*, refusing to react to motor impulses.

With my brain fighting for a toehold on normality, I was dimly aware that I was expected to finish the shell, and *make a speech*. I drank through gritted teeth, but still the liquid went down. I looked around the clearing. The same twenty faces continued to smile. The thought went through my head – it was all I could think of – *they drink this every day. Every day. Several shells of it.*

I sat up. I think I was swaying: I felt like the drunk at the embassy cocktail party, half-aware but unable to care. I supported myself on a log in the middle of the silence they were expecting me to fill. Eventually I found my voice, and a long time later I heard it roaring across the vast green gloom of the *nakamal*. Something I had read about the Tannese returned to me. Unlike other Melanesians, they believed that loud speech spoiled the *kava*. Across the island men talked in hushed voices, debating the village's concerns, arranging marriages, discussing the planting of the taro and maize and the faults of their neighbours; or they were silent.

But if I tried to lower my voice, nothing came out at all. Ringing with commonplaces, full of unmeant thanks for the *kava* and wretched platitudes about the need to appreciate *kastom*, I continued to shatter the clearing's peace. Unable to judge when I had said enough, I went on and on, until the drug, almost imperceptibly, began to loosen its grip. It may have been fifteen minutes. It could have been the same time next day.

Strangely, the ceremony had pleased Chief Kawia and his men. Grinning, they took me on a tour of the village about which I remember almost nothing: an airy collection of messy eating huts and sleeping houses, the men's and women's houses segregated. At some point the women returned from collecting firewood and shrank away from me, more at the shock of seeing a white man than to cover their nakedness. The chief's boy slipped away again and came back with a black cockerel, which Chief Kawia presented to me. It was an honour of which, I learned later, I was completely unworthy, only one step short of the pig that Prince Philip had received.

The clearing where the truck was to pick us up was, as I had expected, empty. We started the walk back. The lingering effect of the *kava* – the loss of volition and a mild but long-lasting sedation – made the afternoon pass uncontroversially and without much consciousness of time. I remember the warmth of the cockerel's black breast feathers under my arm; relief at the remoteness of Chief Kawia's village, which meant it might stay as it was for a while longer; the chiaroscuro of sun and shade; and Jack walking and dancing like a puppy ahead of me, asking over and over again for Prince Philip's phone number.

Khan sat, fuming, on the verandah of the rest-house. The driver of his Land-Rover had failed to collect him, and he had had to walk back to Isangel, in addition to which he had hardly seen any bushmen, therefore no data.

'This country is hopeless. It would collapse if it was not for the Overseas Development Agency.

'These people are too disorganised! This country has *no* income! The schools were closed because the teachers couldn't be paid! You see the lawn in front of the rest-house here? It is getting smaller and smaller because there is less and less kerosene for the council's lawnmower. Soon the mango grove will be overgrown, and all that will be tended are the marigolds at the edge of the path. Am I not right?'

26
White sands, black sands

The tall MP, Daniel Iamiam, bought his cigarettes in ones. He took the crumpled Benson & Hedges from his shirt pocket, lit it and pulled on it with the careful appreciation of a man enjoying a luxury. After a suitable silence, he came to his decision.

'I shall not be standing at the next election. I don't want to be in politics any more. I'd rather just go back to farming. Politics in this country is becoming too dangerous.'

I had hitched a lift from Philip Shing in the government Isuzu back to Daniel's constituency at Whitesands. Daniel could have been picked out in a crowd instantly: his face bore the frown of a man with too many concerns. His B & H burned in silence as the pick-up slid between the trees.

The cross-island road, relaid by the Royal Engineers, was a climactic affair that ended in a series of flamboyant military hairpins within the shadow of a coughing peak of ash and lava. At Whitesands, the guesthouse had opened for business that day for the first time, a miracle of local and personal ambition: a house of four bedrooms and an eating area built from hardwood and pandanus thatch with a coral floor. It had been constructed out of economic necessity, the pastor explained. The copra plantations were all but gone in the last eruption of the volcano. Half a dozen kilometres away the mountain rumbled and spat pillars of steam and sulphur gases a hundred metres in the air.

Later, as the air cooled, I walked down the coast to Sulphur Bay with the pastor's friend Gideon, a small, grave, voluble man wearing a teeshirt advertising the ruling Vanua'aku Party.

Gideon had been Vanua'aku's first MP for the area after
independence. He had lost his seat in 1983 because in a burst of
enthusiasm he and a friend had both stood for the seat, splitting
the vote in half.

Gideon was keen to return to politics, he said. Indiscreetly
– as it turned out – I told him Daniel was ready to quit. His grave
expression turned to glee.

'Oh this is very good news for me.'

'Will Vanua'aku win next time?'

He waved his hand impatiently. 'Oh no. Vanua'aku is
finished. Now I am a member of the MPP.'

He saw me looking at his teeshirt, and smiled slyly. 'Yes,
you see I'm wearing this because I don't want people to know
until the moment is right to tell them.'

It was Friday evening, the night of the weekly Jon Frum
assembly. Adherents of the sect drilled with wooden rifles,
awaiting the return of the 'little man with bleached hair, high-
pitched voice and clad in a coat with shining buttons' who would
bring them the liberating cargo of trucks, jeeps, houses, fridges,
tables, chairs and cigars. Every Friday they converged on the
path to Sulphur Bay, carrying banjos and guitars. 'By tomorrow
evening they will have danced themselves drunk with *kava*,'
Gideon said with contempt.

People said the sect's name had come from an American
serviceman who introduced himself as 'John from America'.
The cargo was the equipment of the US troops (many of them
black) stationed in Vila and on Espiritu Santo during the war.
Leading the way past villages where people stood by Celtic red
crosses and scowled, Gideon dismissed the whole thing as
nonsense.

His mood changed. He had decided to impart a secret.
'Jon Frum,' he said proudly, 'had nothing to do with American
cargo in World War Two. My father in 1935 was one of the
original three that Jon Frum appeared to in a vision.' He went on

to say that all the cult's predictions – which he had earlier also waved away – had in fact come true. Federation ('the southern islands would join to form one land'); cultural revival; polygamy; independence: it had all come about. When Jon Frum finally arose at the day of reckoning from his city of the dead deep inside the volcano, at the head of his army of 5000 souls, you could be sure that Gideon would say he had known it was going to happen all along.

The success of Jon Frum could not have come about without the help of the British district agent through the Twenties and Thirties, a man of extreme stupidity called James Nicol. Recognising that the cult was as much a reaction to European rule as to thou-shalt-not Protestantism, he arrested its leaders, fined them money they did not have and exiled them to other islands, where the cult spread. By the time the US forces arrived with their planeloads and shiploads of wealth, Jon Frum was ready.

His supporters foresaw the potential riches of the earth. The methodology to acquire them was easy. The same methodology – appeals to supernatural power, the correct ritual properly applied – had served the villages well at times of storm and pregnancy and crop-planting. It was a short step from there to celebrating the leadership of a prophet with bleached hair dressed in a coat with shining buttons (a memory of a bewigged officer from HMS *Resolution* 150 years before?).

For the moment they were still waiting.

This part of the coast had an uneasy atmosphere. Whether this was because of its position, sandwiched between the ash plain of the volcano and the cliffs, or because of the people's long-standing suspicion of Europeans, I couldn't tell. But around the crosses, some Celtic, some square like medical insignia, the villages were seedy and closed and depressing. Brand-new Toyotas parked in front of filthy huts increased the feeling of walking in a ghetto. The uneasiness deepened. At Sulphur Bay, a

stockaded village that ran the length of a deserted crescent of
black sand, the chief was in mourning for two of his brothers
who had died that week from dengue fever and he refused to
admit us.

The love of controversy and mischief had been replaced by
the low vitality of resentment and covetousness. I had the feeling
that if I cut my finger, septicaemia would be inevitable.

In a purple twilight I walked back across the expanse of the
black ash plain, where the lava had drifted into dead dunes and
petered out. Pandanus palms a metre from its edge flourished as
if nothing had happened, but thousands of palms downwind of
the volcano, poisoned by sulphur clouds and roaring hot ash,
stood headless like trees after an artillery bombardment.

The pastor had boiled up some chicken and rice. I said:

'Did you know that Gideon has joined the MPP?'

Astonishment showed on the pastor's broad trusting face.
All evening, while the volcano streaked the sky orange behind
us, he kept coming over to me to say, 'Are you sure? Are you
sure? I can't believe it. Did Gideon really join the MPP?'

The next day, accompanied by the pastor's brother, I walked the
fifteen kilometres to Port Resolution in canicular heat, nourished
by green coconuts and tiny wild bananas. At the headland
beyond Sulphur Bay I looked down over a quiet, narrow-
mouthed inlet and tried to imagine Cook's arrival in the *Resolution* in 1774: the exhausted captain and crew, the tired ship that
had spent months in the Antarctic, the islanders who had never
seen a European but immediately engaged Cook in a trial of
strength. Port Resolution had a strange, deserted lightness that
revived the historical associations – you could picture the hard-
used barque appearing, tall and pale-sailed, rimed with salt and
weather, for another small but fatal impact. We found the young
banyan tree Cook had tied up to, its trunk now a massive knotted

cable. The pastor's brother said a cruise ship would be stopping in the bay for the first time a few weeks hence. Standing on the black beach edged with palms and she-oaks, I half-hoped that the islanders would be there to greet the passengers, courteously enquiring whether they ate human flesh, and that, seeing a couple of snowy-haired Melburnians on the headland watching a dugong fishing for turtle, they would inexplicably revert to their eighteenth-century diet.

On the way back I took a short-cut across the volcano. Four hundred metres up, the raking smell of sulphur was everywhere. As I stumbled, I put my hand to a place where the crust had broken away and it was scalded by salt steam. On the lip of the crater, Jon Frum's refuge, deafened and choked and with your eyes streaming from the fires two hundred metres below, you could understand the passion of the vulcanologists – all those Victorian philanderers who debauched their way around Europe and then got science – for the furnaces of Hell.

I slithered down the soft ash on the other side, sending up a pair of swamp harriers nesting on the slope. At the bottom I had a furious row with two boys who demanded 1600 *vatu* as 'guides'. We went back to see their chief in one of the Jon Frum villages, who accused me of prevaricating: 'Yu no wantem pay, yu say strait.' It was no use pointing out that I had had no guide, and 16 dollars was too much. I looked around the filthy village compound with its new Toyotas, at the crowd of sharp-faced villagers who all wore belted purses, and I paid.

The pastor was upset. The price for guides was set by Philip Shing's office, and the collection of cash was supposed to be for the benefit of all the villages impoverished by the last eruption (none of it of course had been distributed). But the Jon Frumers had begun to be visited by tour operators, whose clients would pay whatever they were asked. This process had removed the last obstacle to the loss of their moral sense. Now there was nothing in the way of the cult's members to stop their becoming the spiritual equivalent of the emergency plumber or the Soho peep-show barker.

'They don't agree with us,' said the pastor's brother. 'In fact they hate us. They know we own the volcano, all of us. Do you remember the big banyan tree on the hill? It was eighteen generations ago when our ancestor Apupu appeared from the ground, and he was the first, and the tribe grew and then these people came and they chased them to Whitesands. They know we came from the volcano and they didn't, that we are the children of Apupu and the banyan tree. We don't trust them.'

I would have had sixteen dollars on his saying what he said next.

'We are Vanua'aku Party,' he shrugged, 'and they are MPP.'

Three days later, on the terrace at Rossi's, the heavy night air had brought out the insect metropolis. I had bandaged a cut on my leg but three flies clustered to it like cloves to orange peel. Cockroaches the size of moles swaggered across the tiles. In his tight black trousers Albert's haunches seemed to pout as he wiggled and turned and turned again around the tables, spraying the invisible thousands of mosquitoes waiting just outside the light. Judging by his eyes, which glittered like coals from the volcano, his last *kava* session must have been only a couple of hours before.

Six waiters in turn asked what I would like to order. There was a sweetness to this, since every one forgot out of politeness to show me the day's menu. I settled for a sirloin steak and a glass of Côtes de Beaune. Somewhere in the Rossi's kitchens, somehow preserved, like the taste for coffee, was the pre-independence memory and ability to cook Charolais steak fast enough and hot enough to equal any restaurant in both hemispheres.

At the next table an English couple lingered over their reunion and their Laurent Perrier. The woman turned to Albert and said, 'Albert, we loved your Valentine's Day dance. When's the next one? Old-time dancing doesn't mean everyone's going to be frightfully good, does it?' Delighted to be addressed with such deference, Albert said no and preened and gavotted away with his can of insecticide, his lips and haunches pursed in a businesslike way, a man possessed by the sudden beauty of the night.

Vila was as undemanding as before, quiet and not so civilised that it drove me out. There was nothing to do in the town, but the heat was so constant – the place was as hot as a casserole – I hardly wanted to move. I wanted to see Walter Lini, but I found the prime minister's private secretary had fobbed me off: Lini had gone away on an official visit. He and Barak Sope seemed to be on each other's tails, as the latter went to Nouméa in search of French subsidies, and the former followed him there in an attempt to renew ties with the people who had opposed independence. (Cash was on his agenda too, it went without saying.)

I dithered, the way I dithered in London. I read my mail, ate lunch at the Plantation *pâtisserie*, enjoyed the waiters' fine treble voices and pondered the question of what to do next. There was nothing specific I wanted to do, but I couldn't make up my mind to leave. The port of course was empty. (One day a white cruise liner came in like a ghost, dwarfing the bay for twenty-four hours and filling the town with smiling silver-haired Australians, then it was gone.)

In the end I decided to fly north to Espiritu Santo, to the lost continent of Quiros and the scene of a small war at independence. There was another port there, at Luganville, that shipped supplies in and copra out, and there might just be a ship heading east. My plans involved a lot of hunches that turned out to be illusions. I was caring less and less.

Albert had been delighted to see me. He insisted I join him on the last evening for a session at the Red Laet, one of the dozens of *kava* saloons scattered about Vila. Why did I agree? I think he had the charm – in his case an impeccable francophone campness – that always holds out some undisclosed promise.

I wasn't disappointed. At six-thirty he turned up at the Rossi in the shortest, tightest white shorts he could have worn.

'Not bad for fifty,' he twinkled.

After undergoing a brief flirtation on the bus, I realised that if there was any sexual intention on his part, politeness was such an article of faith with him that propositioning a stranger was out of the question.

We bought orange juice across the street to wash away the *kava*'s taste. *'Pour le goût – eech!'* Albert said. The absence of any enjoyment in the taste of the stuff produced an illicit air in the flimsy saloon: the operation of drinking the contents was accompanied by so much grimacing, hawking and expression of disgust that most drinkers preferred to do it in the narrow alley behind the saloon. All evening the steady factory-noise of people spitting could be heard through the tin walls at the back of the two *salles*.

After two shells the familiar feeling of lethargy descended. While Albert was gone to buy the third, I wandered into the other room and fell into conversation with an Australian. He was a livestock manager who, it turned out, knew Khan, the UN statistician. Was Khan as prone to melancholy as he seemed? His melancholy was hardly surprising, the man said, since the government statistics department was a joke. It was impossible to gather correct data because half the time the ni-Vanuatu farmers said what they thought you wanted to hear and the other half they didn't know the answer. In the case of the cattle, it was impossible to do a head count, because the locals killed their animals with spears and as soon as they saw a human being they fled into the bush.

Khan's temperament was also worsened by his having acquired the Bangladeshi habit of litigation. (Many middle-class Bangladeshis measured their status by the number of court cases they had going at the same time. One of the favourite forms of civil conflict was a land dispute, in which a piece of land would be sold to one man, and then another would appear offering more money, so the vendor would sell it to this man too, predating the bill of sale. Instantly there were the makings of a drawn out and costly action.)

I thought of Khan's desire for strangers to admire how young he looked, and I pictured the statistician at odds with the messiness of life: 'You see, even with the passage of time, and the burden of having to fight for what is mine in the courts, I'm more than a match for them.'

The cattle industry was enlivened by similar quarrels between the French and the Australians. The French had decided they were going to have the best, so they imported Limousin and Charolais and gave them to the farmers; most of them died. The Australians had brought in hardy shorthorns and Brahmans and now they had some superbly well-adjusted tropical herds. Still the French had refused to have anything to do with them. 'The Charolais means Mother France,' the man said. 'They get their Charolais semen flown 20,000 kilometres from source without thinking twice.'

He sank abruptly into *kava*-induced silence. I went to find Albert, who offered me another shell. It was more polite to go to the back and pour it away than refuse it.

Two hours after we arrived, all conversation had ceased. European and Melanesian drinkers stared into the trees and the parallel shadows on the tin wall, or sat as motionless torsoes, their heads in their hands. I tried to clear my head by an effort of will and failed. Albert's red eyes rolled mischievously, but he said nothing. All I could think was that the existence of two separate drinking-rooms in the saloon, a *salle anglophone* and a *salle francophone*, was a bizarre detail in a scene of such speechlessness.

27
Espiritu Santo

I came to the lost continent of Quiros. In 1768, 162 years after the Whitsun fancy-dress party, Louis Antoine de Bougainville, running before the south-east trades, curved through the passage to the south of Quiros' New Jerusalem, and Tierra Australis, the Southern Land of the Holy Ghost, was no longer a continent.

Mysteries remained here. Pygmy tribes that no one had seen still lived in the deepest bush. Mount Tabwemasana, the highest peak on the island at 1879 metres, had never known a recorded climb – although in his 1937 book *Savage Civilisation* Tom Harrisson recalls standing on the summit, looking 'across a chaos of peaks and tangled ranges – higher than Ben Nevis – to the sea on all sides, studded with islands of every shape'. The bush sprang back as soon as you cleared it, hung with snakes and exploding with birds and spiders and lizards. In its variety, maybe it was a continent.

The wet season was on again. In the mornings you could stand on the hill at the site of the old British Paddock, looking across the Segond Channel at the perfect hall-of-mirrors repetition of the light tradewind clouds and then, around midday, watch them drawing up and closing into a canopy of bruises. Every afternoon the Channel, its surface shut and stippled, was swept by rain that fell and fell and fell.

Luganville, the island's main township, had had its transformations. It was the Wild West of the Pacific, a town with an unerring sense of vacancy, a post-goldrush town where you half-expected to see men in stetsons with glazed expressions, all passion spent and only the inertia of an obsession left.

The first town had been a settlement of gabled French houses on the far side of the Sarakata River. In the war 100,000 American troops with a future president among them had reclaimed the marsh at the Segond Channel's edge and built three bomber and two fighter airfields (from jungle to first takeoff took them six days) and a new town. Then the Coconut War of 1980, a maladroit attempt at secession incited by French settlers and American interests, had turned a place of minor charms into one shunned by the government and with little to savour but gentle, undeviating decay.

Now the main street was a half-deserted highway strung with occasional Chinese trading posts that looked as if it had suffered a raid by JP-233 cratering bombs. Japanese pick-ups wove drunkenly along its length, followed periodically by huge, rusting flatbed trucks loaded with sagging logs that crashed through the ditches. At the far end, by the Sarakata River, was the site of John F. Kennedy's wartime PT-boat station. On the north side of the street the bush-tangled humps of Quonsett huts stretched into the distance. For thirty years the town had hovered, resisting just enough to continue, on the brink of utter dilapidation.

'I'm a demon for the drink. That's all there is to do.'

J.J. was an engineer. We were in the Hotel Santo, the haunt of all the expatriates. J.J. loved the sea, and he had built bridges from Guam to the Solomons. But he knew exactly how long – seven months and four days – he'd been stuck in Luganville.

The government in Vila had relented, and commissioned a new wharf for the town; the present one dated from the war. Santo was the granary of the country. Two-thirds of the beef, ninety per cent of the copra and all the cacao went out through Luganville, and the politicians had seen the folly of neglect.

The wharf was a $12 million project financed by a soft loan from the Asian Development Bank. The ground survey and soil report by French surveyors indicated a limestone shelf twenty-four metres down, J.J. said. The design was for pilings to be sunk to thirty-six metres, twelve metres into the shelf, and for a concrete floor to be laid on top.

J.J. had been called to the project as site manager. Four months after he arrived, the first piling was sunk. It disappeared into the sand, along with the second and third and every other test piling.

The limestone shelf didn't exist.

No one really cared, except the engineers stuck on the job. The design had eventually been modified, to one using much longer – seventy-two metre – pilings in a friction hold on the sea floor. The cost spiralled and the schedule stretched to inifinty. The longer pilings would cost another $2 million, and J.J.'s company had had to order a bigger crane to sink them. J.J. dreamed of getting away in his boat, which he was restoring in his spare time, or of being called off the project to build a bridge somewhere else. He knew about bridges.

'But now you can get on with the new design,' I said.

'Yes. The new design is fine. Friction pilings are terrific' – and J.J. got out a smile, balling his fist – 'except in earthquake areas. Like this.'

This was the night I met Pascal and the Texan:

Pascal was surveying a dam site for a small power plant on the Sarakata River, and the job – which meant employing twenty bushmen to cut down bush that grew back overnight – was another one where the weeks had lengthened to months. He was a wiry Frenchman from the French Antilles who had fallen for Tahiti during his military service, and lived on a hill above Papeete.

He had an ability to relax that the other expatriates didn't. He stood apart from them at the Hotel Santo. There were three Australians who nightly tenanted the bar; their conversation always returned to the sexual characteristics of the local women. Pascal said disgustedly, '*Les Australopithèques!* The seventh level of humanity, after the toads.'

When I told him I was a tourist, interested in seeing how life matched the picture people made of it in Europe, he guessed I was lying. I conceded I was writing a book. He said, 'This book interests me. But the book I want to read is the one you don't write.'

The Texan materialised next to us, a man with a basketball player's physique and a farmboy's face that exuded an incongruous, urban self-confidence. He introduced himself at the bar. Both his name – Mark Preuett – and his manner suggested that he was at a cocktail party at which he was the guest of honour. He had a Rabuka moustache that jutted straight out over his lip and stayed quite still as he began complaining about his hotel across the street.

'It's dis*ger*sting. You guys know any better?'

'You can try the bungalows up at the British Paddock,' I said.

'How merch would that be?'

I told him.

'Sounds gerd. Where you guys been hanging out? Taheedi? I've been therr, it's okay. You been to Hawaii? Oh man you gert to go to Hawaii. You gert to go to Oahu. The surfing therr is so fahn. Wherr else? Fee*jee*? You gert to go to Malololailai. Therr's jerst the most fabulous dahving therr. The dahving herr's too expensive. This is serch a ferny place. I'm not sure if I like it. The town sherr is inneresting. Bert everything is so ex*pen*sive. I gert to find sermwherr to change my merny. I gert no *vatu*. Could you guys stand me a beer until I find sermwherr to change my checks?'

The beer came. 'That's real good of you. Bert the beer here is more expensive than across the street – you notice that?'

Later in the Club Asia, Luganville's disco, next to the cockroaches and Chinese gamblers of Preuett's hotel, Pascal was dancing with a ni-Vanuatu woman called Rosine. The low room was thick with the stale smell of the oxidised copra oils that clung to the men's clothes. I was watching their dancing – they shuffled shyly, unused to the music – when Preuett came up to the bar.

'What are you drinking?' he shouted.

I thought he had managed to change some money at the Hotel Santo.

'I'll have a lemonade. Thank you.'

'Why are you drinking that?'

'I drank a lot earlier this evening.'

'Yup,' he confirmed, 'I can smell the alcerhol on your breath.'

I think I would have hit him, if I hadn't been distracted. Another fight had just started at the far end of the room. It lasted only a few seconds, harsh muscular shadows against the wall. The music covered the noise.

When the figures melted into the crowd, Pascal was struggling to his knees and the girl Rosine was crouching next to him. Blood dribbled from his nose and his spectacles were smashed.

'So what happened?'

He shrugged. 'They're from Rosine's village. We were talking, and then they started drinking and they didn't like me dancing with her. It happens.'

By the time I stood up to look for him, Preuett had gone.

I liked Luganville. But it was better as a concept: the town that time forgot. I could see myself slowly transforming into one of the drinkers in the Hotel Santo, the men Pascal had addressed with a sweep of his hand, saying:

   'Tu vois. La bière est la seule réalité.'

In practice the town's straight main street, a symbol of purposefulness, conveyed only lethargy. Its colours and textures irresistibly disappearing, unmourned and unrenewed, the place was like a slowly fading picture. There was one building I often walked past that enshrined this fugitive quality:

Diary, 12 March: The Three Bears is a picture of business in decline. Carmen, the beauty of Luganville, has not been seen for a while. I have knocked on the door every day, but there is no answer. Scattered buildings last whitewashed years ago, padlocks whose signifier is not security, but that the answer has been no for a long time, the dark red roof-tin lying askew, invite only one conclusion. The beauty of Luganville, once seen every morning on her bicycle, always immaculately turned out in black and white, has given up her profession.

Early this morning, driving past in the rain, I saw a light on the verandah. I got the taxi-driver to stop. Through one of the barred windows, I saw a bed that might have been slept in last night. Had she regretted her decision to settle down? Maybe there would be new whitewash, new brown paint for the bears carousing on the front wall, a new front door. I knocked on the door once more, but inside there was silence.

So the bears will carry on fading into the background, smiles rubbed away, well-fed bellies dissolving onto rainwashed, foot-thick concrete laid down fifty years ago, when Carmen was a young girl. I wish I could find her. The idea that there is a woman in this town who – surely she was – was young and lovely when Kennedy was here, nags at my curiosity.

When Pascal suggested a journey in his LandCruiser to the
northern cape, I was relieved at the distraction.

Preuett had somehow got wind that something was plan-
ned. He was in the hotel dining room at breakfast.

'Howdy. Where are you going today?'

'Nowhere.'

'I sherr would like to get out of this town for a day. I was
going dahving but I decided against it. You don't get too many
vatu to the dollar and it's *merch* too expensive on your own. Are
you interested in dahving? We could share the costs. Or maybe
we could go to Million Dollar Point.'

Pascal muttered, 'Who is this son of George Bush? I am
going to kill him.'

I said, 'As a matter of fact, we *were* thinking of going to
Million Dollar Point.' Pascal scowled, and Preuett's face lit up.

At Million Dollar Point thousands of tons of matériel had
been dumped in the sea by the departing American Army. They
had offered the equipment to the settlers at knockdown prices –
everything from earthmovers and jeeps to construction materials,
mudslats, Quonsetts – but the settlers, figuring the equipment
would have to be abandoned anyway, turned the offer down.
Piqued, the Americans had built a ramp off the beach, throwing
into the concrete all the ballast they could find, including live
ammunition, and driven everything into the sea.

I said, 'But we're in a bit of a mess. Pascal's LandCruiser
has got a flat, and the spare's no good. We were going to rent a
jeep but the stupid thing is, neither of us has got any money.
Now that you've been to the bank, maybe you could – '

'That's rilly terf,' said Preuett quickly. 'I'd rilly like to
help you guys but,' getting up and opening his wallet (an object
neither of us had seen before) to pay for breakfast, he said, 'I
think I may jerst go to the dahve shop and see if I can find

someone else to dahve with. Have a good day.'

He was gone. It should have been obvious to us, of course: his wallet had rilly contained *merch* more money than either of us expected.

The road, which had been atrocious, ended at Port Olry. I had not exaggerated much about the LandCruiser's tyres. The thing was a typical Pacific jeep and they had as much tread on them as a bar of soap. In the end Pascal gave up trying to steer around the coral potholes and drove straight at them, drowning out the jarring and protests of the crippled suspension by yelling French marching songs, 'L'Artilleur de Metz', 'Jean Gilles', 'Le Hussard de la garde', one after another.

Port Olry was a Catholic settlement on the coast, francophone and more airy and graceful than any village I had seen. The cows that grazed under the palms were the colour of unrefined flour, the same as the sand, and on the beach, half-concealed like an aluminium crab, lay the silver engine and wings of an American fighter that had crashed in 1942.

The priest had just returned from mass in a village two hours' walk away and seemed burdened with more than distant parishes. He welcomed us with a basket of fruit, garlanded with hibiscus and frangipani blooms. He warned us about the forest people, who did not know white men, and hoped we had a good jeep.

We found Rosine's brother, Gaspard, and made a start. Nowhere so far in Vanuatu had the bush been so close you couldn't walk through it. It had been almost European, the way I imagined a medieval wood, patches of thick obscurity that gave way to motes of insects flirting in the sunlight. North of Port Olry there was a succession of echo-filled clearings which we exited by driving under Gaspard's instructions straight at a wall of greenery that parted at the last minute just wide enough to let

the LandCruiser through. The world resolved itself into a muffl-
ed green half-light and the directionless sounds of uncut bush.
Lianas hung down everywhere; trees with leaves that burned the
skin brushed the bodywork. The ground changed to rock and
then for a while so did the forest walls. The wing mirrors went,
the roof tore, the crankcase kept hitting outcrops of rock. I
prayed for a sump shield, and Pascal continued to sing:

> *C'était un grenadier qui revenait de Flandre*
> *Qui était si mal vêtu qu'on y voyait son membre...*

The rock became swamp and there was a fork in the track.
After taking the wrong turning, the LandCruiser had to be dug
out twice with mats of branches. Gaspard said again and again,
grinning and holding up his index finger, 'Only one more
kilometre.'

'*Allez*, Gaspard, stop fucking around,' said Pascal.

'No no, I promise you now, only one more kilometre – Cap
Quiros klosup, klosup.' But a walk to a place that was 'klosup'
could be twenty kilometres.

Time and distance were not scarce resources. Land was
different. Gaspard swivelled on the bench in the back, saying as
he waved his arm at walls of bush, 'That belongs to us.' Then
suddenly it belonged to the next village ('we have to be careful
here'). Man-Santo, like man-Tanna and the Kanaks – and the
Aborigines they were descended from – was as rooted to his land
as the banyans that sheltered his *nakamal*. The European
emphasis on power and influence that fluctuated with fortunes
and currency had not reached here, where land was the source of
life: producer, protector, servant, master. It was fought for – an
enemy meant a trespasser – and it was the focus of most ritual.
In a measles epidemic, man-Santo had dug a hole in the ground
and climbed into it, covering himself with soil to ward off the
disease.

The passion for land had been at the heart of the Coconut Rebellion. The rebellion had had hardly a chance of succeeding. Its aims were too great, its foundations were compromised, its leader, Jimmy Stephen ('President Moses' – the last of the ham visionaries), was unable to divorce its financial resources from his personal needs. Beginning as a *kastom* movement, with all the respectability of any campaign to return alienated lands, by the time NaGriamel supporters started smashing bungalow windows in the British Paddock at Luganville on the night of 27 May 1980, Jimmy Stephen was being backed as Santo's secessionist leader by a farrago of expatriate property speculators, libertarian ideologues and French settlers ready to go to any lengths to hang on to their property.

Near Port Olry and Cap Quiros Eugene Peacock, an American developer, had bought tracts of land to be sold in parcels as paradise retreats to Vietnam veterans. The *Saigon Post* in 1971 had advertised his plans: 'Your Vietnamese wife will feel at home on the fabulous island of Santo.' Before the Condominium government retroactively finessed his plans, he made $5 million. Afterwards he smoothed Stephen into supporting his campaign against the new legislation, telling him: 'Our interests lie on the same path.'

Michael Oliver, another millionaire, had survived four years in a Nazi concentration camp. He deserved a biography to himself; his imprisonment produced lasting eccentricity in his view of freedom. After the war he had become infatuated with the economic theories of an Austrian economist named Mises. Liberty lay in the untrammelled practice of capitalism. By the 1970s the United States – the United States! – had sickened and was dying at the hands of socialism. He converted all his stocks into gold and began to cruise the world looking for a suitable territory for his 'unhappy Americans'. After failing in Tonga and the Bahamas, he came to Espiritu Santo. For four years he was the *éminence grise* behind Jimmy Stephen. He suggested secession and urged Stephen to work with the French. Santo suddenly flowered with US libertarians, buying plantations and writing enthusiastic letters to Stephen and each other about the new state.

When it came, two months before Vanuatu's independence, Stephen's armed revolt and declaration of an independent republic were an *opera buffa* composed by Oliver. Oliver's driving force, his four years in a concentration camp, was Jimmy Stephen's nemesis. Arrested, Stephen was tried and sentenced to fourteen and a half years in prison; he was still in the old French gaol in Port Vila.

It was past midday. Through the rain there were huts, and beyond the screen of mangroves the traces of the sea's refulgence. Gaspard returned, saying the people had nothing against us visiting the cape.

In the downpour we walked along the scimitar of white sand. Between squalls, it merged with the optical perfection of the aquamarine sea. Ten metres out, a fat hermit crab bowled over the soft underwater dunes in a chipped conch shell: you could see its stalky blue cartoon eyes waving. As we sat and ate the priest's fruit, the weather worsened and the glassy surface of the sea shattered under the onslaught of the rain. Deserted, wet and cold, it was still one of the loveliest places I had ever seen.

Pascal said suddenly, 'I shall never tell anyone I came here.'

At Cap Quiros you could see why white men had the fever for desert islands. They wanted somewhere – all of them, Quiros and Higginson, Oliver and Peacock, planters, settlers – to bring their psychological baggage and dump it. Espiritu Santo was beautiful and enigmatic and rich, like the neurotic's perfect woman, and they longed for some sudden paradise to flower there, some sudden liberation from neurosis and desire. What was interesting was that Espiritu Santo had resisted nearly all the white men; by circumstance or mischief or the working of local magic, hardly any of them had succeeded in gaining any purchase on its mysterious surface.

On the way back the LandCruiser sank to its axles in mud, and it took us two hours – the winch was broken of course – of singing and bush-cutting to coax it out. By the time we got on the road to Luganville the moon was up, a silver curl on a blackout cloth. Pascal drove at breakneck speed straight at every pothole. I stood it for a while, then asked if he could try to avoid some of them.

'Why avoid them?' As he threw up his hands in exasperation, the jeep hit another hole and careered violently to the left. 'You see? The holes are the only reality.'

28

A single man on Malekula

One evening in the Hotel Santo, Pascal had said there was a French planter in a stetson who sometimes came to town. I wasn't surprised when he called him 'the last of the great adventurers', but suspected a French version of Robbie Lepper.

Two days later I tracked down Gaby Grilhault des Fontaines. He lived across the Bougainville Strait on the island of Malekula. His agent was one of the Chinese traders on Luganville's main street. In the back room of the store the voice crackled over the VHF link:

'I got where I am because I have no politics. Meet me in the restaurant across the road at midday.'

Monsieur Grilhault des Fontaines had the bowed legs of a horseman and a habit of speaking his mind. He was wearing what he always wore – a stetson with a broken crown, check shirt, jeans and riding boots – and kept his cocoa-coloured eyes on me. When the French were about their futile secession conspiracy, he had stayed out of it.

'I'll tell you straight. The English were not such bloody fools as we were. They never opposed independence, they didn't put their money on that fool Jimmy Stephen. Now look what's happening. For every minister in Vila there's an English adviser. They knew that after independence they would be able to pick up where they left off.'

Born in 1926 in Cochin-china, the grandson of a magistrate and son of a colonel in the *Garde indochine*, he was the last in a line of colonists who went back to the days of Louis XV, almost to Cristobal Colon. He had grown up in planter society. 'At twenty,' he said, 'my brother had 500 coolies under him. He knew how to impose his authority.'

But after the fiasco of Dien Bien Phu he had had to leave everything behind. He fled to Australia. In Queensland he turned stockman and mustered the trainloads that roared through Eagle Junction. For twenty years he had ridden the boundaries. He had come to Malekula in 1977, three years before Vanuatu's independence. Now he was sixty-four. By an historical irony he was the director of a plantation owned by what had once been the Banque d'Indochine.

He was returning to Malekula the next day and suggested I stop there on the way back to Vila. 'Unless you are worried about being threatened by a ni-Van with a knife.'

'Who's doing the threatening?'

'They sent us four of their prisoners from Vila because they didn't want to look after them. But we haven't got a gaol for them, so they walk around all day and now they've got some knives from somewhere. I've phoned the Minister of the Interior about it.'

Before I said yes, I went to see J.J. at the wharf. He was

waiting for the big crane to arrive and was looking down in the mouth. I was another hunch down. There were no ships due in for a fortnight, he said; if there had been, he would have joined me.

Pascal drove us to the airstrip outside town. His theodolite was waterlogged and he had no idea how he was going to finish the surveying. 'So now you are abandoning me to the *Australopithèques*,' he said.

Monsieur des Fontaines suggested he come with us for a day or two's holiday. He shook his head. 'I have my job. And I have to stay with my Toyota. *Seul, on n'est pas fait pour durer.*'

I didn't want to leave Pascal behind. He had a talent for organising adventure that I lacked, he didn't need the bar-room company of the others to be himself, he was an outsider who wouldn't settle into their drink-fever and depression.

Seul, on n'est pas fait pour durer. After taking off from Luganville, scattering Charolais cows off the runway and pitching out over the blue-black strait, I knew that phrase of his would outlive most other memories of the place.

Two Englishmen lived on Malekula within a decade of each other, and summed up the island's character.

In 1912, to escape the tedium of Edwardian school-mastering, Robert Fletcher went to the South Seas ('12 pounds for 12,000 miles') and ended up on Malekula as a planter. For seven years Fletcher stuck at his island life: it became the hammer of his personality. Beggared by isolation and the climate, dogged by malaria attacks, he turned to his whisky decanter and an island girl who had his child. (He wrote home to a friend in London, Bohun Lynch, and without asking his permission Lynch published the collected confessions of loneliness, hatred and miscegenation in a book called *Isles of Illusion*. Fletcher experienced the horror of a man who did not want the world to see him as he was; but the book was a bestseller.)

Despite his inbred conservatism – he could not imagine bringing the child-bride back to London – Fletcher's letters are the words of a civilised and tender man outraged by black-birders, colonial officials, missionaries, traders and 'Orstrylyuns' (he could not believe the other planters never bathed). The letters are also a meticulous account of gradual giving-up.

In the autumn of 1916 Fletcher wrote to Lynch:

> Man, I'd give you three weeks to be sick to death of the most lovely island that ever had sea round it. I have read gushing descriptions written by steamer trippers of the wonderful, etc. (you know the adjectives) beauty of the New Hebrides. Thank you. I have had some. At the present moment I feel that I should love to be in the Club Uruguay at Montevideo (it is about apéritif time) with the atmosphere thick with the smell of Brazilian tobacco and absinthe and some joven distinguido with a shocking accent reciting Verlaine. Of course that wouldn't last long. I have no real love for decadents and never had very much. Only some 'decadent' people are distinctly amusing; as long as one doesn't probe. But no more nature unadorned for me. Given a really nice climate and heaps of books and leisure, I could easily do without other folk. I may say that I detest other people. But solitude without health or wealth or books or cooks is not compensated for by the marvellous beauty of a palm tree hanging over a coral reef. Wait till you've cursed the sun for sinking to an empty horizon minutes on end; till you've felt excited at the approach of a canoe with two or three dirty natives from somewhere else – a glimpse of the outside world. It is the knowledge that one is 'right up against it' that is so appalling; that one is bound to go on living this rat's existence for months if not years to come.

For health Fletcher did remarkably well. The only ailment he feared was something that started out like malaria and showed itself by stealth. 'Too much quinine spells "black-water",' he wrote.

Bernard Deacon was less fortunate. He was twenty-three in January 1926, when he arrived at South West Bay on Malekula. Introspective and exact, in just over a year he absorbed the substance of the graded societies that constituted Malekulan life so well that half a century later the ni-Vanuatu were turning to his volume *Malekula: a Vanishing People in the New Hebrides* to find out what *kastom* had disappeared.

Deacon was tall and thin and had gypsy looks. Margaret Gardiner had met him in Cambridge when he was reading anthropology. It was a passionate, inconclusive romance: he could not decide if he loved her. But his letters from South West Bay showed that his existence was throwing his feelings into sharp relief. Margaret was certain that he loved her. Eventually he himself realised it. They were to be married in Sydney as soon as they could both get there.

'I want only to be together,' he confessed in his last letter.

Three weeks later he was dead, from blackwater fever.

(Fifty-six years after his death Margaret visited Bernard's grave on Malekula and heard another explanation. The story was that Bernard had been refused permission to go to the sacred village of Melpmes. He went anyway and photographed a ritual. The same evening he fell sick of the illness from which he died. Did he catch blackwater fever, or was he poisoned? It was impossible to say. But Bernard's last request had been that he should be buried with his head facing south, and his feet facing north – towards Melpmes.)

. . .

Gaby des Fontaines' plantation at Norsup was fifteen hundred
hectares of whispering palms, with a small town laid out among
the groves where nothing was replaced until it wore out. Beyond
the line of wooden workers' houses was the unruffled bay. On
the other side were the dock and the store, a square and a church,
the copra and cacao driers, the petrol station, workshops and the
flaking plantation office. The settlement had the dusty fascination of a piece of machinery that should have stopped working
years before.

Gaby said, 'There is not a plantation as successful or as
little changed in the islands.'

The days when copra had been competed for by traders and
the Nobel Explosives Company had gone. But Gaby stabbed his
finger at me. 'Remember. The rich countries have to keep copra
going. There is nothing else. There is a great race to see who can
do most for these islands. Vanuatu is a woman who will sleep
with anyone. And the customers are queuing up.'

The director's house was a beautifully preserved clapboard
bungalow at the top of the hill with a verandah that ran the
length of two sides, and a cookhouse adjoining it. The light
danced between the white wooden jalousies. Gaby would not
have fans or air-conditioning in the house, but the breezes were
never absent.

Gaby and Hélène greeted each other like long-separated
lovers. He returned to the dock to check the loading of his barge.
Hélène had sensibly cut hair and spectacles and the look of a
headmistress. She made a pot of French tea and launched into
the story of their marriage.

They were both divorced: Gaby's first wife, Hélène said
contemptuously, had been an adventuress whom Gaby had
pardoned for the children's sake. They had met in Nouméa when
both their households were teetering.

'We almost ran after each other. Suddenly there were
sparks.'

They had married in Vila, and then the uncertainties of
independence had kept them apart for ten years – she in New
Caledonia, he in Vanuatu. She had only joined him last year.

'We knew,' she said. 'It wasn't easy, but we knew it was
our destiny to be together.'

At dinner Gaby appeared, showered, and his stetson was
off for the first time.

'If I had my life over again, do you know what I would do?
Biology, or something like it. To *discover* things, the molecule,
the universe in yourself, the dead stars whose light hasn't
reached us yet, all those questions. If you end up not asking
yourself questions any longer, it's all over.'

Over coffee he and Hélène had a huge row. She accused
him of being too generous to the workers.

'You give them money out of your own pocket for their
children's school fees.'

'Well, think of our grandson. Twelve years old and he
already has a motorbike.'

'And what about that apprentice of yours? 80,000 *vatu* so
he could buy himself a wife.'

'40,000. And I only lent it to him.'

'And were you surprised when the pastor at South West
Bay wrote a letter for him saying he couldn't come back to work
after the marriage?'

'I did it for my own pleasure.' Gaby shrugged. 'I liked the
boy. You'd do the same for your granddaughter. Anyway, it all
happened while you were in Nouméa and I was on my own.'

'For anything else, fine. But to buy him a woman, Gaby –
no no no.'

The bickering went on after I went to bed, a murmur
punctuated by the cockroaches ticking across the worn floor-
boards. As I fell asleep, I thought of the two of them facing each
other and arguing, while Gaby's bare foot stroked Hélène's calf
and she made no attempt to move it away.

The cockroaches were a mystery. However many you crushed, there were always more. But the greater mystery was that by the morning the corpses, ten or a dozen of them, had disappeared. I suppose the ants came and had them, but it was something you never saw happening, like people stealing cars or getting rich: you were only aware of it afterwards.

In the morning the sun bounced off the underside of the jalousies onto the bare floor. While Gaby was fetching the Land-Rover, Hélène said, 'It *was* 80,000 vatu he gave the boy, you know. He told me when it happened.'

Gaby drove me around the plantation in a Land-Rover without a windscreen. He harried his men to finish loading the barge and strode to the workshop. The mechanic Luigi, a cadaverous figure whose fingers were moulded into the perfect shape for cradling a carburetter, had been at Norsup for forty years – not quite ready for replacement. He was fiddling with a heat exchanger for another Land-Rover; putting his eye to it, then the air compressor, Gaby thrust it back at him and told him to put it back on immediately. We drove to the cacao plantation at Bushman's Bay: the seeds needed more drying and the manager had run out of sacks and failed to re-order them. Whenever we stopped, he was always first out of the Land-Rover.

Gaby had read Fletcher's book, and as we drove past the French school, he said: 'I want to tell you something. I am from an old colonialist line. But if I hadn't had my European wife, I would have gone downhill too. The planters who come out here on their own have got nothing to keep them on the right path, so instead of bringing their people up to their level, they go down.

'That's what is truly moving about Fletcher's book. He knows he is going into decline and losing his European habits, but he can't do anything about it, even if he tries very hard. It's the isolation, the ease of life, the fact that he can't help it. In the end he's one of the local people.'

I thought about what had upset Hélène. She thought it was a weakness in him. He knew that, without her, however tireless and professional a planter he was, his mind would have had no resistance to going the same way as Fletcher's.

On the way to the airstrip after lunch he told me that, after thirteen years, he was giving up. The knowledge that his achievements were fleeting ones was too much for him.

'If I left tomorrow, output would fall by fifty per cent. Even after saying the same thing to these men a hundred times a day. I want to live without those constraints. I'm going back to Queensland. All I need is a horse, a saddle, a fire, something to eat, the life of a stockman. I'll go to the muster for nothing. Whoever takes me will only have to find me my food and a horse.'

The de Havilland Heron bounced onto the coral airstrip that ran between the groves of palms, and four soldiers got out to take care of the wandering prisoners. A ni-Vanuatu sat on his bag, reading a Livre de Poche edition of *Les Trois Mousquetaires*.

We said goodbye. I remarked how peaceful it was to stand in the middle of the plantation. For the first time the sunburnt face lost its determined expression.

'This is *nothing*,' Gaby said almost angrily. 'Dark and cool, at five in the morning – you should have seen the rubber plantations at Phu-hoa. The trees are twelve metres high and make a roof of leaves over your head. At five in the morning you didn't hear a sound.'

I saw the two ends of his life joined. All his life Gaby had been catching glimpses of the boy on the plantation where he grew up; he had been looking for the silence, the peace and pared-down simplicity of childhood: looking on a ranch in New Caledonia, at the Norsup plantation, somewhere on a dusty boundary in Queensland, for the boy with cocoa-coloured eyes standing in the dark in the middle of a glade of rubber trees.

29
Beach Road

No other destination out of Vila presented itself. I had to go back
to Fiji. From there I could fly north if I had to. It was possible –
it was just possible – that the freighter bound for Western Samoa
had not yet put in an appearance.

In the last couple of days at Rossi's, surrounded by Vila's
cheerful seediness, I remembered Fiji's tidier dishonesty. The ni-
Vanuatu basked without effort in their own mysterious world, a
contradictory but hasteless business of practicality and magic.
Development – the way Europeans have of preventing other
people from living differently to themselves – hardly seemed to
matter. Vila and Luganville, unlike Suva, failed to draw the
crowds because the ni-Vanuatu lacked almost all the material
aspirations of the Fijians.

At Lautoka the old phoney normality hung in the air. I was
sick of the bombardment of transparent courtesies, and I scowled
and talked to nobody, haunting the port for two days like a bad
omen.

On a heavy afternoon I found what I was looking for: an
ugly container ship, the *Forum Samoa*, in from Auckland and
without a curve to her line. She was leaving the next day for
Apia. I hung on the decision of the sandy-haired captain, who
looked bored by the whole business. Sighing, he said yes.

In the ship's hospital was the most luxurious accom-
modation I had had in three months: crackling linen, the first
reliable hot water for two months, a clean toilet (*with paper*), a
shower, a writing table and a small library: Heyerdahl's *Fatu-
Hiva*, with its descriptions of Polynesia that made it sound like a
naturist's holiday gone wrong; the absurd *Pornografia* by Witold

Gombrowicz; and half a dozen Readers' Digest Condensed Novels.

The *Forum Samoa* floated off at dawn like a giant shoebox. On board time passed as featurelessly as a convalescence. There was a consecutive pair of Saturdays as the ship slipped over the Pacific Date Line. I stayed under the spell of the white hospital room and the narrow deck outside. In the afternoons I sat and laughed over Gombrowicz's two vacuous Warsaw intellectuals and their experiment in erotic subversion.

My bad, lazy side was taking over. I should have been getting on. I should have flown north from Fiji, where there was a scheduled air service to the Marshall Islands. Instead I was drifting eastwards in luxury, and I had no idea how I would get back.

I wanted to see Robert Louis Stevenson's grave, at the top of a Samoan mountain; and in the way that the word Turkestan had hypnotised Robert Byron, Western Samoa's name had a hypnotic effect on me: the legendary homeland of Polynesia. (I prayed it would be nothing like Heyerdahl's descriptions.) Neither reason justified a one-way diversion. But being on the move, in this floating Sybaris, made me forget idleness and the loss of purpose.

The ship's officers were a corps of like-minded Germans. Their sense of national purpose was their only common bond. They were courteous and helpful and then about their business in the deodorised companionways. The provisioning was miraculous: steak tartare for breakfast; at midday *Nudelsuppe mit Frankfurter*; and T-bone steaks for dinner. But there was no conversation at meals. As each officer finished eating, he stood and said 'Excuse me' and returned to his own cabin.

On the third morning we raised Savai'i, a green-grey whalebacked outline, and the crew of taciturn, fat Samoans, within sight of the earth ovens that laid a wreath of smoke along the shore, were suddenly full of good-mornings and how-are-yous.

There had been a cyclone six weeks before, and in Apia bay on Upolu, the next island, it looked as if a petulant giant had been playing. The dock was a jumble of empty containers scattered everywhere, and the inter-island ferry, a blue hulk of 3000 tons, had been tossed onto the beach in front of the main post office.

The bureaucracy was back to normal. When the passport officer, with buttons missing from his shirt and hair on his mountainous belly like desert scrub, failed to get his case of soft drinks and carton of cigarettes – the German who dealt with him was new on board – it appeared I had to stay with the ship till the passport office opened next morning. As the one-day flies died out in their millions, the chief mate decided at last to give me some advice:

'Remember. Here you are a *palagi*. To a Samoan *palagi* culture is wonderful, but it will always be just *palagi* culture to him. You are there to give. He is there to take from you.

'We brought out many containers of food in February after the cyclone. They said, "We have no food, no houses, no clothing." Then two weeks later the government said, "No more food and clothing. Just send us money." What can the government do with money when there is nothing to buy, except fill its pockets?'

There are three things I will remember about Apia: the heat – the sun was never less than vertical until an hour before sunset; the flies; and the pace of life on Beach Road, which was just this side of immobility. If you wanted a phone, the answer at the post office was 'Come back at nine tonight'. Lunch took an hour and a half to arrive, long after your hunger had gone. People came to appointments two days late. Everything happened in the end, but your skill at waiting, helped by the heat and flies, was tested to the limits.

My first experience misled me: I only had to wait an hour

at the passport office. The office was a flaking humid place like the ticket office of a rundown country station. Most of the buildings in town were the same, rickety clapboard structures with some decayed English formality about them, and the cyclone had failed to disturb their shabby picturesqueness, even though many of the roofs were gone. The churches up and down Beach Road, a rhythm of gleaming stone and wood spires, had somehow escaped the storm intact.

In a bus from the scorching market to the Seaside Hotel a notice was pinned next to the driver:

> *Six common mistakes often occur.*
> 1. Forgetting to say 'thank you'.
> 2. Keeping people waiting.
> 3. Breaking promises.
> 4. Failing to apologise.
> 5. Being too nosy.
> 6. Political manoeuvring.

The buses, one of the coolest places to be once they were moving, were built like boats; their wooden bodies were modified hulls carved and finished in graceful lines on chassis that had never been new. They were a sign of Polynesia, like the hair the colour of coal in the dark that hung in plaits between the shoulders of the schoolgirls who, as the bus filled, gave up their seats to sit on the nearest male passenger's lap. To each other they shrieked with laughter. If you caught their eye, they turned away, sulking (or pretending) at the familiarity.

In the market the vendors were asleep on pandanus mats on the ground. There was no fresh fruit, and only taro and nuts and palm oil were to be had in any quantity. But despite the shortages of the cyclone, the men were an absurd size, and the women, embodying the Polynesian equation of beauty with surface area, only slightly smaller.

Robert Louis Stevenson had come to Western Samoa in 1889 for his health. Within five years he had written himself to death. His output was mind-boggling. On Christmas Day 1891 he wrote to Sidney Colvin, 'God bless you, what a lot I have accomplished; *Wrecker* done, *Beach of Falesa* done, half the *History*: *c'est étonnant.*' Virtually two novels and half a history book in fourteen months – though in another fourteen months he was 'exulting to do nothing' and in his final year he talked often about giving up writing.

How did Stevenson work so hard, even for a week? How did he keep himself going *for five years*? The daytime temperature was forty degrees and the head-cracking sun robbed you of your energy. Stevenson had constant fevers, colds, 'collywobbles' that did not stop him. Nothing stopped him.

Then, at the age of forty-four, he had a cerebral haemorrhage. When the naval doctor was called to Vailima to examine the unconscious man, he found the women rubbing his arms with brandy. The arms were pencil-thin.

'How can anybody write books with arms as thin as these?' the doctor demanded.

Maggie Stevenson retorted, 'He has written *all* his books with arms like these!'

Stevenson talked and wrote of a land of content. The township of Apia was predictably unpromising: the random piles of unhusked coconuts, trucks abandoned at the roadside where they last broke down, the peeling buildings with their greasy windows, the small fires burning on the lots in between; people getting in and out of Japanese pick-ups, concrete laid on buildings half-begun that would never be finished, the kiosks selling Milo and Coke. I recognised the serpentine habits of car drivers, the silence at midday, the home-sewn pinafores and shorts of the schoolchildren, the video stores and Chinese traders and whitewashed churches and ragged, dusty palms; the sudden softening of all the faults at sunset as the clouds rouged the light and added shadows, and the next morning the noise everywhere of grass brushes at dawn.

It was a backwater of a town where America and Japan had begun to take hold. The pick-ups were Hiluxes with grabber tyres; the Mormon college outside town looked like a high-security garrison. At dinner I heard a Samoan having a row with his girlfriend. He stormed across Beach Road to his jeep. He was wearing a torn teeshirt and Nike Air Jordans. A torrent of angry Samoan issued from his lips, then he shouted in English, 'Ain't nobody goin' to tell me how to comb my hair!'

Something of the Samoans' pride remained. On their *fales* pandanus thatch was replaced by corrugated iron, tailored – as skilfully as tailoring a model dome out of a sheet of paper – to preserve the traditional roof line. Around the wall-less houses the gardens were micro-parks of grass and lilies and frangipanis, dotted with the rough concrete tombs of relatives. And I had a sneaking admiration for their dislike of their part in the service economy. When I got in their taxis young drivers with sleek hair turned up their cassette players and ignored me.

The Seaside was the kind of hotel I'd grown accustomed to, an old rust-coloured bungalow partitioned into a dozen rooms. In the afternoon you could sit on the verandah that overlooked the wharf and ignore the one-day flies that stuck in your hair. Later, at dusk, the flying beetles blundered into you, and the striped black and white mosquitoes were reinforced by emerald green ones, and it was wise to find somewhere else to sit.

On the second evening, at last cool and dark, I walked down Beach Road, past the transvestites gossiping on the bridge, as far as Aggie Grey's. The building, floodlit in the dark, was a disappointment, an insipid remodelling of the original hotel opened by the daughter of William Swann, Stevenson's pharm-acist. It was a sketchy, prettified version of the gabled, dormered tropical house, the kind of place for people who required air-conditioning and fax machines.

Inside, beneath the high roof of the bar, surrounded by thatched suites called things like 'Marlon Brando's Fale' and 'Katherine Hepburn's Fale', was a hint of Hell. Bored Polynesian beauties swung between the tables, serving flowering cocktails to corpulent couples, and the air was stiff with the reserve of the wealthy.

'What will you have?'

The first question in the Tropics: the man at my elbow introduced himself: chief engineer on the *Nivaga II*, a ruddy-looking, affable Scot named Nisbet. The beers came, beads of water flowing down the glasses, and my luck changed.

'There's no regular cargo run north from here. But we're heading up to Tuvalu whenever we can get loaded.'

We had dinner together. There were cabins available, Nisbet said, though the ship – 'due to the pace of work at the wharf,' he said, meaningfully – would not be leaving for a while. 'Come and see me in a couple of days. I'll tell you when.'

I was still thirsty when I got back to my room. I bought a litre bottle of Vailima beer from the kiosk next door, and in the yellow light from the docks I sat and read Stevenson's *A Footnote to History: Eight Years of Trouble in Samoa*. The next morning I couldn't move.

30
Political manoeuvring

'Apia,' Stevenson wrote, 'is the seat of the political sickness in Samoa.' In the 1880s half the town belonged to the Germans, half to the British and Americans. It was a place of rumour, gossip and betrayal. Men schemed absurdly for the limited supply of copra and sometimes pronounced themselves prime minister for a time, before being arrested by the passing captain of one or another of the powers. Apia was a lawless settlement, pursuing the kind of ugly behaviour that stung a Samoan into complaining that he was 'weary of whites upon the beach'. It might have remained so, but for the fact that three imperial powers were engaged in the microscopic affray.

It was the Germans who were most oppressed by patriotism. Behind 'the German firm', the four thousand hectares of the Deutsche Handels und Plantagen Gesellschaft für Süd-See Inseln zu Hamburg, were united the political ambitions of every German planter. A symbol of luxury and repression to the Samoans, with its velvet avenues and fixed-contract labour abuses, to the German population it was a costly and beautiful jewel of colonial industry.

The British and Americans were little better. Offered the opportunity to behave honourably, they declined it. They wanted Samoa because the others did. Puppet kings were installed and deposed, Samoan factions were armed against each other. Merchants, consuls and naval commanders engaged in a moscow of conspiracy. Stevenson was outraged by an ordinance directed at him by Sir John Bates Thurston in Fiji (who with his knighthood may have lost his enlightenment) which ruled that all opposition to the British Consul's policies amounted to sedition.

The savagest wars ended in 1893; the British withdrew their claim to the islands in 1899. Samoa was partitioned into Western and US Samoa. On 29 August 1914 the German governor of Western Samoa surrendered to a New Zealand expeditionary force. Forty-eight years later, in 1962, Western Samoa was the first nation to reassert its independence in Polynesia.

A year after the wars petered out, and a few months before Stevenson's final collapse, the chiefs who had been imprisoned as a result of the fighting came to Stevenson's house at Vailima, 'the five rivers'. He had visited them in gaol and paid for their food. He wanted them to end their fighting for good and he read them a speech on the verandah where the haemorrhage later struck him, warning them: 'If you do not occupy and use your country, others will.'

In Samoa the true champion would not fight, he said, but would stay on his land, plant food trees and gather harvests. He asked:

> What are you doing with your talent, Samoa? Your three talents, Savai'i, Upolu and Tutuila? Have you buried it in a napkin?... I do not speak of this lightly, because I love Samoa and her people. I love the land, I have chosen it to be my home while I live, and my grave after I am dead; and I love the people, and have chosen them to be my people to live and die with. And I see that the day is come now of the great battle... whether you are to pass away like these other races of which I have been speaking, or to stand fast and have your children living on and honouring your memory in the land you received of your fathers...

Tiny though it was, the episode in which Stevenson became involved was fascinating. It had the dimensions of territorial squabbles everywhere. Somewhere in it, in all the farce and heat, you could hear the good Scottish exile talking about Scotland. For Stevenson there had always been a tang of peat and water, earth beneath wood, in Samoa. In one letter he wrote to Colvin:

> It pours with rain from the westward, very unusual kind of weather; I was standing out on the little verandah in front of my room this morning, and there went through me or over me a wave of extraordinary and apparently baseless emotion. I literally staggered. And then the

explanation came, and I knew I had found a frame of mind
and body that belonged to Scotland, and particularly to the
neighbourhood of Callander. Very odd these identities of
sensation, and the world of connotations implied; highland
huts, and peat smoke, and the brown, swirling rivers, and
wet clothes, and whisky, and the romance of the past, and
indescribable bite of the whole thing at a man's heart,
which is – or rather lies at the bottom of – a story.

31
Captain Evans

You could not fail to be seduced by Stevenson the optimist, the
romantic, the sympathetic exile. But for two days, immobile on
my bed, all I could think was that I'd made the seventh common
mistake (after 'political manoeuvring'): believing the romance of
the past still existed. I had kerosene poisoning, from dregs in the
beer. It happened, the hotelkeeper said. The Samoans collected
their kerosene in beer bottles and the brewery didn't wash the
bottles out. Every time I tried to stand up, I fell over. For two
days I could do nothing but fall back into the bed and doze and
listen to the Customs men playing table-tennis next door, and the
sluggish conversations on the verandah outside my room.

There were three Australians in the hotel, come for the
surfing. They complained about the food and the temperature of
the beer, but against that, they had scored every night. One,
John, was a blond boy with terrible teeth. Every time one of the
others asked him to do something, he refused. The exchanges
were oddly soothing:

'Your turn to do the run into town, John.'

'Gut fucked.'

'Your turn John or oil hit you.'

'Oi don't have to go.'

'Wear out of cigs and ut's your turn.'

'Oi said gut fucked.'

'John, oim gunner fucking step on your head.'

'Well oi ain't going.'

'John, *wear both gunner step on your fucking head.*'

John finally went. When he came back in the hired jeep he had a girl with him. (The other two were already fitted out. A couple of Samoan girls plugged into Walkmans sat by them, chewing gum.)

In the night there was another row, full of door-slamming and an Australian voice yelling, 'Fuck off. Fuck off, *now.*'

The next morning only two of the Australians appeared at breakfast. 'Oi still can't believe ut,' one of them said, 'John brunging a tranny back. Dud yer see the look on hus face when she slipped out of her *lava lava*?'

The poison disappeared. Feeling weak, I went for a walk.

I bumped into Captain Evans by chance at the shipping office when he was collecting his mail. He was eighty-two, and slight for a figure of legend.

He said, 'Come and have some lemonade at home,' and we drove straight out of town to his hexagonal lemon-and-vanilla palace in the hills.

A palace, and a memory of the sea. He had built the house himself. The windows leaned outwards like the bridge of a ship. The doors had small brass plaques nailed to them. Outside the 'Captain's Day Room' Captain Evans liked to sit by the rail, looking down over the tangled garden, his bifocals perched on his speckled cranium and his bell-bottomed trousers flapping in the breeze. When he talked his jaw champed between the words in concentration.

His black dog came and lay at his feet. His tame one-legged pigeon hopped over from the verandah rail and sat on his wrist. He was like a character misremembered from *Treasure Island*: the bird had come out as a pigeon not a parrot, and it was the bird that had lost a leg not the man.

Joe Evans had been a sailor all his life, lying about his age to get to sea, and running out of Malaya in the war aboard a minesweeper that finished up like a pepperpot. His stories were spiced with decisiveness and he had a taste for glamour, racing speedboats with Tunku Abdul Rahman in the Thirties and taking to the jungle in the Emergency where he dived into a lily pond and acquired the nickname 'Frog', surfacing stagily with a lily pad on his head and a necklace of leeches.

He had tried England, and bought a lovely house on Rosslare Strand when he retired, but it bored him and back he came to Samoa. The Samoans, he said, had shocking tempers and he had recently had to divorce his wife on account of this. He had three sons; the youngest was six years old.

Now a bachelor again, he often brought a Samoan girl home for the night.

'I've got an arrangement with the woman next door. I feed her children but she does the cooking. Nothing else between us. Sometimes I bring a young thing home for the weekend, and she decides if she likes her or not.'

He took me upstairs to 'The Captain's Cabin'. Above the door he had hung his sword, and his MBE and medals sat by the dressing table. 'The trouble is, invariably they steal so I have to throw them out. For two years one came to me, twenty-three, lovely girl but she stole everything, including my loaded gun, pistol, camera, everything. So I had to get rid of her.'

Lately he had been getting bored. But everybody knew Captain Evans – he had been harbourmaster in Apia for four years – and it was no trouble to fix up a trip.

'It'll do me good to get back to sea for a bit. They've signed me on as a supernumerary. I'll get one dollar a month, keeps me on the books. We go to Suva, Port Vila, Santo, Honiara, Port Moresby, Madang where I was pilot and harbourmaster, Lae, Singapore, Suez, Rotterdam and Hamburg.

'I'm leaving on the first of next month, and I expect I'll be back in four months' time.'

He thought about the future. The future was the thing that kept him going. He had always been ready for change.

'Have you seen all the tombs around the houses here? When I go, I think they'll probably plant me down there, in that little patch of sunlight. They'll give me flowers every day, and the cement will stay hot, so the dog will sleep on it at night.'

The next morning the hotel had no water, and the cockroaches were out thirsting in their hundreds.

I walked at sunrise down the path cut for Stevenson by the grateful chiefs, past the house 'built for angels' at the five rivers. An icy pool ran at the bottom, and I doused myself. The trees were still down from the cyclone all along the steep path up the flank of Mount Vaea; it was a slippery way, climbing over sweaty, fallen trunks and scattering black lizards and hearing the high-pitched *diff diff diff* of the cardinals in the forest roof.

I sat on the tomb at the top and watched the light lift up through the clouds in a sudden burst of chrysoprase, revealing the soft hollow of the valley and the cat's-paws on the reef below. Hand over hand Stevenson's body had been carried this way, half the age of Joe Evans, but sharing until the final blow the same 'unwearied hope of finding something new in a new country'.

Captain Evans would never write for himself a 'Requiem' like the one Stevenson had on his tomb, scribbled in Hyères when, with Fanny, he said, he was the most truly happy:

Under the wide and starry sky,
Dig the grave and let me lie.
Glad did I live and gladly die,
    And I laid me down with a will.

This be the verse you grave for me:
Here he lies where he longed to be,
Home is the sailor, home from sea,
    And the hunter home from the hill.

But Stevenson had known Joe's predecessor, a Captain Hamilton married to a native woman. One night he heard hymns. Captain Hamilton had died. The balcony of his house was full of women singing, and the old man lay in a sheet on his table. Hamilton was a man for whom Stevenson had had a deep brotherly affection. Stevenson's description of the old captain's death would do for Joe Evans too, when the time came:

the girls were sitting clustered at my feet... the captain's hands were folded on his bosom, his face and head were composed; he looked as if he might speak at any moment; I have never seen this kind of waxwork more express or more venerable; and when I went away, I was conscious of a certain envy for the man who was out of the battle.

On the road from Vailima back into Apia, the cab driver surpassed the rest in his indifference. The soul music from the sound system was deafening, and he was only prepared to take one passenger, in the front seat. The rear seat was given over entirely to the bulk of a 100-watt amplifier.

32
The bursting sky

> *Palagi*: the Polynesian for a white man or woman, a
> European, a person from the horizon. *'Pa'* is an explosion,
> a burst of noise or light, *'lagi'* the sky or horizon, hence
> *palagi*, 'sky-burster'

Apia was getting on my nerves. You could have enough of lazy
taxi drivers, a straggling picturesque seafront, an utter lack of
pretensions, the charm of shacks and churches and a nice whiff
of the past. You'd seen it all in two days: after a week it was just
another hot and very idle place where nothing happened. I
longed for Norman to appear, his hydrangea wobbling, and wave
his cane to make *something* occur, or for Pascal's chickenshit-
coloured LandCruiser to come crashing through the potholes.

I saw Nisbet, the chief engineer of the *Nivaga,* again. He
was standing tight-lipped on the wharf. 'We'll not leave before
next Wednesday,' he said.

So there was time for an excursion out of Apia. Stevenson
had talked of a land of content, despite the wars and conspiracies; perhaps because of them: a conflict was something you
could get your teeth into. In a hundred years Western Samoa, to
judge by its capital, had replaced that vitality with a slow trickle
of Western comforts and a lethargic enthusiasm for the all-
eclipsing ideal, a better standard of living.

At lunchtime, after I had seen Nisbet, the editor of the
Samoa Observer finally turned up to our appointment, several
days late. His name was Sano Malifa and he was plump, intense
and suspicious. He had the journalist's contempt for vagrant
writers and he enjoyed his reputation as the bad man of Apia. He
was rejoicing in a piece that had appeared that morning about the
chief of police's son beating up a motorist. We were in Amigo's,
Apia's version of El Vino's: Samoan journalists and *palagi* sat

in dark air-conditioned corners scoffing hamburgers and Vailima beer.

He screwed up his eyes. 'Why do you want to see me? Are you writing a book?'

'Perhaps.'

His fluffy beard shook. 'I know. A bloody tourist book.'

'Yes.'

'You should find out what's going on.' He stared angrily at me. 'Look at this.' He stabbed his finger at a quarter-page advertisement in his paper. ' "There is only one thing better than aid from Japan..." ' he read. ' "The Samoan Rugby Team back from Japan." ' The Western Samoans had just won 37-11 in Tokyo.

'Western Samoa,' he almost shouted, 'was the first nation in the Pacific to regain its independence. So why is it still so undeveloped? I'll tell you why. Foreign aid is a sickness here. They have had two million dollars in aid for the cyclone. Parliament split it forty-seven ways, one cheque for each MP, and they are supposed to distribute it. Do they? Who knows? Every time there is an election there is a huge aid drive. Do you know why the potholes on Beach Road will never be mended? If they were mended, they wouldn't give us any more aid to mend them.'

Malifa was happy to be angry. He had a conflict to get his teeth into. He chewed injustices through his beard, savouring them. He suspected me of ignorance, superficiality, condescension, everything. 'You have to go to Savai'i to see anything. They live like Samoans should live there. They won't get the money for reconstruction. But they have already reconstructed. It's what they have always done.'

On the front page of his paper was another story, about the King of Tonga. At seventy-two the king – so the report had it – had become a born-again Christian under the influence of a Californian sect. Denouncing his opponents as communists, he

believed a coup by the forces of evil was imminent. In addition
he was vexed that some members of parliament had dared to
question him over the selling of around 10,000 Tongan passports
to Hong Kong Chinese. They wanted to know where the money
had gone. He refused to say.

I suggested to Malifa it wasn't wise to print royal tittle-
tattle in a serious newspaper like his.

He shook his head and grinned. 'You're wrong. That's the
best-documented story we have.'

If I took the ferry next morning – the one that had escaped the
cyclone – I would have five days on Savai'i before the *Nivaga*
left.

The boat was supposed to leave at six, but by the time
someone had fetched the captain, drunk from the night before
and sweating like an aubergine, the belt of gold-green light was
broadening fast across the top of Mount Vaea. By nine o'clock
the sparkle and freshness of the day would already be staled by a
foretaste of midday heat. As the ferry sailed, the sun rocketed
into the pale heavens and hung there, pouring so much light and
heat into the sea that the world seemed shocked into immobility,
paralysed by the theft of its shadows.

The owner of the Seaside Hotel had scribbled down the
name of a chief he knew on the north coast of Savai'i, promising
that this was a good man who would look after me. I got off the
ferry and onto a bus. I had no idea where I was going.

The road from the wharf had been turned to sand by the
cyclone and the cracked and broken way led to a distempered
skyline of broken trees. I sat on the bus and thought: You've
fooled yourself again. There might be a residue of the tradition
of hospitality here. Stevenson had written that in the *fa'a Samoa*,
the Samoan way, it was a customary right. Samoans once partied
from village to village, delighting in something called the

malaga: songs announced their coming, virgins prepared the *kava* bowl, and so on.

But Stevenson had also noticed that the language revealed a different side to the *malaga*. The word *sona*, used of epidemics, meant 'to overcome with fire or flood', or with visitors. A 'long call', *afemoeina*, also meant 'to come as a calamity'. And the word that meant 'to hide in the wood' also meant 'to avoid visitors'.

I showed the woman next to me the piece of paper with the chief's name on it. After three hours I was pushed off the bus outside the village of Manase.

There were two *fale*s on the shore, one of them parallelogrammed by the cyclone, both surrounded by drifts of sand and trees splintered by the explosion.

Alosio stepped out of the shade. There were no explanations: it was clear I had come to stay. To Alosio, I was a kinsman home from sea. Hugging me, brushing my cheek with his, he said: 'Come with me. Half my coconuts, half my pigs, half my hens have been blown away.' Small vowels detonated at the ends of his sentences. I had stuffed the pandanus mat I had taken to carrying with food – rice, tinned fish, imported apples – and as I dashed them to him, he gave a plosive gasp of appreciation. He was almost the first thin Samoan I had seen, a devout Catholic, and looked strangely like Little Richard in a *lava lava*, with a crooked smile and a rock'n'roller's quiff.

We sat beneath his half-collapsed roof and talked. His speech was peppered with insults for the 'big crooks – ah!': Samoa's prime minister, for one, who still featherbedded the London Missionary Society, and Joseph Smith of the Latter Day Saints. When I told Alosio that Smith had set up his church in order to indulge his sexual passions and had had at least sixty wives, he threw his head back and did a dance of glee on the sand in front of his *fale*.

Alosio was from Manase but preferred to live outside, on the edge of the sea. The whole family, Alosio's wife and daughter-in-law and his three remaining sons, lived in the two *fales*. Beta, his eldest son Sio's wife, had fine upswept eyes and strong legs and shoulders, but the sensual slowness was turning to fat. The youngest son, Loia, smelt of cinnamon. He was fascinated by the hairs on my legs, stroking and pulling them while he sang to himself. Beta was looking furtively at my holdall, and later some apples were gone. Alosio called her back, confiscating the fruit, and criticised me for leaving my bag open. 'Samoans steal – ah! humbug.'

There were kingfishers at sunset and the mosquitoes rained down. An hour after midnight the tide ebbed. We waded out through the warm water to our necks with the long net. With the first pass six bream fell into the bucket. With the second we caught nothing. Alosio said it was the lightning that had started in the sky. All the time shooting stars dropped like tracer.

I spent four days with Alosio in the *fales* outside Manase. He and his wife gave me their bed, a huge bumpy soft mattress, and brought me cups of tea all day long. In the afternoons sleep was the only escape from the light that bounced off the hot sand. The heat and the strange routine made me begin to think that in sleep and out of it, the experience was a dream, blank and pleasant and effortless. It *was* the land of content. I couldn't imagine how any work was ever done here.

In the last letter Colvin had from Stevenson, Stevenson had said an interesting thing: 'It is the proof of intelligence, the proof of not being a barbarian, to be able to enter into something outside of oneself, something that does not touch one's next neighbour in the city omnibus.'

Alosio wanted to know everything. I told him about Europe, the geography, the weather; I mentioned over the rice and *lupo* – small fried fish – that Europeans ate together (Beta and his wife ate after the men). He kept returning to this unheard-of habit.

He marvelled at the foolishness of people who travelled. He had no desire to move from where he was: 'I think you waste your money when you get in a plane, throw it in the sea – ah!'

On Sunday there was Mass. The Catholic church in the next village was a vision of sugared icing; its white baroque towers, minarets squatting on rolls of glistening stone, soared to the sun. All the churches in the Pacific were too big, but this one was absurdly oversized, a dazzling cake of a thing. Inside the pews were rammed as close as charter-flight seats, and against expectations the Mass had a Protestant dullness about it.

Walking home from Mass, we got a lift in the back of a truck already occupied by three Samoan girls, swathed in white. One was paler than the others and had the face of a madonna, with waves of auburn hair – more Scots blood – and a delicate spoon-shaped jaw. When Alosio repeated the story of Joseph Smith, she started to giggle and, with the jolting of the truck, her white *lava lava* slipped open.

I had not expected to see this: a deep blue field of tattoos – the agonising zigzags and rectilinear patterns cut with combs of bone at puberty – from her calf to the top of her thigh. I thought: This was what had made Cook's men think of mermaids in Tahiti – the sleek flashing flank, blue and bronze. In the engravings I'd seen, these long, dark patterns had seemed foreign and disfiguring. Confronted with the girl's legs less than a metre away, as glossy as japan, I found the effect mesmerising. Submitting to the comb was a sign of nobility; there was some lingering allure attached to the first, ritualised experience of pain. There was no other word: beneath the white cotton, the tattoos were dangerously sexy.

The girl saw me watching her and she snatched her *lava lava* close and turned away, blushing.

That evening Alosio and I walked into Manase to arrange the details for the feast to be given by eight chiefs in Safotu the following day, and I came across the girl again. Her name was Faema. Her father was the talking-chief we had come to see.

Alosio and the talking-chief discussed the feast. Faema's mother, a vast woman with a sharp manner, was unimpressed by *palagi*.

'What's your name? That's a girl's name. You married? Why not? Why did you come to Samoa?'

I looked at Faema. 'I came to marry a Samoan girl with beautiful tattoos.'

'Well, have you found one?'

'No. They won't marry me because I can't climb coconut

trees.'

'Don't worry,' she sniffed. 'Plenty *pehu* here.' She spoon-
ed up a piece of brown sponge cake for me and said, 'Faema,
show the *palagi* your tattoos.' But her daughter stood by the
stove and blushed, and as soon as I looked away she slipped out
of the back door.

The kitchen was well-organised, with a long table cut from
hardwood in the centre and plaited coconut-palm blinds half-
keeping out the mosquitoes. Kittens played everywhere. But the
mother's banter tired me. Alosio looked at me and said, 'You
mata fia moi – your eyes are sleepy.' For the first time I noticed
how red his eyes were in his gentle face, and that he had the
beginnings of cataracts.

On the walk back, the houses lit like children's theatres in
the dark, Alosio laughed and said, 'Faema your *pehu*. I know –
ah!'

I woke at sunrise. There was a pig to be killed, and it
screeched like a truck horn as it was dragged across the sand. It
lay on its back in the sun, white and dazzling, as Alosio and Sio
held a stave hard across its throat. Alosio told me to hold its
back legs, and when it died, its wild heartbeat ceasing, a curly
tail of shit came out, on which a dozen flies immediately settled.
Plucked and washed in the sea, it was whiter than ever.

Alosio cut a square in the stomach and pushed out the guts.
Sio found the heart, cut it out and put it to his mouth to blow it
up, laughing. The pig was washed in the sea again and taken to
the *umu* for stuffing with hot stones and cottonwood leaves.
Steam rose in little clouds from the searing of stone pressed into
the throat, another stone, another cloud. On top went layers of
taro leaves and coconut cream, wrapped fish, fresh brown
crayfish, the whole lot covered in banana leaves until almost no
smoke emerged.

Three hours later, the food was ready. In the chiefs' *fale*
next to the icing-sugar church, twenty huge portions were served

up on plates of chopped banana leaves. The families that had prepared the food, Alosio among them, waited in the *fale* alongside.

Alosio was distant and irritable. His pig, for some reason, had not been served. The feast was for the chiefs and carpenters who had rebuilt the Catholic sister's house after the cyclone, but after all the slavish preparation it was an anti-climax. In less than a quarter of an hour the banana-leaf plates were wiped clean.

Alosio replied curtly to the harangue of thanks delivered by one of the chiefs, then turned to me and said: 'You hungry?' But it was not over yet. Five mats and Alosio's pig, with a box of tinned mackerel, were presented to the chief carpenter. The mats were so finely woven they hung like paper. There must have been six months' work in each of them. Decorated with dyed feathers and long fringes, their possession raised a man's status. Later he would give them away in turn, the currency of a gift that, by Samoan ritual, required to be given. Kings made beds with them: 'you never saw such a couch – I believe of nearly fifty (half at least) fine mats,' Stevenson exclaimed when he paid a visit to one of the puppet kings; 'here I reposed alone'.

The second carpenter, who had been deputed to make the speech after the presentation, hadn't practised enough. The words were delivered at ear-splitting volume to no one in particular across the grass. Alosio's cheerful mouth slumped angrily.

The speech went on and on and on.

'What is he saying?'

'That man bloody fool', said Alosio. 'If I had a gun, I would shoot him here' – pointing between his eyes – 'right in the middle of the head. Humbug – ah!'

His hunger had added to his fury. 'Samoa way is a humbug way. We make the food, and all *we* have is tea and coconut.

'You all sit in London and eat and talk together for a long time. In Samoa they eat after we cook all morning. Five minutes all gone. I like *palagi* way. You don't eat in five minutes, then shout at me for an hour.'

He continued to grumble as we walked to the store. We bought bread and soft drinks, but dignity forbade a chief to eat in the street and there was no placating him. 'I keep thinking about my white pig for that carpenter. You see size of other pigs? That carpenter is good man, but my pig is too much. And they eat *everything* – ah! Nothing for us, nothing left, not even for dogs and cats. You hungry? I think of those fat chiefs and I am hungry.'

Outraged by the injustice, he started laughing; his lick of hair fell forward and quivered. 'And I think of second carpenter's speech too: I could shoot him in the middle of the head – ah! I don't like Samoa way, prefer *palagi* way. *Fa'a Samoa, fa'a* humbug. *Next time* I kill the second carpenter, *not* my white pig.'

We slept later, and when I woke up, the day was heavy and the sun was going down like ragged footlights. I had to leave that night to catch the *Nivaga II* from Apia the following day. I struggled off the mattress and saw Alosio sitting in a chair, looking solemnly at me across the *fale*. He had made tea, and now I was awake he poured it. He knew I was leaving, and there were speeches to be made. But I hadn't expected this speech.

'This is your family in Samoa,' he said. 'In your life you think too much. If you think and think, and cannot make your life work in London, you must come here – ah. I am your second father. If I am dead, you must come to my children. If you come to Samoa again, you must come straight to Savai'i. If you are in trouble, I will pray for you. If life becomes too difficult, you just come.'

The bus appeared at three in the morning under another conflagration of stars. I urged Alosio to go to Apia for his cataracts, and we said goodbye at the steps, God-blessing and hugging each other with the greatest formality. The bus went on to the lava field at the end of the road before turning, and there was another view of his *fale* as we passed back going the right way for the wharf. The small boy Loia had a fever – I had given him paracetamol and antibiotics – and the pressure lamp was lit. Through the blue-painted uprights of the *fale* I saw Alosio's silhouette bending over his son, picked out against the encampment of mosquito nets across the matted floor.

In Manase a woman had got on the bus and sat in the seat next to mine. She had a *lava lava* scarfed around her head against the night air, and she was young and solid. After a while I became aware of her thigh against mine. Then this happened:

Her fingers were laced through mine, and she placed my hand on the inner curve of her thigh. Her voice in my ear said, 'Do you like to have a Samoan girlfriend?'

Half-turning my head and seeing the shine of two plum-dark eyes, I assured her that I thought Samoan women were very beautiful. I tried to disengage my hand. But she was too quick for me, clamping it between her thighs, leaving her fingers free to crawl towards my crotch. Abruptly they stopped short, but carried on squeezing and paddling.

What was supposed to happen? 'Night-creeping' was a Samoan institution, boys slipping into *fales* to have fast sex with girls who were waiting for them. But how did you extract yourself from this kind of teasing with dignity? The girl was giggling silently at my side; I realised too that the pressure from my cock was becoming painful. I managed to move her hand away, and said foolishly:

'Do you live on Savai'i?'

'Yes,' as her hand went back.

'Where are you going?'

'To visit my aunt.'

I moved the hand away again.

'Where?'

Her hand gripped my knee, stroking the hairs just above it. 'Here,' she said, giggling again, and standing up to pull the bell cord. The *lava lava* slipped from her head as she did so. It was the talking-chief's daughter, Fanua.

'Goodbye,' she said. 'Sorry you never saw my tattoos.'

On the ferry I imagined Cook's first days in Tahiti: the working-class captain viewed as a king, the banquets in sweltering uniforms, the taboo impelling Tahitians to pickpocket and steal, the flies that ate the paint off the artist Parkinson's canvas – and the sudden exposure to sex. The captain's reason for being there, to observe on 3 June 1769 the transit of the planet Venus across the sun, paled into insignificance next to the descriptions of the Polynesians on Tahiti, where, in Banks's words, 'both the bodies and souls of the women are modeld into the utmost perfection for that soft science idleness the father of Love'. (Bougainville, arriving the previous year, believed he had been transported to the Garden of Eden and named the island New Cythera, after the place where Aphrodite – or Venus – first emerged from the sea.)

Cook took no mistress, but Banks and the others were ever-ready swains. When the *Endeavour*'s quadrant and tele-scopes proved inadequate to record the exact passage of the planet after seven weeks of preparation, all Cook could manage about the experiment was a couple of lines. His journals however are full of incidents like this:

> Mr Banks was as usual at the gate of the fort trading with the people... the man (who appeared to be only a servant of the two women)... took several pieces of cloth and spread them on the ground. One of the young women then stepped upon the cloth, and with as much innocency as one could possibly conceive, exposed herself entirely

naked from the waist downwards. In this manner she turned herself once or twice round, I am not certain which, then stepped off the cloth and dropped down her clothes. More cloth was spread upon the former and she again performed the same ceremony. The cloth was then rolled up and given to Mr Banks, and the two young women went and embraced him which ended the ceremony.

I loved that 'I am not certain which': accuracy faltering in the face of bewildering sexual openness, as the woman displayed to Banks her tattooed thighs and buttocks. The meaning of 'embraced', however, was clear, even if its conclusion happened later, and it put Banks a step ahead of me. But Cook's landfall at Matavai Bay would have had the same empty beach and tangled palms as Manase, the quicksilver water in front and the bread-fruit trees bright green against the thick webbing of the hills behind.

The real Venus that Cook observed, in the reports that he brought back from his first confrontation with the Pacific, had nothing to do with the shade of another planet trickling across the face of the sun. The real Venus observed was in those mythical anecdotes, of freedom and desire, that men are always astonished to relate about women.

In the afternoon I sat on the verandah of the Seaside Hotel and watched the tugs at the wharf and the ferry beached by the cyclone. I had gashed my knee on some coral that morning, after getting back from Savai'i, and it felt like a knot that was tightening all the time. In the hotel the water main had broken again after another makeshift cyclone repair.

I had become a sunset-watcher. The verandah was a fine place to study them, the way they could go quickly or linger. You needed clouds for the best sunsets, tradewind clouds for the

light to gild, a filter to decorate the spectrum, a belt of strato-
cumulus to carry the final glimmers right round the horizon.
However often you watched, you could never tell exactly how it
would go. Tonight the flying beetles swarmed in their thousands
against a wash of acid yellows and purples. The air was still.
Unusually the whole palette just faded out, with no change, no
final burst of light.

I thought about Alosio and Savai'i. Without expecting it, I
had found in Manase the sense of a beginning, the release of a
pared-down, simple life. Like the smell of Sunday afternoons in
Suva, the days there were another pennant fluttering in the
direction of childhood, a life when days are collections of sense-
impressions, when, without knowing it, you practise the art of
idleness. It was the kind of bolt-hole that Europeans, when they
found it, didn't want, because it was a deception: simple, hot,
boring, and the myth of the Pacific failed to mention all the
hours when nothing happened. But you couldn't hold it against a
life that gave you that kind of relaxation, of mental uncoiling,
that it was boring, because the boredom had the special quality
of a child's boredom in a hot climate, easily lifted by the sight of
a lizard or a homemade stick-and-hoop or a beach where the
pebbles shone like silvered almonds.

For weeks afterwards I could call up Alosio's handsome,
buckled features in my memory, with the missing tooth, the d.a.
haircut, the cataracts creeping across his retinas. In a country
that made you cynical – bad aid, small-scale corruption, children
in the streets shouting 'Give me my money' – he made you want
to laugh. He possessed an unquenchable enthusiasm for daily
events; he defended his chiefly responsibilities, despite their
silliness; and there was his candid serenity by which everything,
including civilisation, interested him but nothing made him
envious. Because he was himself all the time, he refuted
everyone who said the islanders had to change. If I had had any
wisdom I would have stayed at Manase, and drunk tea with

Alosio and courted the *pehu* with the tattoos.

In any case, by the time I got back to Apia, there was nothing to leave for. The harbour was empty. The *Nivaga II* had sailed twenty-four hours before time.

33
Jesus and the Mekons

There are times when the only enlightened thing to do is ditch everything. When I started out, I had thought I would finish up with a kind of composite biography of the South Pacific: a re-writing of the Pacific myths of desert islands and the noble savage, of the gardens of plenty and days of blinding sun, the mermaids and fishermen and kings. The ocean still had its attractions and mysteries, as much as a rich amalgam of states of fealty to the white man as anything else. The surfaces were glorious. But I felt defeated. Venus had not come out of the sea. Many of the places I had found myself in were flourishing states of boredom. And now the shape of the journey had beaten me. I knew what they would say at the airline office: to get to Tuvalu and the Marshalls – *you'll have to fly to Fiji, and then get another flight out.*

Then, late that afternoon, a ship appeared in Apia bay. It was the *Capitaine Tasman*. She was in a hurry to discharge her cargo and head south to Nuku'alofa in Tonga.

There are, as I say, times when the only enlightened thing to do is ditch everything.

Massasso – his first name was Giulio but no one ever used it – was seventy-five and had the deathly pale face of a man who has been left too long under wet towels. He lived on cigarettes and the half-pint glasses of riesling Umberto sold for two dollars. His job, if you could call it that, was honorary Italian consul. The unonerous duties allowed him to pass the day as he wanted. It was a life of almost monastic simplicity: sitting behind a gingham tablecloth in Umberto's restaurant, he invited diners to play rummy with him in a social transaction that was fair and illuminating. He beat you and you paid up, and in return he provided a stream of gossip, rumours and reminiscence, mostly lies, but encompassing the details of forty years in the islands, in a gangsterish English roughened by a career of cigarettes.

Massasso had been the director of Tonga's agricultural college, introducing wheat and strawberries, asparagus and rice to the islands. He was a close friend of the King, who had given him a grant of land for a house, so he could live in Tonga without papers until he died. The two Tongan women who ran the guesthouse adored him, and he had twelve adopted children.

During the war he had driven ambulances, mainly drunk, around the capital. One night he had driven through the palace wall. The hole had never been repaired.

'There was no trouble. They never repair the wall because they not need to. Now recently they repair it.

'I am sorry to say Tonga was a paradise and now it is near a pur-ga-tory.'

Despite the rumours of paranoia at the palace, I couldn't believe him. The climate was as near perfect as it could be. The seafront was all stilted bungalows and straight empty streets and benches next to the seawall, as I imagine Littlehampton or Pevensey must have looked in the Thirties: sunny afternoons, sea breezes and slap-and-tickle. And after weeks of breadfruit, fish and rice, the food at Umberto's was like the revival of a long-forgotten memory.

Umberto was a taciturn Piedmontese, and he got up at dawn to go to the wharf for fish. After a couple of days I was consulting with him about lunch and dinner in advance. 'Today,' he said lugubriously, 'you will have a squid and prawn pizza' (the prawns were the size of bananas); later, 'maybe a couple of crayfish?'; the next morning he knocked on my door and asked if I would like his *gnocchi* for lunch, 'which people usually like very much'. They were the *gnocchi* of a master. I had *bêche de mer* one night in town, a gritty and tasteless thing, and afterwards I never forsook Umberto's kitchen again.

Massasso was there most evenings, eating with a smoker's daintiness. He had not been out of Tonga for years, but hinting at an estate to be settled or a sentimental journey, he was planning a trip back to Genoa. He had had a wonderful boyhood outside the city, growing up on his father's farm and developing his arts of seduction. When I asked him why he was going back, he leered and said, 'Special reasons.'

He had fond memories of Mussolini.

'What makes you say Mussolini was a good man?' I said.

'I am not saying Mussolini was a good man,' he retorted, 'but he made perfect roads, and I was seventeen, and I loved my Guzzi.'

The day I left Apia there had been another report about the King of Tonga in the *Samoa Observer*:

> Rumours come and go in rumour-hungry Tonga. The rumours that have gripped the conversations of most people these past couple of weeks are to do with assassinations, kidnapping, angelic visitations, the overthrow of government, and the takeover of Tonga by a foreign power.
>
> Tonga's Roman Catholic Bishop Finau and the kingdom's leading commoner member of Parliament, 'Akilisi Pohiva, are both Marxists trained to destabilise the country and overthrow the government, His Majesty King Tauf-a'ahau Tupou IV said.
>
> There is a newly-constructed high fence around the

Palace, and the ceremonial guards have been replaced with combat soldiers equipped with assault weapons. A sergeant of the palace guard told reporters they were expecting trouble.

Nuku'alofa was a spacious, unhurried town. The main street straggled conscientiously to the (barred) palace gates, behind which stood a railway station, canopied and tin-roofed, plundered from provincial France. The chainlink fence erected two months before had wide unguarded gaps at each of the side gates and you could walk straight in through the pig and chicken houses.

I talked to a corporal on guard duty at the main gate. 'The King is too fat man,' he said.

Some days the 28-stone King could be seen cycling with his bodyguards, or running at the stadium, or swimming in the pool at the Dateline Hotel. But these were rumours of fitness: he was more likely to be glimpsed, a solitary Mekon-like figure in wraparound sunglasses, speeding aimlessly through the streets of Nuku'alofa with a police escort. (As he passed, all the traffic stopped. It was the law.)

The sunglasses were a royal affectation, copied by his nobles. On Saturday at the rugby game (a hopeless mismatch; the half-time score was 48-0) another Mekon disgorged from a stretched Mercedes sat impassively in a heavy leather armchair while the commoners roared with laughter.

It was Easter Sunday. I put on a suit and walked down Vuna Road to the Free Wesleyan Church behind the royal palace. I had expected solemnity, but the children sat in a white foam of fresh shirts and lace frocks, and the congregation raised the roof. The only segregation was between the commoners and the nobles, who stayed apart in the raised pews to the left of the altar. Something about all this moved me. It was a handsome occasion, with the 750 voices; the unanimity, the noise and gusto and happiness; and as you looked round, the perfect Polynesian outline, a twenty-year-old in a bowtie and blazer, or a girl the same age wrapped in white cotton and satin with the classic features above, a ringlet of hair quivering on a high forehead, everted lips between smooth cheeks, a gaze of black intensity in no particular direction, and the long jet rope hanging thickly over the laundered white frock.

Afterwards the Cadillacs and Mercedes idled to the church steps and bore away the nobles. Unusually the seventy-two-year-old King did not put in an appearance. Maybe it was because he had felt himself the focus of too much attention in the past weeks.

Known in his later years to have developed a lively fad for fundamentalist Christianity, Taufa'ahau Tupou IV had forged links with a charismatic fellowship, the Tokaikolo, established in a church compound outside Nuku'alofa. Hand-in-hand with the new fervour had gone a distrust of democracy. 'It is difficult to control democratic government,' the King had said in a recent interview. He went on: 'The Russian revolution was a democratic uprising against the Tsar. Then the communists changed a democratic government into communism. In Spain the Spanish people democratically elected a communist government and Franco had to change communism back to democracy.'

The King's speeches had begun to smack of the right-wing mumbo-jumbo of American evangelists (the Fellowship was, unsurprisingly, California-based). Recently things had come to a head. A month before I arrived, four New Zealand 'evangelical missionaries' attached to the Fellowship had visited the King and warned him of an imminent coup d'état by the Minister of Police assisted by foreign Marxist support. The Fellowship had put a twenty-four-hour guard on its buildings after claiming on Radio Tonga that a woman member had been abducted outside the royal palace as she left an audience with the King. Only the power of prayer had saved her, the sect said; an angel descending at exactly the right moment had snatched her from her kidnappers, one of whom was a woman in black who was clearly a witch, with powerful computers strapped to her chest.

The Fellowship had the usual targets: journalists, reformers, anyone who disagreed with them. Somehow a Tongan washing powder company had been roped in as a conspirator of Satan, apparently using subliminal messages from the devil in its advertising. So far there had been no coup, though people in their villages were being urged to report anyone they suspected of treason.

The afternoon of that Sunday passed as if it was endless. The Easter silence and the heat acted like a mental eraser, rubbing out sensation and thought. Halfway to sunset the church bells began to ring again. A breeze sprang up, and the air was briefly charged with the scent of frangipani.

I lay on my bed and meditated fitfully. All the charm of the Tongans, aside from their physical beauty, lay in contradictions. No islanders were more religious, but they were always chopping and changing from one Wesleyan sect to another and sometimes to Mormonism and fundamentalism; their piety excused promiscuity; homosexuality was tolerated, but sodomy carried a life sentence; they loved a king who was loopy.

When Abel Tasman set foot in Tonga at the easternmost point of his excursion from Java on 21 January 1643 – the first European to land there – his barber-surgeon Henrik Haalbos provided the only picture of their reception. Haalbos' journal was suppressed for thirty years and was then only published hidden among the pages of the geographer Arnoldus Montanus' *The New and Unknown World*, because of the barber's graphic eye:

> Meanwhile a number of South-landers had come back to the ships: for whom the mate and boatswain's boy blew on trumpets, another played on the flute, the fourth on a

fiddle; the ship's crew danced: at which the South-landers were so astonished, that they forgot to shut their mouths... With the men also came many women on shipboard: these were all uncommonly big: but among all stood out two frightful giantesses, one of whom had a moustache: they both grasped [me] round the neck: each desired fleshly intercourse: whereupon they assailed each other with words. All had thick, curly and black hair. Other women felt the sailors shamelessly in the trouser-front, and indicated clearly: that they wanted to have intercourse. South-landers what people.

The Tongans were always in church, and always laughing. When Cook called there in 1777 he was charmed by their manners and gave the place the name of the Friendly Islands. At dinner, unknown to him, the islanders had chewed over the idea of killing him, abandoning the plot, according to historians, when they failed to agree about the precise way it should be carried out. It seemed equally likely to me that they gave up the assassination because they couldn't be bothered; or that the whole thing was a joke.

Massasso was at his usual place in the restaurant. I lost three dollars to him and he talked about girls.

'Tongan girls are like cherries – you cannot 'ave just one. Me, I kept a little book. Then one night two came when they shouldn't 'ave and there was a third. It is difficult to organise your life.'

There was a German boy with sandy hair listening at the next table. He had been travelling for a year; his complexion had not been improved by the sun – he looked as if he worked in a dry-cleaner's – but his enthusiasm for new places was undiminished. He said, 'I finished with my girlfriend to travel. I am looking for an uncomplicated life away from Germany, eventually with a sexy girl.' His name was Eckhardt.

Sunday was club night. On Saturdays the nightclubs had to close before midnight, but on the stroke of midnight on Sunday they opened their bars again and the bands started and they went on till eight in the morning.

Eckhardt wanted to go to a club called the Phoenix. It was a low-ceilinged room, and extremely polite, in which the band played Tongan mixes of Western dance hits with a strange gentle emphasis on the guitar. At every table they passed, the waiters delicately straightened the chairs, and every half-hour they mopped the dancefloor.

Eckhardt spotted Elena before I did.

'Look at that one,' he suddenly said. 'She is a *mountain*. I bet you will not dance with *her*.'

I danced with Elena to prove him wrong. She worked in a restaurant in town from ten in the morning till midnight, six and a half days a week, to bring up her daughter and pay her school fees; her husband had gone off. She was the biggest woman I had ever seen.

But she moved beautifully, with the sinuous energy of a whale, and we danced again. She gave me some coconut oil for my hair. 'It will make you smell better,' she said, laughing. I had forgotten about the stiffness in my leg with the first dance and she carried me with her movements. We went on and on. She smelt of coconut and vanilla and sweat. From the corner of my eye I could see Eckhardt laughing.

Eckhardt had ended up with a beautiful half-Tongan, half-Chinese girl who sat at his elbow and stroked the hairs on his arm. He was drunk and in love with the atmosphere.

'*This* is what I am looking for,' he said.

I had to sit down. Elena followed me.

'Come on,' she said, 'come on, come on, come on, *come on*.' I looked up at her, exhausted, and shook my head. She leaned over me, and I fixed on the polished surfaces of her shoulders and breasts. The grain of her skin was remarkable, close and delicate and with the stretched smoothness of glove leather.

It must have been about four-thirty by now. My leg had tightened up as soon as I sat. Blood made a growing map on my trouser-leg; I was finished. I was a disappointing date, but I shook my head again.

Elena stood in her gold sequinned frock and scowled at me. She looked like a model for the Empire State Building, shimmering, slope-shouldered and enormously tall.

'I'm not asking you again,' she said in a voice that trailed contempt. 'But I am going to get you a beer, and then you'll dance.'

She came back with another two cans of Tongan Royal Beer, and just before the band packed up, I danced again.

Elena half-carried me back under a lightening sky, though the sea and the empty street were still the colour of steel. The guesthouse was a clapboard relic on stilts. A once-spacious bungalow occupied by a catechist or vanilla trader, it had been cut into a maze of cells painted in strong colours. The black walls of my room had been decorated by Umberto with spreads of Italian opera singers torn from magazines.

Pushing the two beds together was our last act; I don't know who fell asleep first.

Later, as I slept I heard Eckhardt's voice, saying, 'No no no. Get out of here, get *out.*' I realised he had the room next door to mine. Through the wall I heard clearly a woman's voice:

'You have to give me twenty dollars. Twenty dollars. That's the price.'

Only Jesus and the Mekons could save Tonga. Everything else was apostasy or treason. The King's anger was directed at the two 'Marxists', the people's representative 'Akilisi Pohiva and the Catholic Bishop of Tonga, for suggesting that there could be more democracy in the country's parliamentary system. (This apparatus of aristocratic authority, mantled lightly with the notion of popular representation, had worked for over a hundred years, since the first king, George Tupou I, had abolished serfdom and turned the chiefs into hereditary nobles. Now the Prime Minister was the King's brother. His son Crown Prince Tupouta'a, Minister of Foreign Affairs and Defence, was an absentee figure more often found in the hotels of Europe. All eight Cabinet ministers were appointed by the King, and ministerial salaries reached $100,000 in a country where $2500 was the average wage.)

Possibly no dissent would ever have arisen if the King had not become a devotee of get-rich-quick schemes. A few years before, his government had set up the sale of Tongan 'Protected Persons' passports to Hong Kong and mainland Chinese. It had come as a shock to most of the purchasers that the passport conferred no right of residence and was not recognised by most Western governments. 'Akilisi Pohiva had asked questions about the non-appearance of revenue from the sales in the government's accounts, and the pamphleteering started. The King admitted that there was $20 million in a Bank of America account in San Francisco. It would not be given to the Treasury, because the Treasury would only spend it; Pohiva, the King said, was trying to 'sabotage the parliamentary system'.

Now there was a new sales drive, to sell full naturalisation at somewhere around $50,000 – four times the cost of the 'protected' passport – and Pohiva had begun a court action to have the sales declared unconstitutional. Pro-government broadsheets, denouncing him, contained advice on 'How to Identify a Revolutionary Tongan'. The King, for decades, had had the undivided loyalty of his subjects, half (as ever) out of ignorance. Then communications had arrived; reform had followed, and journalism with its mix of serious questions and mischief. Ironically, the King's latest commercial venture had been in the lucrative business of buying up satellite slots over the South Pacific for lease to communications companies. The King was too affronted and too old to adapt; everyone who challenged him was part of the Red Threat, to be fought off with the power of Jesus and his army of loyal appointees-for-life.

I drove out to 'Akilisi Pohiva's small bungalow the following afternoon. Dishevelled and calm, Pohiva lived surrounded by court papers and issues of the reformers' newspaper *Kele'a*. He had an admirable conviction: there was no talk of rebellion and a coup was 'impossible'. The King's accusation amused him:

'After the election' (in which Pohiva had been re-elected with a huge majority) 'there was a fear among the King and his ministers that the people were moving away from the King. By denouncing us he is trying to regain his power and popularity. He knows very well that he is declining.'

He talked seriously of accountability and the danger of reforming too quickly and the importance of education. I could see the danger to the King, not through opposition, but through the fear that a commoner and not he was becoming the symbol of dignity and justice.

I tried to talk to the King. He had once found it entertaining to meet journalists. In the offices next to the royal garages where the King's Mercedes were stabled, his private secretary, a fussy pampered-looking man, said the King could not see me. I mentioned Massasso's name: the consul had been down the week before to try to talk the King out of his strange new mood.

I might as well have been mentioning a new brand of poison I wanted to test on the old man.

The King was becoming the model of the 'funny foreigner'. There were more Mercedes in Tonga than anywhere else in the Pacific, with ministerial plates from PM1 onwards. He and his nobles would continue to be driven at high speed around the streets of Nuku'alofa, wearing the Mekon sunglasses and impassive expressions. But there would be a nagging feeling that they had mislaid something that they wouldn't find again, and maybe soon there wouldn't be quite the same deference: the traffic wouldn't stop for them, and there would be laughter behind hands and gossip later ('how *weird* they looked...').

The next day I paid my bill to Umberto. A trace of wistfulness crossed his features as he pored over the meals he had cooked. For five days the room came to 50 dollars (including breakfast of banana, watermelon, pawpaw); lunches and dinners to a hundred. They would have been cheap at three times the price.

He stood up, his face resuming its normal melancholy expression. The message on his teeshirt read, 'Let us kiss and say goodbye.' We shook hands. Massasso was sitting at his table, smoking.

'You should stay longer,' he growled. 'Umberto needs your money. If he don't 'ave it, he cannot go to Genoa with me. He will 'ave to stay 'ere and 'ear about the World Cup when I come back.'

34
Prescriptions

I thought I had reconciled myself to flying back to Fiji. Then in a dream all my teeth fell out, and as they dropped into my hand I saw they were all etched like cheap mementoes from a Nadi gift store: 'Souvenir of Fiji.' And my knee was slowing me down. It had been stitched in the hospital in Apia and dressed twice a day, but the wound refused to close, and it was a nasty colour, like an acid sunset.

I had to catch a plane back to Samoa, another to Nadi,

then, to start the final stretch of the journey to the north, a third
from Suva. There was a day to kill in Apia.

On the bus into town I heard a speech about the government from a wiry Samoan farmer who exported six taro crops a
year to New Zealand, Australia and Japan:

'I'd shoot that lot of bastards. I had two containers of taro
ready to go to New Zealand when the cyclone arrived. They
wouldn't give me an export licence. They said if people knew
we were exporting food, we wouldn't get the donations. But we
still had plenty of food. It was only the people who didn't farm
who found their few bananas and breadfruit trees knocked down
and had to live on handouts of rice. Then they got their remit-
tances from their relatives in New Zealand and they could buy
all the fish and corned beef they wanted.

'All my taro rotted in the containers at the wharf.

'I'm going to get those politicians. All I need is half a
million behind me, and then a machine gun and the Holy Ghost.
You know the first thing I'd do? Stop all aid, just like that. No –
more – aid.'

I sat with my stiff leg on the verandah of the Seaside Hotel
all afternoon. There was another newcomer, a Polish economist
called Rybowski from the University of the South Pacific. It was
the posting of a lifetime for him. By his well-pressed appearance
and the light of academic certainty in his eyes, he had come to
teach the Samoans something.

'The Pacific nations have had a free-trade agreement with
Australia and New Zealand for ten years. After ten years, the
trade imbalance – the huge gap between imports and exports – is
exactly the same as it was ten years ago. So giving the Pacific
nations duty-free access to Australia and New Zealand has
achieved nothing.'

'Why?'

'I don't know. There is too much reliance on aid. There is a
side to the Samoans that does not want to work. But the country

must be developed. The first thing they need is tourism.'

'Perhaps there is some side to the Samoans that does not want to be developed.'

'Look, I come from a communist country. Everyone has the same, which is' – he held up his thumb, touching the tip of his forefinger. 'It is very well for you to say from the point of view of your capitalism which has gone too far that there should not be the same services here. But that is a sentimental view.'

'They've had longer than any other independent nation in the Pacific to make development work. So why haven't they?'

He shrugged his shoulders. But, brought up under communism, he thrived on a shared secret.

'I think you are not a spy,' he murmured, 'so I will tell you something unofficial. I have it from a *very* good source in the government that they exaggerate the GNP per capita downwards.' He was delighted with the discovery. 'It's true. *They fiddle the books*. The GNP should be over $1000 a year, but they make it something less so that they qualify as one of the Least Developed Countries at the United Nations and get more automatic grants.'

I suggested it might be worth his while to go to Savai'i and see how people lived there. But now that he had discovered the government was cooking its accounts, he was complacent. This secret scandal put everything, including his research into free-trade agreements, in the shade. 'No,' he said. 'I have no time to go to Savai'i so I shall not go to Savai'i. I shall see some villages here and make up my mind. My feeling right now is that these people must change.'

In essence his arguments were the development arguments put forward by everyone. At its best, development was not a free ride. It was a form of medical prescription, which would be painful, but if the nation wanted to get better it had to get on with the treatment. People like Alosio were no use because they had an invisible resistance to the changes that threatened, but they were small in number. Everyone else would, in the end, be sensible.

The reasoning was impeccable. Was it, in the end, all worth it? By the standards of a materialist philosophy, it had to be. If these countries were going to remain debtor nations forever, which they were bound to – the cost of running a developed country wildly outstripping the people's ambitions or resources – that was regrettable. But the islands would not find their benefactors ungenerous. Some of them, as Gaby des Fontaines had said, would take anyone's medicine. And that was the best state of affairs. It didn't matter that the indulgent Samoans hid the bitter pills under their tongues to spit them out later, went on secret binges and only swallowed the sweetest and most brightly coloured elixirs.

35
Sunset and coconuts

I flew north finally, a week later, in an old de Havilland Heron that had to bump-start its inner engines in the air and land again to take the passengers on board. I preferred these small planes. If you were going to crash, you could see why. It was a four-hour flight over empty ocean to Funafuti. The payload was limited to eight passengers instead of the usual twelve to accommodate the extra fuel, and you had all the time in the world to watch the cowlings of the engines flex and listen to their uneven note.

Funafuti: the rambling filament of coral was no more than a prospering shoal, straggling around a lagoon the colour of absinthe.

This was Tuvalu's capital, once the end of the line in the administration of the Gilbert and Ellice Islands, now a busy bureaucracy full of fat men on bicycles. It possessed an hotel, a

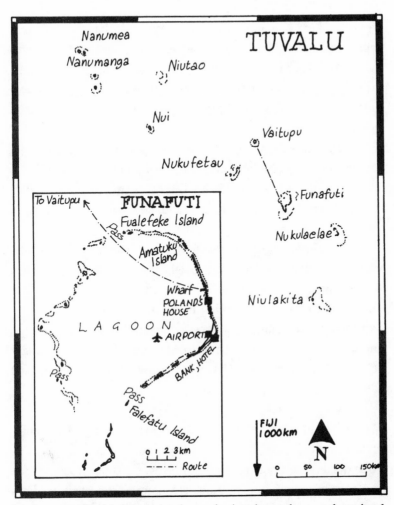

bank, a road, a pocket-sized coral airstrip and a pocket-sized
democracy installed by the British. Its philatelic bureau had just
been swindled by its Channel Islands-based consultant, a blow to
a nation whose only exports were copra and postage stamps.

But neither copra nor philately attained to the importance
of Tuvalu's main industry, 'planning development': the reason
for the ever-spreading bureaucracy. (It should have been 'development planning', but the words had somehow got switched.)
This had produced the following: from the British, a new inter-
island ship, the *Nivaga II* (badly-needed – her predecessor was a

natural sinker), and a radio station; from Australia, a wharf; from Japan, six fishing boats; water towers from the USA; government buildings from New Zealand, the police station from Australia (it might have been the other way round); government bicycles from Taiwan; and jobs for what seemed like every man in Funafuti.

I stayed with one of the planning developers, a senior civil servant who was the husband of the guesthouse owner. He had studied public administration in Chiswick and Torquay and at dinner he sat stiffly, his hair sleek with coconut oil, as if it was a government reception.

The following afternoon I met one of the few men who was not a civil servant. Poland (the name had come from a fighter pilot stationed in the Ellices during the war, just before Poland was born) was drinking Foster's on his own in the hotel bar. He was the country's biggest contractor; he was about to go and oversee a grand extension to the country's one secondary school on another atoll. His eyes narrowed as he smiled and said:

'All your taxes.'

Poland collected me for dinner that evening. The senior civil servant ignored him: Poland was too rough and too rich. Poland's house stood on the atoll's ocean side, broad-fronted and spacious, two storeys high. He ignored the planning laws and kept his pigs, fat and glossy, next to the house; his chest fridge was stacked with beer.

Poland's face was open-pored and irregular, like a piece of brown tiger coral. He had the hooded and directionless eyes of a man used to deals. Builders everywhere come from the same genetic stock: cigarette-smoking genes, beer-drinking genes (extra supplement), a-law-unto-themselves genes, pride-themselves-on-plain-speaking genes.

'Poland. What's the biggest problem in Tuvalu?'

'Too many people. Take another beer.'

'How many children have you got?'

'My wife is carrying her – ' he pulled on his cigarette and thought hard, then held up seven fingers.

'That's a lot for one family.'

'Not for me. I have land on Funafuti, Vaitupu and Nui. Enough for all my children.'

While Poland's children scuttled back and forth to the fridge for more beer, then squatted in front of the video upstairs, we sat on a raised deck at the top of the concave beach watching ropes of breakers roll in and send up a soft evening mist.

There was no continental land for at least eight thousand kilometres, and this was the highest point on the atoll. I felt vulnerable, though not from being exposed. It was a feeling of concealment, the opposite to exposure: a child's cold sensation of being lost in a wood as the sun is going down, too far from what it knows of life. I suppose it was natural that the first sensations of isolation should creep up on me in one of the low islands, on one of these spits of coral concealed in a million square kilometres of ocean, where the light fell like a hammer and the world was the range of an outrigger.

The feeling was reinforced by the infection in my knee. My leg had swelled as far as my thigh and had the proportions of a filaria infection. In my diary I was writing melodrama: 'Couldn't stand this morning. Another dihydrocodeine makes it less untouchable.' The skin was corpse-blue and yellow. I was surprised that people would come anywhere near me.

For ten days I had been pumping myself full of tetracycline and pretending the leg didn't belong to me. But the night before I had lain awake, thinking of Bernard Deacon facing north in his grave after the attack of blackwater fever, and of what Pascal had said: '*Seul, on n'est pas fait pour durer.*'

Out of the uncertainty of the evening, more drunk than I should have been (I was half a dozen cans behind Poland, but had easily drunk enough to lay waste the beneficial effects of the tetracycline), I heard Poland announce that he was going to Vaitupu in two days' time to check on progress at the school, and inviting me to go with him.

I bought a ticket at the government travel bureau. The *Nivaga* left Funafuti at eight-thirty the following morning. I finally walked her packed decks and failed to find the chief engineer. For most of the day the ship seemed caught in an invisible web of light, not moving on the sea.

I sat in one of the first-class cabins beneath a clattering fan with the resident magistrate, dispatched to try a rape case on one of the northern islands. He was rarely asked to leave the capital, he said in excitement; as for the case itself, rape was almost unheard-of in the islands. The certain course of events was that the man and woman had had sex on the usual understanding that marriage would follow, and then the man had simply refused to marry the woman.

The magistrate's adventure had puffed up his self-importance. It was impossible to take him seriously, partly on account of his uncanny resemblance to Duke Ellington, partly because, when I could avert my gaze from his face, it was drawn to his teeshirt, with its design of a palm spearing a circle of yellow and crimson and the words 'South Pacific – sunset and coconuts'. As the afternoon lengthened, he began to look very seasick.

Everywhere on the ship were mothers and babies sitting half-hidden between a hundred washing lines strung between the rails. Some of them could not have been more than fifteen. All were dressed in the bright *lava lavas* that knotted above their breasts. I remembered a young woman I had seen the day before, bathing in the shallows of the lagoon. The water ran off her shoulders like rain off oil. She soaped herself carefully, keeping her *lava lava* knotted under her arms. There was a gymnastic thoroughness about her movements: I thought of convent girls having to bathe in bathing-robes. As she finished and re-knotted the length of cloth, a gleaming Polynesian torso was fleetingly visible, but, suddenly realising she had been seen, she gathered up the wet ends of cloth and fled into the trees.

There was something crazy about this. The Revd Archibald Murray had imported the European male preoccupation with the female breast into the islands in 1865; the prohibitions associated with it (always prohibitions) were more firmly entrenched now than at their source. The Polynesians had got their own back. No European woman in Tuvalu was permitted to swim or sunbathe without a *lava lava*.

The earthquake of Christianity had sent out its strongest tremors here. The islands had each had their guardian deities, balancing white and dark magic – 'darkness is good', the chiefs protested briefly to the catechists – but in less than twenty years these powerful spirits, ancestors and the essence of objects, in some cases overseen by a paramount force in the heavens, regulating every aspect of life, had been swept away. The Church of Tuvalu, still as inflexibly Protestant as the London Missionary Society, was more powerful than the government. Poland had told me a story:

Long before the developed world started worrying about the greenhouse effect and rising sea levels, the Tuvaluans were aware that every spring tide was higher than the last. They began to build coral barrages at the most vulnerable points along the shoreline. They also turned to the Church for guidance. The minister had spoken to the Tuvaluans on Radio Tuvalu; the gist of the message was a reminder that in Genesis, after the flood waters had receded, the Lord had said the waters would not come again. Reassured, instead of speeding up the barrage-building, the Tuvaluans slowed down.

Poland had raised his eyebrows and held out his hands, palms up, in a beseeching gesture. Don't trust anyone, his genes told him: not the planning development office, and certainly not

God.

Shortly before dusk, a huge white church with twin towers rose out of the sea.

36
Pretending to have fun

The church stood at the apex of Vaitupu, geographically and spiritually.

'If a man and woman (unmarried) fornicate in the mission house,' the first pastor's law-book said, they shall be fined two dollars.

> If a young man and a young woman are detected talking privately, they shall be fined one dollar.
> If a man and woman are detected meeting in an out of the way place *with intent to commit adultery* they shall be fined five dollars.

The church law squads were still active. Someone had reported Poland for allowing work to continue on a Sunday. The school buildings were behind schedule; the school was a good cause. But the Samoan pastor was immovable. Poland's good temper had deserted him and he stalked up and down in the unfinished school library, cursing. I sympathised. There was a big completion bonus involved.

The pastors, of course, had been the first traders. The Church had introduced the cash economy. (In the beginning, God had created the profit motive: a number of pastors who became over-motivated had had to be dismissed.) Then, in the wake of their standard conversion techniques, had followed the notion of subscribing to the Church, encouraged by implanting the idea – to which Polynesians could be relied on to be receptive – that the more you gave, the more social esteem you gained. Parents were known to stand up in island *maneabas* and pledge their son's first year's salary to the church without his knowledge. The biggest donors to the Church had their names announced on Radio Tuvalu. The missionaries, here as elsewhere, had been the islands' first materialists.

The village was no more than a cluster of *fales* at the base of an atoll enclosing a violin-shaped lagoon. Half an hour's walk through coconut and pawpaw groves was the secondary school. Twenty minutes down the path in the opposite direction was the house of the man I wanted to see.

Dr Tomasi Puapua was a bulky man with hair that shone like fuse wire. His and his wife's possessions were cleared away in suitcases and trunks at the back of his *fale*. The small wall-less room seemed as spacious as a marble hall. Imported building materials were the first thing a Tuvaluan with any money spent it on; nearly everyone on Vaitupu lived in brick and tin-roofed houses. Dr Puapua's *fale*, raised off the ground and facing the still water of the lagoon down a path edged with lilies, was a fresh place that picked up the smallest breeze.

For eight years Dr Puapua had been prime minister of Tuvalu. Now he lay on the pandanus mats on the floor of the *fale* by the lagoon with Barclay's *World of Cricket* open in front of him. He stood to shake hands, then sank to the mats again. It was ill-mannered of me to call without warning, but he was delighted to get a visitor, and he was accustomed to the coarseness of the British.

The Ellice Islands had only belonged to the Gilberts in the tidy mind of the British Colonial Service. The Gilbertese, who were Micronesian, thought the Ellice Islanders were second-rate. The Polynesian Ellicese thought the Gilbertese vain and violent. A succession of charmless British administrators, out for minimum inconvenience, at first insisted the two countries

remain one at independence. Britain had caved in in the end, but
the settlement was as grudging as could be managed. Princess
Margaret had put the seal on Britain's behaviour by declining at
the independence ceremony to leave her cabin on the New
Zealand warship which had brought her.

Dr Puapua motioned me to sit. I don't know what I had
expected, but not this tolerant, contented, cricket-loving Anglo-
phile who resented the influence of the Church in the country
and admired Henry VIII for breaking with Rome as well as
marrying six wives.

'You know one of the great social problems of today? All
our youth watch action videos and do no competitive sport. The
pastors stopped all that when they first came. All we have now is
a bit of Pacific cricket. Very inferior to the real thing.'

At five he was up to collect his toddy, the sap collected
from the cut flower spathes of the coconut palm; by six he was
fishing for trevally on the lagoon; at eight he went to the taro pit.
He was still leader of the opposition.

The prime ministership no longer tempted him. 'How
could I get my trevally? Here I can lead a little by example.
Since I came back to the island for good, and started fishing
regularly, the young men have seen my catches. They are
starting to fish again.'

As the light went, a wind came up and it began to rain. Dr
Puapua's wife brought in a tray with a Sèvres-blue coffee
service and cake on it. The mosquitoes came with the rain. He
handed me a switch.

He had constructed his *fale* with his father just before his
father's death. 'Every scrap of it is built with island materials.'
He ran his hand over the mat floor. Six cruxes of hardwood held
up the roof, thickly thatched with pandanus; around the edge was
an apron of coconut stems lashed together with coir. It was a
building of grace and solidity, unstuffy, cool and tension-
absorbing.

'Why doesn't everyone build *fales* like this?'

'They don't have to rethatch their tin roofs. And everyone thinks anything that is foreign must be good, anything *palagi* bring us must be better.'

He was right. The two most pretentious buildings on Vaitupu were the church and the new bungalow being built (by Poland) for the bank manager from the capital.

Dr Puapua went away to rummage in a suitcase and came back with an unopened litre of whisky. Without pouring a glass for himself, he said, 'Have a Scotch before you go. It will keep out the cold.'

Relieved of power, Dr Puapua was relieved of the duty to be plausible. The last thing he said was:

'Development is like a wave that is washing over us. We get three times as much money in aid as we make in a year. Once people have these expectations they cannot lose them.

'Once the people have brick houses, then they want electricity for fans to keep them cool. Once they have a taste for beer you can't take it away. When you have beer, you have to have a cold store. We are lucky on Vaitupu because the ship only comes once every six weeks. Of course the men get drunk on fermented toddy, but at least they have to do a bit of work for that.

'If an island like this is worth living on, it's because it provides everything for a plain life. You can't pretend to live a white man's life here. I like cricket and I like you British. But why are we trying so hard to be somebody else?'

The government ship was touring the northern islands and would not return for – no one knew exactly how long.

After two days on the atoll, I believed Dr Puapua. Land was scarce, but the ocean teemed with fish; there was fresh water in the coral lens, coconuts, breadfruit, bananas, pawpaw, taro, wood and thatch for the *fales* and for boatbuilding. For a plain life it had everything.

I stayed with Poland in one of the brick *fales* that belonged to three families and reeked pleasantly with the smell of fish and Gallagher's Irish Flake that the men smoked in rolled-up pandanus leaf. They cut their copra and toddy and fished and dug their taro pits. They worked harder than most other families, who purchased their corned mutton and rice from the trade store and only fished when the money ran out.

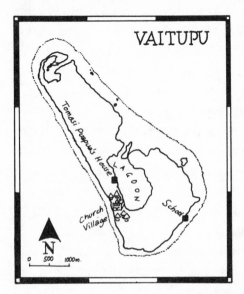

I enjoyed Vaitupu's plain pleasures. I fished for trevally and surfed with the boys. I cycled around the atoll, trailing my leg, with the two small girls from Poland's family. They were remarkably beautiful. Everywhere I went there were these young loose-limbed Polynesian angels, bursting with health, who would grow into fat middle age on breadfruit and taro. By some trader's decision to offload this or that product here, Poland's girls ran around all day wearing only French knickers of dove-grey satin.

I picked my way among the pools of fish at the edge of the reef, green and madder, and limped along the shore on the ocean side. The sand was blinding. The fairy terns, spiralling and flapping in the wind, shone like white neon sculptures. I was awed by the height of the clouds and the empty, unanchored beauty of the shore. It was, in a technical sense, paradise, a *hortus conclusus* or a watered garden.

And no Western upbringing, I suspect, could have prepared me for the monotony of it.

If I had been a painter, there would have been that light, perpendicular, bouncing back at the eye like the light in the bottom of a goblet, to draw; and the animal beauty of the place. But I had read Matisse's letters home from his excursion to French Polynesia. Having worked for forty years in European light and space, Matisse had dreamed of other proportions to be found in another hemisphere. In February 1930 he left for Tahiti via the USA. (He sketched shoals of flying fish on his way to Papeete, to discover the next day that they were common terns.) At first he marvelled, but after six weeks he woke feeling depressed, feeling as if he were in a steam bath. He could not paint and he wrote home: 'I see clearly all that is exceptional here, but I've quickly grown tired of it... It is alarming to have the day begin with a dazzling sun that will not change until sunset. It is as if the light were immobilised forever. It is as if life were frozen in a magnificent stance.'

I did what I could. I spent time at the school. I was ignored by the boys; the girls flirted with me. Their complaints about their lessons hid their pride at attending the school. They all wanted to go to college in Australia, but talked about it for the pleasure of talking about it, without believing it was possible. Australia was too far.

One of them, Fakatalinga – her name meant 'waiting' – fourteen and straight as a she-oak, was bored and walked with me, her hand on my arm and full of school gossip, whenever she saw me. There was an American writer, she said, whose wife taught at the school: he was avoiding me. And all the girls were in love with Gordon, the Scots-Australian teacher.

Boredom continued to creep up on me.

'All right. I came here by mistake.'

Gordon was part of the Australian volunteer programme, posted to Tuvalu after applying for a teaching post in Africa and finding there was nothing going there. An administrative blunder had forwarded a request from Tuvalu for a teacher when the school had no need of one (it sounded like the planning development office). Gordon had made the journey from Sydney to be met at Funafuti by the pained expressions of the welcoming committee. No one in Funafuti knew what to do. In the end the headmaster had offered Gordon a job that did not exist.

As a result, Gordon taught English some of the time but spent most days on his own. He was about forty, with the angular warmth of the Highland Scot. It was obvious the girls would fall for him. But now there was a not quite natural jauntiness about him. With nine months of his year still to go, he lived in a sparsely furnished cabin on the shore. A hammock sagged between two palms, and inside his three kittens ran after moths. Gordon had wanted the job in Africa because the girl he had fallen in love with had been accepted for a job in a school in Botswana. He wasn't needed here.

'Why don't you go to Africa?'

'I don't know. I can see a whole new set of problems if I just turn up there.' He was determined to see his year through, but you could tell by what he didn't say that the isolation was getting to him.

Gordon showed me his girlfriend's photograph above his writing table: a laughing, good-looking blonde woman against a country background, looking unreal in the way lovers in snapshots do, their passion nowhere in evidence.

My gaze wandered over Gordon's tidy writing table. A cheap blue exercise book, headed 'Subject: Dreams', lay next to an unfinished letter to his girlfriend on foolscap paper in which he had come to page thirty-one. I had never seen a free man more enthusiastic about the idea of a sentence of exile.

Two days later the *Nivaga* reappeared, bobbing at dusk outside the reef like a toy boat in a bath. In the narrow pool of the ship's lights the trans-shipping of passengers from the workboats was a chaotic affair. As the boats fell away from the ship's flank, fat islanders were pitched onto the deck as if they were sacks of copra. On the beach five hundred islanders watched until the white ship turned south. After five minutes, all I could see from the deck was the ghostly silhouette of the church.

The chief engineer appeared at my elbow. 'I heard you were on board,' he said. It was as if this was where we had arranged to meet.

Nisbet had been in Funafuti with his wife for two years; he intended to stay for three. I mentioned Gordon to him.

'You don't know the first thing about the Australian volunteer programme.

'Perhaps it's them, perhaps it's this place. There were two came before Gordon. The first took one look at Vaitupu and decided he was taking the first boat home. The second was different. The usual problem with male school-teachers without enough company of the opposite sex, as you know, is over-familiarity with their pupils. Not this guy. It was the *wives* he was after. Staring down blouses and the like. Then he got up on a chair and started preaching religion. He became such a nuisance they sent the police over and took him off in handcuffs.'

I imagined the scene: in the middle of the village, next to the white church, a thin, hunched figure standing on a school chair, radiating a mad pathos and received in respectful silence by the islanders; afterwards, with the methodical passion that besets the appetites of evangelists, visiting the women of the village one after another while their husbands were collecting toddy or fishing.

Nisbet pushed his mouth into a gesture of sympathy. He repeated what he'd said in Aggie Grey's: 'In a way I kind of admired him. Crazy he may have been, but he wasn't like the rest of us, pretending we were having fun.'

On the return journey to Funafuti the preacher had given his guard the slip and run to the stern of the *Nivaga* and jumped off. 'We had him back on board in three minutes. Good thing he did it bang in the middle, or the twin screws would have had him.'

Nisbet was another good Scots exile. A combination of dour charm and a wife had preserved him from the absurdist details and the settling tedium of the place. In this huge ocean you had to have someone with you to survive. I knew that if I stayed any longer, I could with absolute ease finish up lecturing the Tuvaluans on what was wrong with their lives and peering, with the pale glare of lunacy, down the blouses of married women.

37
The Paradise Club

Life, far away from the conscious motivated mind, the self-directing forces of will and character, is an immersion in the gods' game of appetites, biochemistry and time, which can only be described   as aesthetic or unaesthetic. There was another plane, an Airline of the Marshall Islands 748 that rolled off the runway like a field-piece; a British aping of the American enthusiasm for finning, polish, horsepower, the seats wrinkled, the air dirty, the rackety interior drumming against the fuselage; and another island group, another step towards the equator and the Marshalls, the first two atolls disclosed as lonely bursts of coral and sand, radiating an endlessly shaded collection of turquoise, aquamarine and green, the ocean crashing like heavy furniture on one side, the barely emerging islets rising – or sinking – infinitesimally on the other.

The scene was full of possibilities that you, still, carefully, tried to select: to ignore some, the unusually morose immigration officers, the ugliness of South Tarawa atoll at ground level, overcrowded and drab, the stiff, foul-smelling leg irritated by the humidity of a sudden squall; to linger instead on the neat thatch of the island houses that brushed the ground and the sweep of the vast sail-shaped lagoon, on the children shrieking as they kicked up muddy puddles.

Somewhere in the Gilbert Islands, it was said, were intimations of the ideal atoll life. The cacique of Ocean Island, the weak-spirited Arthur Grimble, had celebrated the islanders in his charming, patronising book. They were all porpoise-callers, magicians and octopus fishers if he was to be believed. Stevenson had said that the Gilberts – Kiribati now – had the perfect ocean climate.

And yet the exercise failed to work. You could not pick and choose. I found myself prejudging the place on an instinct. It had the seediness of a Pigalle nightclub in the middle of the afternoon, feeble, tedious and undramatic, and with no loucheness to moderate it. I was sure from the start that Kiribati's capital was not somewhere to discover; it was not a place to exercise your will or fulfil your intentions. It felt like an authorial intervention over which I had no control. I had stepped into someone else's plot device.

Here they all were again, in the bar of the Kiribati Hotel: the German who looked like Gielgud doing a performance of a tourist whose baggage had been sent to the right place while he had been lost en route; the chain-smoking insurance agent, a professional disagreer, always with a whisky in his hand; another mild Englishman whom alcohol had taken the other way, leaving him gentle and watery-eyed and hopeless. And half the population of Kiribati lived on Tarawa, thirty thousand people on a string of islets, Bikenibeu, Bairiki and Betio, drawn by beer and electric light. (They imported and drank three million cans of Foster's a year.) The beaches, still littered with the skeletons of American landing craft from the war, were a dustbin of aerosols, old tyres, engine transmissions, disposable nappies.

At the limit of the Japanese advance in 1942, the Gilberts had been captured from the British. In one of those military decisions in which the planning, overlooking a single element, incubates a spectacular disaster, the American assault to retake Tarawa on 20 November 1943 had taken place at low tide. The Marines were faced with advancing across hundreds of metres of unprotected water after their landing craft were hung on the reef; three thousand were killed or wounded by the Japanese. For its main tourist attraction, overlooking in its turn another detail – that war-grave tourists were dying off at an accelerating pace – the government had just spent $24,000 of aid money on restoring an eight-inch Japanese gun on Tarawa's southern shore, where it gleamed in the wind, unvisited.

Over breakfast an Australian named Perry who had come in on the plane to take over the Toyota dealership suggested going for a drive to the other end of South Tarawa.

'This kind of job is a real challenge, it's what I'm good at,' he said.

Forty kilometres later, beyond the abandoned fish farm, the torpid half-deserted settlements and beaches full of garbage, Perry sat shaken and hunched forward, with both hands on the wheel of the car.

'This is the most primitive place I've been,' he said, 'in fifteen years in the islands.'

In the evening I wound up at the Paradise Club, a hangar bespattered with murals of tropical sunsets, from which knots of murmuring i-Kiribati boys who had run out of beer-money

spilled into the darkness. As I walked in, a voice said in English:
'If the priest sees you, he will refuse you communion.'

At the bar Foster's was a dollar, cash in advance. A dozen
i-Kiribati crowned with neat flower garlands sprawled along the
counter in attitudes of Hogarthian relaxation.

Mariano was the only i-Kiribati without a beer; he was
shocked to see a white face.

'What made you come here?'

'I want to avoid communion.'

'You don't want to believe that. The priests threatened me
once, but not any more.'

He had a guileless fresh face, and steered me away from
the continuous scuffles at the door into the hall. I asked why he
was drinking Coke.

'Last year I drank many, many beers. Every week I
fought.'

His girl was dancing with someone else. She came, dark
and laughing recklessly, wearing a Fifties dress, and took him
away to dance; after two dances a heated argument started. He
came back. 'She says I should drink beer. She is very sexy but no
good.'

He insisted on walking me home through the hundreds of
i-Kiribati converging on the club. When they were drunk, they
had no manners, he said.

He left me outside the hotel. The hotel roof and the crowns
of the trees were plated with silver. I had slept in dirty sheets the
night before. They still had not been changed. I went downstairs
to find George, who ran the hotel.

Two chambermaids sat in his room, watching a video.
They did not hear me come in. The cassette case was on top of
the television – 'George's Special Song Collection Vol. 4' – and
the picture was scratchy and worn: two women lying back, one
licking the other's breasts, while a man flicked his tongue like a
lizard over the blue-pink lips of her vagina. The chambermaids

looked up at me and giggled, then one of them sauntered to the set to switch it off.

So that was it: trash and overcrowding, boys getting pissed on a Saturday night, fighting and porn videos. It was just like England.

38
Strange manias

I dressed my knee. The skin was so swollen the stitches had started to tear. I swallowed four tetracycline. Belief in antibiotics had turned into a superstition. I had to go to the hospital.

Outside, the *fales* were quiet, a scene of elements that had survived. There was a small spotless area swept clean, in the middle a neat cairn of stones beneath the sparse breadfruit and palms; a slim girl in a black and white *lava lava* drawing buckets of water from the well; a tired woman picking lice from her sister's hair; and a tethered suckling pig, to be killed that day, snuffling unsuccessfully on the tidy barren surface.

On the way to the hospital I stopped at the Ministry of Home Affairs, a U-shaped bungalow from an early edition of the development building catalogue. I was shown into an office with an academic-looking i-Kiribati sitting behind a large desk in Bunterish tortoiseshell specatacles. He spoke progressively more quietly as I asked him about the people's health, and over-crowding and the state of the beaches. 'We had a clean-up, a voluntary one, in the Seventies when there was a cholera out-break, but this is a traditional use of the beach.' When I asked how much of the government's budget was spent on health, he referred me with infinite relief to the Ministry of Finance.

The cheerful British economist running back and forth between the computers on the first floor suggested we go back to his house to talk. He jammed on a hat like an Edwardian bonnet.

'Have you heard about the deputy foreign secretary? He went fishing with his cousin and another man a few days ago, and they didn't come back.'

It didn't mean they were lost for good, he said.

'The i-Kiribati know how to survive at sea: they can always get fish to eat, and for fluid they drink the fishes' blood. One boat washed up on a beach in the Solomons, nearly 2000 kilometres away, the whole crew in good health, five months after it disappeared.'

But the deputy foreign secretary was a decent man, and it was still worrying.

At home the economist had a sleek overfed cat that sprawled on his table, and walls decorated with magazine pictures of cities at night – London, Tokyo, Stockholm – and northern landscapes in winter. We surprised his housegirl and another girl watching the television. It was another porn video, or another part of the same one – they were all part of the same one – a girl on a sofa sucking two cocks alternately. There was the same giggling, and the economist sent them off and said:

'Oh that. I lent a video to some friends, and they've sent the wrong one back.'

He had lived for six and a half years on Tarawa and he was cheerful about everything, like a boy who has found a mechanism to halt the business of growing up. Being away from England had enabled him to perform the expatriate trick of keeping the world tidy. He talked enthusiastically about the country's abysmal health record, the high infant mortality, the vitamin A deficiency that caused infant blindness and was the worst in the world, the people's life expectancy ('around their mid-fifties; Catholics, for some reason, do better than Protestants') and the bad diet. The people ate neither green vegetables nor pawpaw, though both grew, and now that *kamaimai* – coconut toddy syrup – had been abandoned in favour of white sugar,

their historically sweet tooth had pushed the diabetes rate
through the roof.

He was looking forward to his new posting. He thought it
could be Saint Helena. He was a very happy man, with the
beautifully organised happiness of the statistician.

The i-Kiribati painted their minibuses with the names of
video characters. I took a bus called 'Romeo' out to the hospital.
(This was as close as the buses got to sex. I felt obscurely cheat-
ed not to see 'Black Stud' or 'Swedish Nymphet' pulling up at
the roadside.)

The hospital compound was dusty, with hardboard buildings at the edge. I filled in a form and put Britain as the 'island
of origin'. The doctor had the unkempt, harassed look of casual-
ty doctors. A smell of alcohol that was not surgical lingered
around him.

There was a slight difficulty of diagnosis. I didn't find out
the true reason until later, but he peered blearily at the knee,
swollen like a wineskin, and kept his distance. (It turned out that
touching a white patient was taboo, something of a disadvantage,
I thought, in the case of a broken arm or a gynaecological
examination.) Why did I believe in his peering and his prescription – the same old antibiotics and dressings and zinc sulphate
cream? Maybe the doctor's faith-healing in reverse, the not-
laying-on of hands, would work where everything else had not.

At the dispensary, among the official notices, there was a
supplement to the conditions of service for Kiribati Government
employees, headed 'Missing at Sea':

> F40 (a). An employee who goes out to sea in an open boat
> and who fails to reach land within fourteen days of his
> departure shall from that date be deemed to be 'missing at
> sea'. From that date:
>
> (i) The first thirty days will be regarded as sick leave
> on full pay;

(ii) Further days will be regarded as annual leave to the employee's credit; and

(iii) Thereafter no salary is payable.

The faint note of impatience said there must be absenteeism. Men went off to other islands to hide out with their mistresses. But was the deputy foreign secretary – assuming he had no mistress – giving a corner of his mind to how many days' leave he had left?

With nowhere else to sit, I sat in the bar of the Kiribati Hotel, at a table with plastic flowers shoved into a cardboard tube that had once held duty-free whisky. Perry was at the bar with a hard starter; Gielgud sat bolt-necked at another table.

Gielgud's plane had had engine trouble. Because he never talked to anybody, he had not known what the whole of Tarawa knew the day before. He had gone all the way to the airport in the morning, his heart soaring at the prospect of leaving, before he found out that he was stuck for another four days. I avoided his eye: I did not see how a man could stare like that without being on the point of setting off some murderous reflex in himself.

Some i-Kiribati dancing had been arranged at my request in a *maneaba* beyond the Paradise Club. I had a couple of hours to kill before Mariano came to collect me. This was (at last) an interesting possibility. Given the keenness with which it had been agreed to, if it was mediocre I could not complain; if it had any of the supposed quality of such performances, it might arrest the failing perspective I had acquired on the place.

There was a seaman's school on Betio. The German commandant came into the bar with a tall i-Kiribati who ran the Atoll Development Programme. The man was broad-shouldered and handsome: he got his physique from fishing, diving six metres down off the reef at night with a spear-gun and torch for snapper and wrasse and crayfish. He had dived most of the sixty-five-kilometre reef from Betio to North Tarawa; when his relatives came to South Tarawa looking for handouts, he took them fishing and they sold their catch instead.

He had the look of health about him and the knowledge that life was difficult. 'I see what we have lost on Tarawa. I see what people on the outer islands still have: health, few social problems, a balanced way of life. We are at the mercy of the donating states, who say you need this, you need that. For them it is easier to get us to follow their example than to let us go our own way.'

Of course it wasn't quite true. It is always easier to be the way someone else tells you to be. Kiribati seemed to me like a demoralised partner in a marriage who allows themself to stay ensnared by the other's will for the sake of security. But in one sense he was right: the developed countries were the ones with enlightenment, you supposed – until you saw what they got up to.

No inter-island ships were going anywhere for at least a fortnight. How could I get out of Tarawa? There was an atoll called Tamana to the south. I could fly there, if I had time... 'There it is completely unchanged. As an i-Kiribati, even I was shocked when I went there. They have very little, it is all survival on fishing and what they can grow, aid has not reached them, and the people are the healthiest and happiest in Kiribati.' On Tamana, he said, there was a byelaw that confiscated a man's canoe and hung it in the *maneaba* for six months, if he was seen to lose a fish; a tuna that got back to the shoal, they said, could disturb the shoal so that it disappeared for good.

Mariano arrived, with an immense sailor in a singlet in tow. On an impulse I braved the killing stare and suggested to Gielgud that he come. He nodded absently and came out with us into the dark.

Children hung like photo-sensitive insects from the screen-ed windows of the *maneaba*. Girls – perfect lithe Gauguinesque beauties – changed into black-dyed skirts and pandanus-weave brassieres and put on pandanus armlets and bandoliers of shells; two wore elaborate crown head-dresses. None of them was more than fourteen. The men, all older and with the powerful physique of fishermen, came in in mat skirts tied with blackened sinnet. There were twelve dancers in all, standing in a square, the white bars, stripes and crowns decorating coffee-coloured skin.

The dances were the first exciting thing I had seen in weeks. Most of the movement was in the scrollwork of hands, a constantly changing rhythm of beckoning and dismissal, with short savage interludes in which the men jacknifed at the waist and the girls suddenly quivered, their hips shivering. Calling, stamping and clapping, the dancers allowed their tension to flow out under strict control.

Mariano had disappeared. In his absence Gielgud and I were handed beer after beer by the fat sailor, who seemed to be the host. His interpretations, muttered at first, became louder and more incomprehensible, interspersed with more recognisable references to the beauty, and single status, of the girl dancers, and one in particular.

After the performance there were the usual speeches; the formalities over, the fat sailor's generosity, stoked to new heights by more rounds of beer, turned to the question of my bed-partner.

'Any one you want to fuck, you say,' he said encour-agingly.

It was apparently a necessity. In my thanks I had said how beautifully the girls danced, and so young; hospitality now required that I be supplied with company. The best of the danc-ers, a willowy thirteen-year-old whose temples were beaded with sweat, was called over and sat to one side of me.

'Very fuckable,' the sailor whispered.

It was difficult to know from the girl's expression what she felt about this development. Her hands were folded demurely in her lap, and she cast me a glance from between sweeping lashes, a look that could have been detached interest but could equally well have been apprehension under perfect control.

Light-headed from beer and neutralised tetracycline, I was flagging and, though the sailor was undoubtedly right in his appraisal, I had a vestigial Western prejudice against her having no say in the matter.

In the end, it came down to vanity. I couldn't see either of us being much entertained by further developments. And in the state I was in, I could see the eventuality of her not being entertained at all. The fat sailor continued to encourage me with sly smiles and nudges, but the night was over.

I had absorbed some of the demands made by life in the islands. Waiting; sleeping when you felt like it; the shocking light that blanked out energy and emotion; the monotonous food; the way the days succeeded each other in a dreamlike mood of lethargy and serenity. All the places I had seen were remarkable in some way (if only for their special quality of boredom), and I still shared the European fascination for an ocean where life was not a European taste.

But I could not get off South Tarawa. Every morning for the next four days I took 'Conan', '007', 'Rambo' or 'La Bamba' to the airline office, a down-at-heel travel agency donated, I suspected, by the British with its flyblown listlessness intact. Each day the uniformed i-Kiribati women told me with mounting impatience that all the inter-island flights were full. Only one plane was airworthy, and the airline was without its chief engineer, an Indo-Fijian who had given up in desperation a few days previously.

The first morning I had gone on from the hospital to the

airport to see if I could get a standby seat on the flight to Tamana, the atoll that had been praised by the tall i-Kiribati in the bar. In the queue I stood behind a Peace Corps volunteer swamped by four swollen cardboard boxes and a pink bicycle. She had the dazed stare of a blast victim that you see on the faces of Fifth Avenue shoppers. The plane was full and she had no money for the excess freight. She kept pushing a strand of hair back behind a small sunburnt ear. In her *lava lava* and a *lei* of frangipani blooms she was the picture of assimilation, but I suspected that without her boxes and a Sears catalogue she would be lost.

I had been on Tarawa for a week. Nothing was moving. The most animated creatures were the huge rusty Micronesian pigeons that strutted around the fish market, between hoop-shouldered women with trays of chromium-flanked tuna and the fatigued expressions of Greek bronzes. I stumbled over the beaches, trying to imagine what they might be like without the nappies and sardine cans and car tyres every few metres. The i-Kiribati were friendly but incurious; if they *were* curious, their curiosity was like a wall, a shore, a border they stared out from but never crossed over. This perishable curiosity seemed to lie in their insularity. What was imagined or thought possible – or wished for – stopped short at their daily needs; and everything that was wished upon them, they accepted.

The trait was already there in their creation myth. The islands, the myth went, had been fashioned by Nareau, a great spider floating in space; but if you listened carefully to the story, the truth was that, curiosity spent, Nareau had wandered off and left it to his son to do the dirty work of separating earth and sky.

Returning to the hotel, the menu shrank daily – no fruit juice, then no milk, then no potatoes – and there were no green coconuts or pawpaw to be had in their place. In George's office the chambermaids carried on watching his Special Song Collection, and the beer, miraculously, was exempt from all shortages. I

glimpsed Perry hunched over the wheel of his Toyota, his face
set like Yves Montand's at the wheel of the truck full of nitro-
glycerine in *The Wages of Fear*. And Gielgud had slipped back
into his catatonic state in the hotel bar, leaving the hours to
trickle past until the Saturday flight came in which would take
him to Honolulu and the relief of Europe.

With the foresight of cowardice, I should have decided to
leave, but there were always temptations – always culs de sac –
to find out more. One afternoon I got over to North Tarawa, an
outrigger ride between lagoon and ocean, and walked briefly in a
different world of exquisitely built houses, shady paths and utter
quiet. Boys were playing *kapwane*, a game of almost unnatural
skill in which a falling feather – substitute for a lazy frigatebird
– was brought down with a weight on a string.

On Friday I failed again at the airline office. Afterwards I
walked to the Bairiki Club, a tall shady *maneaba* across the
dusty triangle of the fish market. I-Kiribati sat piling empty cans
into the middle of rickety card-tables. There was a dartboard in
the corner, and two Englishmen, drunk but formidably upright,
were playing three-o-one. A beer lasted a game, and they played
six games in three-quarters of an hour, never going lower than
double-twelve to finish.

At one table some old men with juicy faces began to sing,
short, breathy harmonies with a captivating charm that were
accompanied by formal, swinging arm movements. One of the
songs was about a man's love for his housemaid and the
question of whether he should divorce his wife: it had been
written by Grimble, who had always considered himself a poet,
in a funk of desire. Eventually he had turned back to his wife's
affections, but the old men, roaring with laughter and clapping
their thighs, mimicked his compliments about the girl's beauty
and youth with unmistakable irony. The language was the old
Gilbertese, hardly understood by young men. These men were
the last of their generation.

The dartboard was an ordinary circle of pulp and wire, the yellow and black a bit faded, the high numbers blown. I saw Captain Pape flapping his hand dismissively at the wall, as he had in the *Tasman*'s mess, and saying in his funny emphatic voice: 'This *dart*board signifies the strange mania of you British, wherever you go, for games and nostalgia. *No other atolls in the world* have bars with these things.'

Without the dartboard, I might have stayed to find out more. As it was, it seemed to complete the formula to which the place had been constructed, that of a gloomy realist novel set in a secretive country town from which none of the characters ever manage to get away.

One of the tight Englishmen told me a story: Grimble's grandson had come to the islands to write a sequel to *A Pattern of Islands*. He had an allowance of $300 a month. For months he stayed on the outer islands doing nothing; there was no sign of a book getting written. Reports came back that the limitless hospitality of the i-Kiribati was becoming frayed. As time went on, the man would appear on Tarawa looking more and more dishevelled. The scrupulously clean islanders were offended that he rarely washed. His father eventually cut off his allowance. When the government had asked him to leave, the High Commission had had to pay his fare home.

I felt a thrill of satisfaction that a Grimble had had his comeuppance. But it was impossible not to have a sliver of sympathy for him.

The next morning the blue and white Marshall Islands 748 with the egg-like chromed engines stuck on top of the wings emerged from out of a thick, marbled sky, and I ducked through the hissing screen of rain to board it.

39

Ground control

Tiredness was getting harder to shake off.

It had taken Robert Louis Stevenson and his wife Fanny two and a half months in 1890 to sail from New Zealand to the Marshall Islands and back again on the *Janet Nichol*. I had spent four months just getting there.

I should have felt elated. Stevenson had called the capital Majuro 'the pearl of the Pacific'. Blame it on exhaustion, or drugs – I was practically a tetracycline junkie by now – or too long without a lover. Blame it on the writer. Blame everything on the writer. Majuro was the most unspeakable dump I had ever seen.

Dropping out of clouds of clay into the greenhouse mist of a wet Pacific afternoon, I saw a tarnished serpent of tin-roofed shacks and trailers slithering away on a highway to nothing. On the ground high tides and storms had left the buckled tar-sealed road awash with water the colour of milky tea. Seawalls of old axles and transmissions towered along the shore, and other heaps and pools of rubbish eked out their half-life between the shacks, leaving no room for vegetation. The garbage collectors had given up in despair. I took a taxi into town. Under dripping billboards advertising Winston cigarettes Marshallese sat with their baseball caps pulled down over their eyes, and in this apparently pedestrian-free and parentless environment the procession of cars swerved slowly to avoid the naked children playing in the muddy puddles.

The next morning I drove to the American Embassy.

If I was going to see anything of the skyworks of the missile testers, I had to persuade someone here to get in contact with the base at Kwajalein for me. I had requested permission to visit Kwajalein in London and had an encouraging answer from the State Department, but I already saw a bureaucracy preparing to deploy one of its built-in capabilities, that of allowing a decision taken at a distance to lose its force by the time it reached the point where it was supposed to be implemented.

The Embassy was one of the few buildings, along with the President's house, that had any pretensions to normality. As a result it was absurdly over-opulent, an elaborate cream-coloured hacienda planted in the middle of a huge lawn and surrounded by a chain-link fence.

Major Moore, the military liaison officer inside the Embassy, was a model office soldier: a tight creaseless uniform, near-slaphead haircut, and translucent skin from spending his life under artificial light. We sat on the edge of a sofa in a reception room that looked out over tennis courts and the ocean, and Major Moore took several notes. He grinned and whistled through his teeth.

'I'll gin up a memo to the base at Kwajalein first thing in the morning. The base is a day behind us, so it's still Sunday there,' he said cheerfully. 'I'll call your hotel tomorrow.'

He stood up and we shook hands. Unreasonably, out of fatigue, I saw Major Moore's helpfulness as inversely proportional to the likelihood of reaching my objective. The impression that for a person with the right credentials few things were easier than a visit to the US Pacific missile range left me obscurely depressed.

I rode back into town, to the Bikini Atoll office. Jack Niedenthal was behind a desk covered with papers, talking on the phone. Behind him, pinned to the wall, were more papers and a satellite photograph of a broken necklace of islets and shoals – nothing like a bikini – on a blue velvet cushion.

Niedenthal was the co-ordinator of the Bikini clean-up campaign, an athletic-looking man with the air of a long-distance runner. He was labouring under the consequences of yet another attack of grounditis. His charter for Thursday was on the rocks. He put the phone down.

'I can't get you to Bikini,' he said. 'I *may* be able to get you there for half an hour on Sunday while the plane turns round, but it's almost certain the answer's no. The Bikinians have just been voted $100 million by Congress to decontaminate the atoll, and the plane is full of islanders who want to go back and see the place. Not to mention the scientists.'

The news, which should have been a blow after coming so far, did not disturb me. The pessimist in me expected it. I had seen a lot of atolls, empty, familiar, haunted geographical features. The contamination at Bikini was invisible. Whatever there was to see, the only people there would be scientists crawling all over it. Niedenthal's decisive refusal was almost as cheering as the major's helpfulness had been dispiriting.

It had taken forty-four years for the exiled Bikinians to be awarded compensation and a chance to return. For most of that time the islanders had been settled on Kili, a tiny coral crust 800 kilometres to the south.

'Can I get to Kili?'

It was not in Niedenthal's nature to be unhelpful. But these places had become more than his expertise over the years. They were his territory.

'If you can get permission from the Outer Islands Office, it's okay by me. But *only* if you get their say-so.'

I needed some peroxide for my leg. I walked across the street to the Robert Reimers supermarket. Everywhere there were signs in shop windows that said, '*Yes*, we're open!' – to which the question presumably was 'Is that place open – because I really *have* to buy something any minute now?'

I found the brown bottles of antiseptic halfway down the store. The well-stocked supermarket was a forgotten concept. I stood there enthralled by the bounteous necessities of life. Toothpaste, shampoo, hairspray, nappies, suntan lotion on one side; to the left were the soya-substitute beef and the hostess fridge containing every legitimate flavour of ice-cream and

something called twinkies. All around were the answers to other
tricky questions:

Can't sleep? 'Try Compoz – 38% faster!'

Can't stay awake? 'Be alert with NoDoz caffeine tablets!'

Want to give up caffeine? Try caffeine-free Coca-Cola!

Worried about your weight? Take Lo-Cal sweeteners with
saccharin!

Worried about saccharin and cancer? Try saccharin-free
Lo-Cal!

I bought a couple of teeshirts. Amongst all this affirmation
it was odd to find a pile of them at the back of the store with an
orange mushroom printed on their back, and the words:

'BRAVO SHOT: Bikini Atoll – March 1, 1954. First deliver-
able Hydrogen Bomb, 15 megatons – 1000 times more powerful
than Hiroshima Bomb Drop. Test vaporized 3 entire islands and
blew a crater 1 mile wide, 440 meters deep. This Nuclear Test
contaminated the entire northern Marshall Islands.'

In the hotel, above the Down Town restaurant, I turned on
the first t.v. I had seen in four months. A woman in a lycra skirt
spun round and said, 'Look. Dexatrim: it's a dream come true. I
wanted to slim. I thought, there's a drugstore across the street
from my apartment, and the guy there suggested Dexatrim.
Dexatrim: a dream come true.'

Across the street from my hotel room was Charlie's Bar.
Two red lights shone over the plush studded doors. Inside there
was another Hogarthian scene, booths cast in dull blood-red
shadows and Marshallese sprawled in odd attitudes, their eyes
blank with the effects of Bud. One was roused by the sight of the
pizza I had ordered; he sat on the stool next to me and tried to
talk, but couldn't manage it, so I gave him some pizza that he ate
half of before slipping off the stool. A few minutes later, I went
to have a piss; at the back of the bar was a concrete cell lit by

powerful fluorescent lights where a dozen silent one-armed bandits were all in use by young Marshallese, with others waiting their turn.

I regretted not buying the Compoz. All night I had indigestion from the pizza and rain roared on the tin roofs above and all round. Next morning I went to the Down Town for breakfast. It was served on melamine crockery by one of the girls I had seen in Charlie's. Next to the till there were seven green health certificates taped up, one for each staff member: '—— of the Down Town Restaurant, Majuro atoll, has been examined & found free of communicable diseases, Jan 1990.'

I had read that the Marshall Islands had the highest rate of syphilis in the world. The thought occurred to me that the certificates were more reassuring for the women behind the counter than for their customers – unless they had been examined too.

What has happened in the Marshalls in the past fifty years can be seen as the logic of Cold War strategy. Captured from the Japanese in the final months of the war; subsequently administered by the United States as a 'strategic trust territory' by virtue of their location in the mid-west Pacific; by virtue of their remoteness successively adapted to the needs of the Pentagon's nuclear weapons, anti-ballistic missile and anti-satellite programmes, the two chains of atolls in the group have seen the most spectacular military activity in any time of peace.

Bikini's name was so well known that its significance was virtually forgotten: twenty-three atmospheric nuclear blasts from 1946 to 1958. Another atoll close by, Enewetak, was the location for a further forty-three tests. The actual testing had been restricted to these two places.

Rongelap, 150 kilometres to the east, had a different history. It had never been used for any weapons test or strategic installation. But the week before I arrived the senator for Rongelap, a gentle Marshallese dentist, had put the cat among the pigeons in Washington. In Washington he had disclosed the existence of one of those pieces of paper that lie around for years in classified files, evidence of the lunatic fringe of government.

The senator's office was a suite above a diner overlooking Majuro's lagoon, where they were running out of money and paper and toner for the photocopier.

'Even after all this time it came as a shock to me,' the senator smiled slowly, his eyes hidden behind tinted spectacles.

His name was Jeton Anjain. He had been fighting the US Department of Energy and its predecessor, the Atomic Energy Commission, for eighteen years: a hero to his people and an outcast in his own Senate for jeopardising the $55 million a year subsidy from the US trustees.

After years of unrewarded persistence, travelling, speaking, facing the hostility of US government departments and his own, he had the appearance of an infinitesimal weariness about him, tempered by patience and extreme courtesy.

The secret memorandum he had discovered was written in 1982 with the florid obscurity of bureaucratese. It recommended that the radiological and health monitoring programmes in the Marshalls, for which the Department of Energy was responsible, be transferred from its environmental department to the defence department. The argument was simple: that the DOE's activities in the islands were 'largely weapons-program related' and that much of the DOE's field effort was 'an exercise of the expeditionary capability... to resume atmospheric [nuclear] testing'.

(This capability – one of history's more major pieces of fine print – was one of the four safeguards requested by the US Joint Chiefs of Staff in 1963 when the Limited Nuclear Test Ban Treaty was signed. Safeguard C effectively kept America's options open by declaring an intention to 'establish and maintain standby facilities for the resumption of nuclear testing'.)

I had read the story of the disclosures in the *Marshall*

Islands Journal. Giff Johnson, the paper's editor, said, 'Go and see Jeton. You'll like him.'

He was right. Anjain was transparently honest, unembittered by governmental obstruction. And he had the best story. He was a small man against a monster.

'I am so glad you have come to talk about these things. We need to tell people and my English is not so good,' he said, smiling again.

His English was faultless. 'Do you know, the DOE memo was written two years *after* we signed a compact with the United States in which they agreed not to conduct any further nuclear tests in the Marshall Islands?' He spread his long, slightly trembling fingers flat on the desk. 'Unfortunately we have known the Department of Energy for a long time. This makes things in the past much clearer.'

The monster's breath had first breathed on the Senator's people on 1 March 1954. In the morning of that day, on Bikini, Operation Bravo was detonated. It was twice as powerful as the designers had expected. In the afternoon white ash drifted thickly down onto Rongelap. Children played in the ash, which fell on into the evening and turned the well-water yellow. The islanders were evacuated by Americans wearing protective clothing seventy-two hours later. The islanders' hair and fingernails fell out; later there were thyroid cancers, leukaemia and stillbirths.

Three years later, the Rongelapese were allowed home. In the mid-1960s DOE scientists ate pandanus and coconuts from Rongelap under controlled conditions: their intake of strontium-90 in a week was twenty times higher than normal, of caesium-137, sixty times higher. The islanders were allowed to stay. The DOE refused to allow any independent health survey, and not until 1978 did it conduct a radiological survey of the northern Marshalls, which showed the average concentration of plutonium in the soil of Rongelap to be more than twice that on

Enewetak.

'I was using all my salary by this time, asking for my people to be re-evacuated. On every occasion I was refused. I don't know the exact medical figures, but the normal rate for thyroid cancer is one in 100,000. Out of eighty-six people exposed on Rongelap, twenty-five got it. Today we have paralysed children, children that do not grow, children who do not speak.'

I asked why he had been refused. He picked up a thumbed, heavily re-xeroxed document. 'This is the first radiation report on Rongelap by the DOE.' His finger wavered over a line at the end of it. 'Their conclusion was that "the habitation of these people on the island will afford most valuable ecological radiation data on human beings".'

In 1985 the Senator had done what the DOE never expected a Marshallese to do. He took the initiative. He contacted Greenpeace and had the *Rainbow Warrior* – a month before she was bombed – resettle the islanders on a remote island, Mejato. The DOE were furious at their long-term radiation monitoring programme being upset, as the Senator had suspected they would be.

'You see, the Rongelap people are unique, not like the people of Bikini who were evacuated. They are an exposed people. But we will do what we have to do.'

He would go on fighting and telling the truth until the monster gave up. He expected it to exhaust itself on its own lies, and perhaps he was right. In eighteen years he had not spared himself, acquiring the kind of frame pared down to accommodate only the cause he was pursuing. He gave the impression of being not just single-minded, but single-bodied.

I asked him if he he felt optimistic about the future.

He smiled and did not hesitate.

'I will tell you, if you can tell me the meaning of the word optimistic.'

40
From Rita to Laura

Gene pointed at the silted weedy lagoon and said, 'See this. This is my swimming pool. This would cost you twenty million in Hawaii.'

In the morning the sun had come out, briefly, and I walked to Rita at the northern end of Majuro. Among the shacks were the odd flamboyant with its blood-of-Christ flowers and a dusty breadfruit tree or two. At the tip of the island, in the usual garbage of engine blocks and axles, a flotilla of black-winged butterflies, polka-dotted and tinged with violet, settled and rose in small playful clouds. I climbed the water tower. From the top I could see the straggling, tarnished roofscape following the rusty curve of the lagoon, animated by three hulks swinging at anchor.

There was less overcrowding here, but the same population explosion of glossy young faces. It was another eerie fact, along with the incidence of syphilis (which many of the children could expect to have inherited), that the average age of the Marshallese population was fourteen. Fighting the idea of nuclear extinction implanted in the hypothalamus, or following the ordinary ghetto pattern, every fifth girl – every *fifth* girl – between fifteen and nineteen was having a baby a year.

The Marshallese couldn't see the point of contraceptives. The ingenious solution to the population problem, favoured by the President (a hugely overfed man called Amata Kabua, whose face reminded you of an overripe pineapple in sunglasses), had been to import fifteen million tonnes of California's domestic garbage to create lagoon landfills, a brilliantly simple scheme in which the government would be paid $140 million by grateful waste disposal companies and potentially end up doubling the land area of Majuro island. The President was a paramount chief and in the Senate he rarely lost a vote. The plan had suffered a momentary setback when another secret memorandum from a waste company was uncovered that mentioned the possibility of slipping in some low-level nuclear waste with the municipal garbage, but parliament had passed the necessary resolution, ignoring the estimates of half a million gallons of leachate, containing heavy metals, asbestos and solvents, that would seep into the lagoon every year.

Kabua was not such a fool. His government was already collecting more than $1000 for every man, woman and child each year from US subsidies. The waste would double the Marshalls' annual income. What could be better? He couldn't be bothered to organise proper garbage disposal for the 20,000 people living on Majuro, but in ten years' time he would be able to say he was president of the biggest garbage dump in the Pacific. It reminded me of a joke I had heard in Charlie's bar. Overcrowding and cash and supermarket life had produced some of the highest rates of heart disease and sugar disorders and infantile malnutrition in the world. Mothers in Majuro fed their children on Coke and ice cream. The quickest way to get rich in the Marshalls, they said, was to sell doughnuts to diabetics.

At the hotel Amos, the Marshallese-Irish manager, said he was going to Laura, the settlement at the other end of Majuro. He knew I was fretting about the answer from the Embassy and suggested I went along.

We picked up Gene, a paunchy amiable American with a haircut that curled over his collar who talked non-stop, and drove out in the rain past the burned-out power plant, the pool hall, the docks, the President's guarded villa, and the sweltering pools of trash. Beyond the airport were the occasional houses of senators and American exiles and a couple of buildings from the Japanese occupation, water dripping from their delicately carved, rotting eaves.

Amos was building Gene's dream house. It was half-finished, a concrete bungalow just beyond Mile 22. Gene had had his fingers in a lot of pies, first on the east coast and in California; then he had moved to Hawaii, and now he was here, as far west as he could go. He was the picture of enthusiasm. There were no business permits for Americans, no tax below $80,000, he said: '*no* reporting to the IRS.' He capered around in the rain in his white shorts and rose-tinted spectacles, saying, 'I'll have a deck here. Don't let them cut down that pandanus, Amos. Grass all round. Sliding doors straight out onto it and my own private beach.' As we left, he turned to me.

'You can tell people about the Marshalls,' he said. 'But tell them hotel rooms are five hundred dollars a night.'

When I got back there was no call from Major Moore. At five I called him. He was his charming, helpful self, saying he had better news than he expected: the public affairs officer had arrived from Kwajalein that very afternoon in Majuro. His heartiness was another indication that things might not be easy. The PAO had received Major Moore's memo that he had ginned up. There was a pause. Just before he hung up, he said what I had known since I met him. 'But you ought to know, Mr Evans, this may not be a shoo-in.'

Don Michael prided himself on efficiency. I met him in the Robert Reimers restaurant, a place that served the blandest salads in the world, and he had a file full of faxes and memos about my visit. He hung over the edge of his clothes; he had a neat moustache and the appearance of a serious country-and-western fan. Internally the PAO was what, externally, he tried hard to be: compact, disciplined, serious. Was I interested in technical things? Did I want to take photographs? What was the reason for my wanting to come to an installation like US Army Kwajalein Atoll? 'The base is purely a testbed, you know. A measuring station without political significance.' As bland as the food, the mild, searching interrogation could only be answered by a performance of equal blandness. I said I was writing a book about the Pacific: the base could not be ignored for its size and its importance as a collaboration between America and the Marshallese.

In the end he was reassured. The problem was, he said, that other journalists' misconceptions preceded me. They came and wrote about the country-club atmosphere and the contrast between living conditions for the Americans and the Marshallese, who were all housed on a dormitory island at one end of the atoll. He hoped I would describe what I saw fairly and remember this was only a technical scientific establishment.

We were both satisfied with our performances. He pushed his salad aside and ordered another plate of fries, the Army official on duty recast as the reasonable guy trying to keep his weight on the right side of 10 kg over and allowing himself a little weakness. What were the chances of my seeing a mission come in? His answer was non-committal. Things were real busy and he couldn't promise anything. But I should arrange to be on the morning flight to the base in ten days' time.

Daily life in Majuro required a special quality of endurance. There was a direct relationship between fatigue and the size of the obstacle to be overcome. I came to need a sleep before gathering my strength to go to the airline office to change a reservation.

After twenty-two taxi rides and three further visits to the Bikini Atoll Office to persuade Jack Niedenthal to let me go to Kili unescorted, I had tickets, and permission, to go to Kili and Kwajalein.

No place I had seen rivalled Majuro for the uncontrolled impact of one culture on another, but with all the resources it possessed America had been unable to replace the Marshallese way of life with anything worth having.

The food everywhere was terrible. And apart from eating there was nothing to do except go to the supermarket and watch t.v. I spent a couple of mornings in the library, a small, well-stocked but largely deserted room; but to go out – to walk – anywhere fuelled the boredom. The downpours continued, nourishing the tonnes of oxides on the shore, attended and succeeded by a racing wind. The days were lit by a directionless low-wattage light source of sputtering intensity, and on the main street the seamless loop of traffic circulated without apparent destination. Out in the lagoon the three rotting hulks, barely afloat, turned at anchor like disembodied clock hands showing time dispiritedly, at random.

I had forgotten that there were still stitches in my leg. At Majuro hospital the doctor took time to get to them, hidden by the swelling. There might be a bone infection, he said. I didn't believe him. After six weeks I knew that the cut had just become a constant companion. In dry weather it closed up slightly. In this humidity it deepened and made the leg stiff. It wouldn't go away until I no longer needed it. Until then all I had to do was dress it twice a day, pack the hole with antibiotic cream and forget about it.

The tiredness I felt was due, I knew, to solitude. Even your feelings get tired when you're alone with yourself too long. Solitude becomes a sensation of invisibility. The Marshallese fostered this sensation, as much among themselves as with strangers. Was it because of what had happened to them? Was it something inborn? As soon as they stopped being children, they seemed to take a vow of semi-silence. As I walked past the close-built plywood houses there was no noise of conversation, no heckling, just a strained quiet among the unbroken rumble of car and truck engines. Uninterested in contact with Europeans, a face that returned a smile or answered as an equal hardly existed. My feeling of invisibility became so uncomfortable I felt I should wrap myself in bandages from head to foot; would they notice me then? But they didn't really even notice each other.

Why had I come to this crazy, horrible place? I began to see the journey, and its end in the Marshall Islands, as a penance I had imposed on myself. This was the other agenda, unadmitted by the slippery ego: a pilgrimage in reverse, not to Bikini or to the heart of the American military machine, but to force myself into contact with the meaning of solitude, under the tropical sun I had known as a child. Now I had found it where I hardly expected to, without the sun, in the darkest, ugliest place I'd been. And there was nothing good or nice about it – except that it was a good reward for a coward, a nice episode for a pilgrim. Splashing through the streets day after day in a filthy temper, bored and exhausted by everything I saw, angry at my invisibility and other people's cheerfulness, I had got onto intimate terms with solitude. I was face to face with the inside-out passion of solitude.

At last the penance was over. At last, after ten days of watching slimming commercials and mooching through the supermarket four times a day, it was time to go.

41
Return to Bikini

At eight the next morning the air was clear and damp from three more storms in the night. How did anyone sleep in this town? The tin roofs amplified the rain to a roar. It came suddenly, waking me every time, the soft static burble of overflowing drains replaced by an untuned radio at full volume. I began to see the point of new Compoz, 38% faster. You had to get to sleep fast in order to get in as much sleep before the switch was next thrown in the heavens and you woke up to the rising smell of mould from clothes that became wetter every time you went out and somehow, despite the air-conditioning, stayed that way indoors.

The plane for Kili was late. The young Bikinians made perfunctory conversation. Their mouths glinted with gold when they laughed. Older men with crocodile complexions sat immobile, the brief enjoyment of someone else's joke their only sign of life. A man in his sixties wore a baseball cap with a heat-moulded picture of a plane on it. This was Blackbird, the SR71, the Americans' first radar-evading aircraft. The Marshallese were suckers for product placement. Across the hall another man wore his 'Dive Bikini' sweatshirt. The lagoon whose floor was scattered with the wrecks of ships sunk by the first nuclear blasts, was being promoted as the location for the most sensational diving in the world. Clutching a three- or four-month-old baby, a young emaciated mother sat down with an economy-size tin of Planter's Cheez Balls and two cans of Fanta Red Cream which she fed steadily to the child.

In my notebook I scribbled:

Further notes on incuriosity of Marshallese:
1. Children, naked and less than a year old, play in the road.
2. Adults sleep with every other adult, get syphilis, get treated, sleep with everyone else again.
3. They accept unquestioningly the US gifts, influences and aid, even though under the new compact of association the money is going to stop in ten years' time.
4. They have as many children as they feel like.
5. They eat all refined food – flour, rice, sugar – and feed their children on Cheez Balls and Fanta.

There is something missing, some path in the mental process, an awareness of the conditional, an ability to envisage consequences, the conditional intelligence that motivates imagination, speculation, the control of the future. If this is right, if the Marshallese don't possess the ability to say 'what if...?' or 'if... then...', then they and the Americans who have succeeded in treating them as children for so long must be made for each other.

Kili was a small forested blob with a brushstroke of an airstrip down one side, maybe three kilometres long by one wide. I don't know what I expected, but not the prisoner-of-war camp buildings, the lack of food, the pretence at normality. They had a prisoner's joke: there was one main settlement, Downtown, and a smaller knot of houses, Chinatown, half a kilometre away, so called because it was so far. Nobody walked between them: the distances were so short that going by car was the only way to inject some interest into a journey from one to the other or to the scrubby coral sportsfield or the airstrip. The ninety houses of tin and plywood were all prefabricated to a uniform five-room design and painted a drab peach colour. To every three houses there was an insanely loud generator. After five in the afternoon the island throbbed and smoked like a place under bombardment.

Hearing the racket of the generators for the first time, you could imagine the conversation between two officials arguing over what was to be done with the evacuated islanders:

What do we do with them? Simple. We give them another island. What do they need? You're making difficulties. So they can't fish, because the reef is too dangerous? So the island's too small to support them? We fly food in, we build a sportsfield and an airstrip, a church, a school, a dispensary and a restaurant, give them water tanks and electricity. We build them all houses. They'll have everything they need. But they like their old *fales*. No, we've got a prefabricated design, a huge improvement on those. And once they've got electricity and running water, and food on tap so they don't have to go fishing, they'll be really happy. They'll be thanking us for hugely raising their standard of living.

And so on. What a wretched place it was, a Panglossian creation where the chthonic thump of diesels meant everything was normal. The people of Bikini were living fulfilled lives because every peach-coloured house with square windows, a tin roof and a water tank had electric lights and power for an icebox or video. And the thing most often forgotten about the island to which this dismal watered-down version of Americanness had been imported was that, left to their own devices, the Micronesian navigators who had first settled these islands had decided that Kili was not fit for habitation. The coastline, too rocky to fish, was unprotected against storms, the land area too small. It was a real desert island.

Uraki Jibas was at a loss after showing me the guesthouse and driving me around the island. He was the acting mayor (who could blame the mayor for never being there?) and there was nothing inhospitable about his welcome. I was garlanded with frangipani and shown Downtown and Chinatown and the sports-field, over which hung an ambiguous banner that celebrated defeat as much as survival, announcing '44 years progressing towards the return to Bikini'.

But there was the incuriosity again. He drove me along narrow tracks between overgrown palms, staring straight ahead. He seemed uninterested in why I had come. I sympathised. If you lived here, what point was there in being interested in anyone else's life? The near-700 Bikinians were a closed community. White men never came here. The Bikinians saw a stranger, and acknowledged him with a big wave and a smile, a gesture that seemed learned, not spontaneous, like the hesitant way the Marshallese on Majuro blurted out 'You're welcome' when you said thank you.

I was hungry. I asked Uraki where I could get something to eat. He seemed relieved there was a new task to perform, and with something approaching enthusiasm he turned back to the 'restaurant', a large empty replica diner on the far side of the sportsfield.

The owner, a narrow-eyed man in a baseball cap and a Robert Reimers teeshirt, leaned against the pillar outside, smoking. He didn't feel like opening. He wouldn't look at Uraki; I had reverted to complete invisibility. Eventually, half an hour later, after an argument in the kitchen, a chicken leg with white rice and sweetcorn on a melamine plate, along with a glass of Kool-Aid, were slid in front of me.

That night, in the guesthouse, I had a prisoner's dream: a real dinner on a white tablecloth, wine, little currents of perfume from the other tables. It was a dream I had dreamt with increasing frequency recently. You know the one: the all-important date, the rage of glorious anticipation, and then – she doesn't turn up, and you sit foolishly in the crowded restaurant among the contemporary prints and the waxed ferns, eating alone. The food, an anchovy and pepper salad and a salmon steak with a bottle of Meursault, just about makes up for it; then, at the end, you put your hand to your wallet and it isn't there. This time there was a variation: the waiter came to the table to say that, since I couldn't pay, I would have to spend the next forty-four years on Kili.

At six forty-five Uraki arrived to take me for breakfast.

'Where are we going to get breakfast at this time?'

'The restaurant will be open.'

It was Sunday, and I didn't believe him. When we got there the place was shut. He sat in the car outside the shuttered diner, his knees shaking steadily, picking his nails and his nose and spitting out of the window every thirty seconds.

'I don't think they're going to open.'

'They will in a little while.'

The word 'food' had been imprinted on his mind by my question of the day before, a new concept in attending to a visitor. It had made him so eager that he had woken me up an hour early.

'Uraki, there's no one around. It's seven o'clock.'

'We wait five minutes more.'

'Uraki, it's kind of you to take me for breakfast. But I'll have a shower and meet you at the church later.'

Sulking, he drove me back to the guesthouse. With a child's reasoning, he believed the restaurant would be open because he wanted it to be. Cause and effect had no regulatory status in his thinking.

If he thought the restaurant would be open because he wanted it to be – if the Bikinians believed everything they wanted to happen would happen because they wanted it to – it would explain why they were still waiting on Kili forty-four years after they were exiled.

The church in a tropical town has one useful purpose. Even for the non-believer it is the one spot of coolness out of the vertical sun. On Kili the church was just another prefabricated building supplied by the US government. At ten o'clock there was no escape in the quivering heat. The ushers sat nervously in their Western-cut Sta-prest; behind the altar the American flag was furled next to the sand-and-palm colours of the Republic of the Marshall Islands. The sermon was in Marshallese. English words emerged, 'malnutrition', 'baby-sitter', 'Mother's Day': there was something about family responsibilities.

But the room was gripped by a baffling oddity. From every windowsill emanated the sweet perfume of disinfectant. Their surfaces were crammed with bottles of Clorox and Pine-Sol and Joy! cleanser. Camay was piled along the altar rail and held down the corners of the lectern cloth. On the altar stood packets of Trend soap powder. All through the service my eye was caught by the red and blue packets. 'Compare and save! Compare and save!' It was like a rewriting of the Bible: God's mercy was insufficient for everyone, it was better to go for selective salvation. Who would be saved? The Americans, obviously. Which of the Marshallese? It was all relative. God sounded like Henry Kissinger, when he was questioned about the effects of nuclear testing: 'There are only 90,000 people out there. Who gives a damn?'

The air continued to heat up. It was hard to see any sign of uplift in the congregation. The older men, their faces engraved with resignation, stared through a cataract haze. The women did better. All day they had their hands full with children and preparing food and washing. There was little time or energy for discontent, and they radiated a kind of tired tranquillity. Among the young men there was the same jiggling of the legs that I had noticed with Uraki, a repetitive muscular tic that went on constantly and reminded me of male polar bears in a zoo, pacing up and down, sitting and rocking back and forth, shaking their heads: stereotyped neurotic behaviour caused by removal from their snow caves and plains of ice.

A few hours would have been enough in so tiny and barren a place. Any landscape is a state of mind. You owe your melancholy to the Black Mountains, your arrogance to the Castilian plain, your bureaucratic heart to a canton in Switzerland, your happiness to Suffolk. On an atoll the still heart of the lagoon pulls you away from the ocean. The beaches on the ocean side are gorgeous ribbons of desert. Houses and life face the other way, to the blue glassy water, to the balancing, tranquillising power of the flooded crater. Here there was no still heart. Ocean in front of you, ocean behind you; there was nothing to fall back on.

Nothing to fall back on, until the plane arrived the next morning. In the heat of the afternoon I walked in a circle round the shore of the island: nothing to see but the tide-worn eighteen-cylinder engine of a Japanese fighter embedded in the sand beside the airstrip and the Downtown beach littered with used Huggies.

Going round in circles: it was what everyone did. The four survivors of the evacuation that I met as the sun ripped away over the horizon (it was an illusion, but the sun seemed to want to get away, casting none of the slow melting shadows of Savai'i or Vaitupu) all said the same thing. They would not let the Americans do the same to them today, but they still trusted the Americans to take care of them. The Americans were good to provide food and help – as if the help were something separate, unconnected to the situation the Americans had put them in in the first place.

They sat on the steps of their plywood houses. The three men's faces were cracked, like old deflated footballs. The fourth was Uraki's grandmother, only half-visible in the shadow. They hardly talked. Between sixty and seventy, they had the stubborn lethargy of children. Sorry Lang had the features of a Mongol king, all slack lower lip and square skull, and the hands of a canoe builder.

He had been taken back to Bikini briefly.

'I was happy then, remembering when I taught my sons to build and sail their canoes.' The pale half-blind eyes looked at me, then flickered away to the ground.

Uraki's grandmother moved out of the shadow. She had never been happy here, she said. When I took out the camera, she suddenly brightened. The picture I took was a perfect lie, of a face that was once beautiful, the angle of eye and cheekbone perfect, momentarily, misleadingly alive.

The story was going to have a happy ending. Could you start again after forty-four years? It was impossible to tell. If they had lived lives of wild anxiety, you might expect some sudden enthusiasm that it was all going to be over. But this reticence was different, an infinite depressing fatigue like that of people wrongfully gaoled.

Had I misjudged them? Maybe their reticence wasn't
prison lethargy, but something else, the deliberate putting-aside
of confrontation and rancour which was a Marshallese sign of
dignity. Their thought processes weren't circular or contradictory either, but part of the same restraint. What chance had
seven hundred people had against the aims and needs of a continental power?

Then I remembered Jeton Anjain, and Kaiekieki Sigrah
poring over millions in compensation in his airless office on
Rabi. You only need one man. And obsession is preferable to
restraint.

I went back to the guesthouse. I took another shower while
the generator drilled into the wall, and walked into the bedroom
to the minor clatter of the air-conditioner to find my last clean
shirt. In the pokiest buildings in the Marshalls, lacking every
other comfort, there were always air-conditioning units, another
bizarre token of normality, clattering and shooting out cold stuff
at you.

But there was something else. My notebook was open on
the table. I had scribbled some footnotes to the survivors' comments. They thought of themselves as America's children. After
having their home vaporised and plutonium-enriched, they still
trusted the Americans to show them a sense of purpose, and
were grateful for the compensation and the Bartletts Pears, white
bread, Spam, Ketchup, Kool-Aid, white rice, white sugar, chick-
en pieces, sweetcorn, canned vegetables, corned beef, canned
tuna; the Toyotas, 24-packs of Huggies, Jell-O, Winstons,
Bensons Menthol, Taster's Choice coffee, Hong Shing Ramen,
Aloha Maid Guava Drink, cans of Iced Tea with Lemon and
Levi's Sta-prest. All the world's talk had gone on over their
heads since Operation Crossroads in 1946, when the US Navy
set up on Bikini, among other things, a makeshift bar called the
Up and Atom for the accompanying press which an Army B-29,
the next day, atomised with its load. The world – that rigmarole

of men in suits and motorcades and t.v. cameras – had moved on to other things. The Bikinians' place of exile, their placidity, allegiance and state of mild ignorance had not altered. But in two respects they were remarkably modern. At the end of the notes I had written:

'Today they think America's enemy is Japan. The phrase "the Cold War" is meaningless to them.'

42
To Venus

We came in off the ocean in a tremorless glide, the sea below decorated by a necklace of slender islands that made its way to the line of the horizon and vanished. The twelve-seater Dornier landed without a murmur on the white concrete runway. After the brutal braking I was used to on short coral airstrips, the plane seemed to be taxiing for hours to the terminal building. Through the window on my left I took in hangars, piles of oil-drums and equipment, low-rise offices with fat white vans with fat black tyres parked outside, a hovering helicopter and two more on the ground, and against the sky there were three white radomes that looked like enormous golfballs.

Out of the right-hand window I saw coconut palms and a knot of men in shorts and baseball caps, talking as they walked between them. There wasn't a great deal of room between the runway and the ocean's surf – it really was one hell of a landing strip – but my eyes did not deceive me. On this side the men really were trailing golf carts, and what they were trailing them over really was a nine-hole golf course.

The policeman on security duty grinned and said: 'You have a real nice time.'

Don Michael was waiting, with itinerary in hand.

'I suggest you get some breakfast, and I'll pick you up around ten-thirty for a briefing.'

He loaded my bag into one of the white Dodges and left me at the hotel.

I walked down Ocean Road to the Pacific Dining Room on Eighth Street, a clattering white and chromium hall where people sat far apart from each other in order to be alone with their breakfast. For $4.25 you loaded a tray with as much as you wanted: pawpaw, cereals, yoghurt, grilled bacon, sausages, tomatoes, eggs easy over, beans, fries, hash browns, toast, and then a little cheese or a couple of oranges to finish off with.

After twenty weeks of a diet that lately hadn't varied much between fish and breadfruit and coconut and more fish, I had no stomach for any of this, and picked up a slice of pawpaw and some toast and coffee.

It was nice to know that the capability to satisfy that kind of appetite was there if you wanted to use it. Plenty of people did. Most of the diners, in huge horrible Babygro tracksuits, beat the Polynesians for size; they could have trampled a Sumo wrestler underfoot. They walked back to the line for repeat orders of sausages and a second double shake (and later in the day I saw three of them in the cafeteria down the street, making just as swift work of two beef subs and a pizza). As they ate, they had a look of watchful, possessive concentration on their face.

Kwajalein was all about capability. The range briefing was given by Lt-Colonel Harrison, a genial man in spectacles and combat fatigues who was on crutches from a bad case of jogger's ankle. (At Kwajalein base, apart from golf, you could play almost any sport you cared to. Tennis, softball, volleyball, basketball, handball, and there was an eight-lane bowling alley. But what everyone was involved in, one way or another, was the major-league baseball of governments – more world-series than the World Series. They called the atoll, or more accurately the lagoon it enclosed, the catcher's mitt. The pitcher was in California, at Vandenberg Air Force Base. The ball reached speeds of up to 16,000 kph, and the only play they were aiming for was a strike.)

'Kwajalein became the US Army's major range in 1964,' Col Harrison started. Since then, anything between 300 and 600 unarmed intercontinental ballistic missiles – he wasn't sure – had been test-fired from the west coast of America at its lagoon. When it was not using what Col Harrison proprietorially called 'one of the most extensive collections of radars and computers ever assembled' to play baseball with Minuteman, Peacekeeper and Trident missiles, the range did not sleep. 'It is a key component of Pacific Command's satellite defence and space surveillance network. Kwajalein is also a testbed for the space interceptor weapons of the Strategic Defense Initiative.'

Pacific Command's size beggared belief.

'320,000 troops of the Army, Navy, Marine Corps and Air Force; the Seventh Fleet and Third Fleet; long-range bomber bases; early-warning systems and space tracking stations; attack submarines on permanent rotating patrol.'

If you were CINCPAC (the commander-in-chief, Pacific Command), I thought, you were liable to be almost as powerful as the President.

The Pacific was America's destiny. Ever since she had won the war in the Pacific – a war she kept her allies out of – she had seen the Pacific as her great western frontier. All through the late 1980s, while we were being told that the apparatus of the Cold War was being dismantled, the US President (who played a baseball star or two in his time) and his Navy Secretary John Lehman were *increasing* the size of the Pacific Fleet from 200 to 300 ships. And naval nuclear weapons, particularly the US Navy's real hotshot armaments, the hunt-in-the-dark, hide-in-

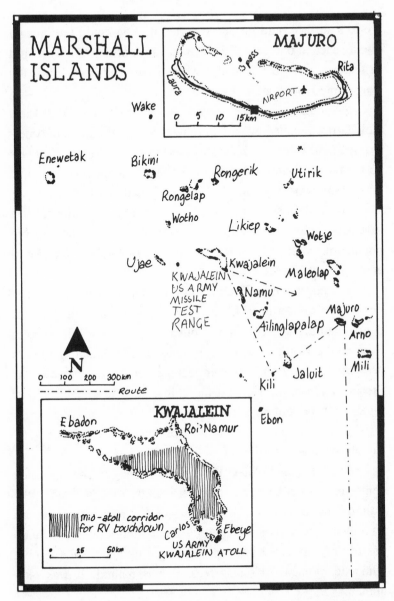

the-dark submarine-launched ballistic missiles, were being kept right off the agenda of all the arms talks, despite Soviet suggestions to include them.

This was the ocean's most interesting characteristic. You could do all of this, set up a sphere of influence over half the world's surface, and no one reported it. You could talk noisily about peace in one part of the planet, and continue quietly to arm in another, and no one said a word. Peace had been brilliantly transformed into another PR concept.

Although Kwajalein was west of the Pacific Date Line, Col Harrison explained, and thus a day ahead of mainland America, the atoll followed the same calendar as California. This was so the men at Vandenberg and the men at Kwajalein were quite clear about what day a mission was supposed to go off on.

'Kwajalein's attributes as a target are unparalleled,' he said. 'Its position in relation to launch points; its isolation from population centres; and its versatility as a tracking and intercepting point.'

In Majuro Giff Johnson had said: 'Listen. In any war, missiles will be subject to all kinds of unverifiable assumptions about their reliability and accuracy. Both sides' weapons will have to fly over the North Pole, for one thing. The joke among missile designers is that *if* the US ever gets itself into a nuclear war, the President can be sure of just one thing: he will be able to blast the daylights out of Kwajalein Atoll.'

'Did you hear about the Peacekeeper mission last night?' Col Harrison asked.

I had. I already knew that I wasn't going to see a mission come in. I wasn't surprised or particularly disappointed. Why should I be surprised? The keepers of the range, so generous with their time in passing on all the theory and foreplay of weapons testing, preferred to keep that single intimate, split-second, climactic moment to themselves. It was natural. It was only human.

But the maintenance man at the hotel, Randy from Tennessee, had seen it.

'Boy, it was real neat,' he said.

'That mission,' said Col Harrison, 'took twenty-seven minutes from launch to impact, a distance of 8000 kilometres. Its

ten RVs splashed down in prearranged sectors of the lagoon and
ocean, monitored by long-wavelength tracking radars and short-
wavelength imaging radars. The phased-array Altair radar, with
its dual field of vision, one of only three in the free world, can
spot with a single millisecond pulse a metal object the size of a
basketball 4800 kilometres away. Then, when an RV gets close
enough, we have the Tradex radar, and that will give you a
gnat's-ass view of it.'

RV was short for re-entry vehicle, the piece that was
bussed off the main body of the missile in mid-flight and re-
entered the atmosphere in free fall to hit the target. Each RV,
when armed, carried a 330-kiloton charge. Trident II, the 'silo-
buster' which would supposedly destroy Soviet missiles before
they could be launched, would carry eight RVs – each with a
charge of 475 kilotons.

A missile was a mission. A warhead was a re-entry vehicle.
330 kilotons was twenty-six times more powerful than the
Hiroshima bomb: you called something carrying the equivalent
of over 3 million tons of TNT a Peacekeeper. You changed the
terminology and you avoided the real significance of things. To
the personnel on the range – most of them were scientists and
contractors rather than soldiers – this epistemological leger-
demain was second nature. They were happy with the euphem-
isms. They didn't think about it. They were – they all were – real
friendly and real polite. No one ever used the 'n' word.

The base was clean and it was nice and neatly laid out,
spacious and airy. The wind blew all day and dropped its wings
at dusk; the temperature/humidity was a constant 85/85.

Off Ocean Road, to the left of Eighth Street, was the
sportsfield, with the athletic spire of a Nike-Zeus missile from
the Sixties mounted on one edge and the open-air movie theatre
on the far corner. Between Sixth and Eighth Street you could
find everything else you needed: the Pacific Dining Room, post
office, Macy's department store, the library, Bank of Guam and

the golf pro shop. In a trailer next to the cycle racks was the Surfside beauty parlour. There was a theatre, a club and a video library called Tape Escape that took $14,000 a month in tape rentals at a dollar a tape. To get to the beach you went down Lagoon Road, right for the family beach, left for the bachelors'.

The brick officers' houses, shadowed with palms and frangipani trees, stood in quiet streets with children's bikes lying in the front yards. The high school was here too. On the tip of the island stood Silver City, 250 stainless steel trailers that some residents just lived in and others had lavished verandahs and patios on and the occasional Doric colonnade or conservatory.

Kwajalein was tidy, quiet, ordinary: suburban trailer-park America at its best. (No Marshallese lived here of course. The Army paid rent to the landowners and sent them to Ebeye, the next island along, from where they commuted to the base to work.) It was *better* than America. No private cars were allowed; people cycled or took the bus or even sometimes walked. And the residents felt comfortable and safe. It was so homey some of them kept renewing their contracts. In Macy's I met a jelly of a woman in a pink tracksuit who had been on Kwaj (rhymed with Dodge) for eleven years.

'It's real nice here. You know there's no drugs, no violence, no street crime, no rape. The high school is terrific. It's a great place to bring up the kids.'

You heard this everywhere. *Real nice*: they became scary words. For a place at the heart of America's military future, which had probably contributed more to the arms race than anywhere else on Earth, Kwajalein's greatest triumph was its niceness. It was true. The base was calm, beautiful, friendly. In the club at lunchtime, a place where people stuck to soft drinks and ate huge salads with the taste frozen out of them, the conversation was about contracts (to renew or not to renew) and girlfriends (just renewed) and the weekend.

I had lunch with Don.

'Don, what is the worst thing here?'

'I'll tell you. The worst thing is the way the video store has killed off ballroom dancing. Entertainment can be a serious problem. One of my biggest headaches is getting entertainers to come out to Kwaj. There was talk of Elton John coming on his world tour, but it looks as if we're going to have to make do with the Miss USA troupe.'

'Do people have problems with isolation?'

'Oh, people cope with the isolation, one way or another. Of course it's a pain when you can't have an argument or a date without the whole range knowing. Sure, there's some stress. You see how much people eat around here? You see how many fat people there are?'

I realised what Kwajalein most closely resembled. It was a Fifties s.f. movie, something in the tradition of *Fire Maidens from Outer Space* or *Robinson Crusoe on Mars*:

Flight to Venus
A Universal Picture

The apocalypse has come, but a small community has escaped off-planet to start again. Twenty-five years ago, five hundred men and women – a collection of extra-ordinarily talented scientists – climbed aboard a rocket in the final frizzling moments of Planet Earth and blasted off for Venus. Everything they have on the new colony has been salvaged and painstakingly recreated: in twenty-five years they have founded a kind of Utopia. The planet's atmosphere is surprisingly beneficial, and the population lives in near-complete harmony. (Some dramatic licence creeps in. The club never runs out of beer; and somehow there are always fresh steaks to be had, even though there are no animals. But this is balanced by a little discord, a fight in the bar, the occasional argument over a girl, to provide the correct note of verisimilitude.) All references to Earth but one are forbidden to prevent homesickness, along with the word 'nuclear'. Meanwhile a group of senior scientists constantly monitor the dead planet they have come from for signs of recovery. The only concession to memories of home is the big t.v. set in the colony's club. Somehow a single t.v. transmitter is still functioning in their old, unhappy, burnt-out world. The timescale is odd, but time has funny habits in these post-apocalypse days. The non-stop reruns of the David Letterman Show, which are all this thing transmits, give people a reassuring feeling of normality.

43
And Atlantis

The next day I was supposed to go to Ebeye, but that evening I went back to the club. Outside, a fat blonde girl said:

'So you're a newspaperman? You be careful on Ebeye. Are you staying the night?'

'That's the plan.'

'Are you crazy? Don't mix with those women. They are *diseased*.'

'What do you mean?'

'They're mudhens. You go to the club there and you'll *catch* something.'

The policeman from the airfield came past.

The blonde girl said: 'This guy's going to spend the night on Ebeye.'

The policeman grinned at me. 'I thought I'd go tomorrow.'

The blonde girl turned away. We were both crazy and sick. 'Oh yeah, I forgot. He's got a mudhen.'

Inside the club, with the salad bar rolled off the dance floor, you socialised in deep brown armchairs. Everyone danced with everyone: it *was* real nice, to begin with. The sound system had everything from Tammy Wynette to Lisa Stansfield and Marillion. The favourite cocktail was a B52 – vodka, kahlua and Baileys. Trays of tumblers filled with the murky drinks went forth with impressive frequency.

As I watched from the bar, gradually a change came over the room. The air began to be filled with suppressed bad behaviour; the dancing was terrible, as wooden as your parents' parties.

I turned back to the bar, a line of single men in baseball caps. Wendell was a hard-featured man in his fifties. He was also a policeman. 'Nuthin to police.' Humpbacked cowries were his obsession.

Wendell introduced me to his friend Rex. Rex asked me what I was doing. He had a thin face scored by nerves, and a moustache. He said: 'Yeah, I did some writing a while ago, maybe ten years. Won a competition in *World of Poetry*. Bob Hope presented the prize.'

Wendell guffawed. 'Rex, you never said you were a poet.'

Rex was injured by the scorn.

'What about your damn shells?' he said and turned his back on his friend. He was out of the Army now but he had done two tours in Vietnam, one in helicopter gunships, one in charge of a reconnaissance platoon. Bombing Cambodia was no bad thing. He didn't blame Nixon, he blamed the generals. There was a line of trucks waiting to go in and get the VC, but they were never allowed to.

'Have another beer. I've learnt some fascinating things about the Marshallese. I've decided I should learn some of their language.' He spent most of his free time in the library. 'You've got to do something. I've been here forty days, and I tell you I'm climbing the wall.'

There was no need to ask about Vietnam. It kept cropping up. Another couple of helicopter pilots, one white, one black, both vets, stepped in. I had one in each ear, on the balls of their feet, wired.

'America's pulled a lot of small countries out of a lot of tight spots. What *I* want to know is, who ever helped out America?' said one.

The other one said: 'You know what nigger means, man? N-i-g-g-e-r. You hear what I'm sayin? It don't mean *nuthin*, because I can still keep the Commies out, black or white. And I'll tell you sumthin else. I never took no fuckin newspapermen on my missions. They said, "You gotta." I just grabbed their notebooks and stomped them in the mud.'

Fifteen years later, after a handful of B52s, the nerves and reflexes were coiling up all over again. The war was still on, it could be won. Kwajalein was just R & R. The pilots were thinking about air sports, hover-cover, shoot them if they freeze, shoot them if they run. We've got to keep the Commies out.

Maybe it was the B52s. Anything that tasted that disgusting couldn't be good for you.

The military build-up in the Pacific was not a one-sided phenomenon. During the Eighties the Soviet Pacific Fleet, based at Vladivostok, had been augmented by two new aircraft carriers and the transfer of guided missile cruisers and destroyers. Soviet attack submarines had begun deployment in the northern Pacific. The Soviets were also said to be developing a counterpart to Trident II.

Pacific Command's answer to this lay in strategic denial: operating forward bases and deploying its forces actively to keep the Soviet fleet in port. The US Navy was spending more time at sea than it had during World War Two. The Department of Defense's idea of the balance of power in the Pacific had always been to keep one step ahead, to seize the initiative and force the Soviet Union on the defensive. It was a policy enshrined in the phrase of Admiral James Watkins, a former chief of US Naval Operations: 'We can get inside their knickers before they find us, and they don't like it.'

This was an interesting idea, reducing global conflict to unsolicited heavy petting. The latest of these third-base activities, of course, was Star Wars, the means by which the bad-ass jocks at the Pentagon intended to secure what, in sex-slang, you would call a home run against the Soviets. In the place of arms talks which would include sea-launched missiles – the Soviet suggestion – the Pentagon preferred an anti-ballistic missile system that was supposed to knock out the missiles as they came in.

At the far end of Kwajalein they were building the GBR-X ground-based radar which would guide the first generation of interceptors. Testing of ERIS – the exoatmospheric re-entry vehicle interception system – was due to begin later that year. Many military men privately viewed it as an excessively expensive and complex way of setting about the ultimate hot date.

With the Star Wars defences in place, the wisdom went, the picture would be complete, and Americans would be able to sleep easy in their beds. Trident II would be out there somewhere silo-busting, and if some of those Russian missiles did somehow get through, they could just let ERIS and its associated weapons take care of them. They had all the bases covered.

The problem with this reassuring conclusion was that although all kinds of tests and rehearsals were going on all the time for this particular World Series game, no one had actually played it. So much of what would happen was the hypothesis of men in baseball caps with gold braid on them standing up in the bleachers and yelling for the home team. On the basis of experience, all kinds of things could malfunction seriously. Trident II had a miserable test launch record: two of the first three test launches in 1989 had failed. Peacekeeper, after eighteen successful launches under controlled conditions, had had to be blown up in mid-air on its first operational test. And since atmospheric nuclear testing was banned, no one had been able to quantify the effects of a nuclear blast on radar signals in the atmosphere, although it was known that any blast ionised large volumes of air, blocking or severely distorting radar transmission. With most missile systems and eighty per cent of military communications carried by radar and satellite, it began to look as if the guys in the bleachers – it went for both teams – were suffering severe perceptual dysfunction. Not only were the balls they were playing with way too big for the game, they could also end up zapping their own boys.

I took the landing craft to Ebeye in a downpour. I half-suspected what I would find. To create Kwajalein, they had also had to invent Ebeye. Ten thousand Marshallese lived here on an islet of forty hectares. The children were as thick as flies, the plywood barracks so close you had to sidle between them to get to the shore.

The shore: the density of garbage gave it the appearance of a clumsy land reclamation project. Everywhere there were oil-drums, old trucks, earthmovers, the carcasses of cars, freight containers, transmissions, tyres, split bags of household waste, beer cans, disposable nappies. Among the bonanza of waste, the children crawled and played, grinning, their faces streaked with rust.

What had I found? Nothing that people wanted to talk about or look at or visit, unless, like the easy-going policeman, they had a mudhen here. But why shouldn't ugliness take on mythic proportions? I had stumbled on another new Pacific myth, man-made like the thunderbolts the islanders watched overhead. Almost treeless, sanitationless, overrun by children under fourteen, it was no earthly island. It was the lost slum of Atlantis.

The rain sluiced down the walls of the barracks as I stumbled to the office of the mayor, Alvin Jacklick. He was said to have achieved a lot for Ebeye, along with the Kwajalein Atoll Development Corporation. The sewers no longer backed up into the one-room houses. They had desalination and power plants. The streets and sidewalks were paved. Hepatitis was no longer endemic.

But his lugubrious optimism in the future was unjustified, as he conceded, by the facts. They had around $21 million a year in lease payments, wages and income tax. Instead of luxury, the appearance of the place was a sort of joke tribute to the unfettered application of cash. The Marshallese landlords were failing to distribute the rent income among their people. The overcrowding was worse than ever. The super-slum conditions had brought about a conformist promiscuity.

'I can tell you,' Jacklick said, 'that *every* man is seeing, apart from his wife, at least three other women.'

Who was to blame? Everyone was screwing everyone else with gusto. What else was there to do except despair? The Marshallese were passive but not browbeaten. The children laughed and scrambled over hazardous garbage, their parents (whoever they were) caught the landing craft every day to the base and got on with their lives. The Americans had not intended to create Ebeye the way it was, even though they had ignored for years the biological time-bomb it had become and maintained rigorous apartheid at Kwajalein for health and education facilities. I thought of the woman in Macy's: 'Kwajalein's a great place to bring up the kids.'

There was nothing to be done. The clock couldn't be turned back, Ebeye couldn't be cured. Small improvements would occur, but nothing that would be allowed to disrupt its chief purpose as a segregated labour reservoir for the base. Of course if the Americans hadn't come, wishful thinking said it would be as it was: an ordinary, undisturbed coral island. But wishful thinking was more the province of the Americans than of the Marshallese.

Nothing, not even a suppressed lust to shake off the real nice atmosphere at the base and be crazy and sick with a mud-hen, could have induced me to stay the night. I ran through the pouring rain to catch the last landing craft back to the base. On the way I passed a small Marshallese girl. The rain had collected in a rusty oil-drum outside her rotting barrack. Bathing in the water sloshing in the bottom, her wet head was just visible over its rim.

You couldn't say the Americans were evil. But they were terrifying.

I walked to breakfast down Ocean Road for the last time. The Pacific Dining Room was full of people beating anxiety with the $4.25 breakfast.

Past the baseball diamond, I noticed something I hadn't seen before.

There were no coconuts on the palms. The familiar clusters of swollen ochre and green fruit were missing. When I happened upon him later, Don was surprised I should ask about them.

'Oh, we get the Marshallese to cut all the coconuts down. They truly are a hazard. Can you imagine what it would be like if one of those mothers fell on your head?'

At lunchtime I went to the club, then packed my bag. My laundry had been done and I took a scalding shower. As the jets of water smacked my shoulders, I had a bizarre pang of regret. Why should I mind leaving this spruce and beautifully organised colony of scientists? Was it the expensive bed, or the gentle shush of the high-grade air-conditioning, or the shower – this wonderful high-pressure shower – one of mankind's greatest inventions? But there was also all this security and enfolding warmth. Immobility; ordinariness; being in someone else's system and not having to think; some power bigger than you (the Bomb – a Christian creation); oh, the relief of the same comfortable life to look forward to tomorrow.

Movement saved me. Don arrived in the Dodge. At the airfield the Marshallese in transit to Majuro sat in suspended animation on wooden benches. We walked out to the picket fence and watched the plane for Majuro drop gently out of a pearl-powder sky.

Don had dug out some mementoes for me from his office at the control tower: a calendar, a brochure about the Strategic Defense Initiative, and a Kwajalein baseball cap. I thanked him, and for ten minutes we talked nostalgically about England, where he had spent four years stationed at Lakenheath.

I had found the best souvenir in the club at lunchtime. I had trousered a handful of the club's paper napkins. These showed a cartoon of the sun rising behind the silhouette of a palm tree. From the lagoon next to it, a baby black missile leapt joyously, like a spawning salmon.

44

Last journey

I had nothing left to do.

On the way back the Dornier pilot threw the plane through the clouds to find his position and brought it out banking over the shoals of yet another atoll. For forty kilometres he followed the thread of islets, the shadow of the fuselage and wings weaving over brakes of palms and the harsh sapphires of the lagoon. I couldn't find the place on the map. There was supposed to be only ocean between Kwajalein and Majuro.

Then the Dornier made an unscheduled stop on a green speck at the far end, the wheel-struts flexing hard on the coral. There were no glinting tin roofs and no radomes or trailers, hardly any *fales* either, and I made a snap decision to let the plane go without me.

I walked through the bronze gleam of the coconuts towards the lagoon. As I came out onto the path, a bald smooth-skinned man walked up to me.

'What is your purpose?'

'I saw your island from the plane. Can I stay?'

There was no way of leaving, in any case. His name was Airi and he swaggered in front of me, enjoying the prestige of having found the unexpected visitor.

On the shore it was a relief to see *fales* with space between them and smell the sweet, stuffy smell of copra drying again. New pandanus thatch rustled in the wind; the painted surface of the lagoon was hardly moving.

The island's king had left on the Dornier. The people had been up all night cooking for him. An old man was being wearily teased by some others on the steps of the palace, a clapboard house of peeling cream paint once, before the war, a Japanese trader's. The old man had lost to the king at draughts, out of deference, and now he was getting it in the neck. Airi gave me a green coconut and some breadfruit. Where had the king gone? 'To Majuro,' Airi hinted darkly. 'To the bar.'

I slept in the hospital on a bed with missing springs, surrounded by boxes of Unicef drugs. I looked for antibiotics from force of habit, before I realised that the swelling in my leg had gone. All night the rats shuttled down the wall to collect the remains of the breadfruit, then disappeared back into the thatch.

During the night a mermaid stood at the end of the bed, whispering to the rats to send them away and holding a draught-board. She had long dark hair and a model's flawless complexion. I could see parched salt glistening on the pale down in

front of her ear. The dream was a strange one. The draughtsmen
turned out to be tiny turtles, and, impatient with the game and
the turtles' squiggling onto the wrong squares, she smiled and
picked them up in her small fingers one by one and dropped
them into her mouth. Then Monsieur Dubos appeared. 'You
didn't believe me. But you see they do exist,' he crowed.

When I woke up, she was still there. She stood by the
window in a loose blue cotton dress with tiny daisies on it and
smiled again.

'They told me there was a visitor.'

Her name was Cathy. She *was* a model — had been — and
was now a Peace Corps volunteer. She had been teaching
English on the island for eighteen months, in a classroom past
the flaking palace. Later that morning I stood in the doorway.

'He is a careless skier,' Cathy read from the textbook. She
paused. 'He skis carelessly.' Twenty children repeated, 'He – is
– a – careless – skier.'

I laughed. At first I thought it was a model's trick, but she
had a cast that made her pale blue eyes under their high orbits
come slowly to rest on you, like the sweep of an arc light. She
turned and laughed too, lifting her chin, then gave the class the
next example. They intoned back: 'She – is – a – skilful –
checkers – player. She plays checkers skilfully.'

The island was a miracle of neatness. The banana gardens
were dug and there were lines of pawpaw trees. Around the well
and the houses were swept squares of broken coral. At its eastern
tip a towering coral-head sat on a declivity of sand that unwound
onto a shallow reef swarming with moorish idols and damselfish.
I climbed the coral-head and sat watching the long feathered
edge of palms separated from the water by a belt of white sand.
The beach was magnificently empty and rubbish-free. Here there
were no more than two hundred people on an island the same
size as the dormitory-slum at Ebeye; no cars or electricity; cutting copra, harvesting the fruit trees and fishing were the only

activities. Three outriggers sat on the surface of the lagoon. From the shade of the trees I watched for an hour, maybe two, the hunched backs of the fishermen pulling in their catch, before the spreading heat of the ground forced me to move.

After lunch – more coconut and breadfruit – I dozed and, through the doorway, watched Cathy sitting with the island women, gossiping in Marshallese. She had only been back to America once since she had come here: I marvelled at an adaptability I was incapable of.

Airi marched into the hospital. The boom-boom would come the next day, he announced. He mimed a big diesel boat. It would take me fifty kilometres across the lagoon to another airstrip.

There was no food aid for the island, but the islanders traded copra for ground coffee and cigarettes that they plugged into elegant holders with hardwood bowls and stems of dried plants.

Airi ran the store. His covetousness and bald obsequiousness amused me. At dusk we drank the sweet coffee beneath the pandanus trees outside his house and he chummed up to me, introducing me to his friends and boasting about his new generator and his television. He was the only man on the island with any taste for material things. He strutted up and down on a length of bare sand.

'This is where I will put my speedboat. It will be eight metres long and have two motors.'

The other men smirked at his feverish ambitions. He was up to his ears in bank loans. It didn't matter. In two years he would be harmlessly bankrupt.

Airi threw a dinner party that night. The breadfruit was baked this time, tasting of baked potato and nutmeg, and I had the customary delicacy: the fish heads, sweet meat dug from the shoulders of full-grown bass.

Cathy was in the hospital when I got back. She was reading

by the light of a hurricane lamp, and the mosquitoes had got in and raised red dots on her arms. To see her in the milky glare, sitting easy-limbed on a cushion at the end of the bed, was to experience a sort of dismay. She was the first good-looking white woman I'd seen in months. I was tired and wished she would go away. When she raised her pale murano-blue eyes and settled them on me, I felt like a fool, no longer cool and curious, no longer justified in my intense dislikes. She was – I felt mocked by it – beautiful, and the fragile control I had over the succession of events that had brought me here was slipping away under her gaze.

But she stayed where she was. The hurricane lamp hissed above her head.

'You shouldn't have caught me out in class like that. Sometimes my mind wanders and I read straight out of the book without thinking.'

She was from a tiny township in Arizona; a place wrongly marked on the map, she said, so no one ever went there. Growing up somewhere no one could find was how she had got her taste for isolation.

'I never wanted to be a model, but at high school in Phoenix I got spotted by a guy with a camera and a horrible quiff, and the next thing I knew I had spent eight years in New York. After I gave it up, it took me six months to learn how to laugh again.'

'Was it all that miserable?'

'No, no.'

Her throat came out of shadow as she lifted her chin and laughed at the question.

'When you're a model you have to laugh specially. You open your mouth and throw your head back and say, "Hah." Laughing properly gives you *terrible* wrinkles.'

Now, when her classes were finished, she read poetry, sat with the women and played checkers with the children. The book lay open on her lap: e.e. cummings' *Selected Poems*.

The transition could not have been easy. From $5000 a day she had gone to a Peace Corps salary, and after the reassuring nonsense of men saying 'You look just great' fifty times a day, she had had six visitors in a year and a half.

Her parents had come: her father couldn't bear the heat, her mother had been taken up by the Marshallese women and within a week had gone native. Among the others there had been a writer from Los Angeles, working on his third unpublished novel. He had rarely had anything published, but one way and another he had made a living from his ink.

'There was this obsession with ink. He didn't use a typewriter. He liked to get cylinders of ink, he said, and flatten them out on the page. And he talked about "fictions" all the time until it sounded like a dirty word.'

The writer had had a rucksack crammed with manuscript pages covered in a crabbed blue hand and had spent days talking to Cathy about the skills of writing, how once you had learned about verbs and tenses, you could 'zip into the future perfect, just like that'. It was part of a seduction routine that had worked before, but not this time.

'When he said he loved me at one in the morning, I had heard enough of his fictions. I told him it would be better if he zipped into the future perfect right there.'

I could only remember one e.e. cummings poem. I said:

'since feeling is first
who pays any attention
to the syntax of things
will never wholly kiss you'.

She laughed again. She had the checkerboard behind her cushion and she beat me hollow, three games in a row, while I told her where I had been. She knew about the missile range and quoted, 'a politician is an ass upon/ which everyone has sat except a man'.

It was late, and now of course there was nothing to tell me apart from the other writer. I didn't want her to go.

'How did you cope on your own all this time?'

'I didn't want to hear small talk or compliments again as long as I lived. Then after six months I got over that and had to learn how to be alone again, like when I was a child. Once the women had taught me Marshallese, that was easier.'

She had learnt more in the last year than in the last ten: everything from childbirth to mat-making.

'But I'm a little tired of it now. I need to go back and face people again.

'You can only learn so much on your own, be on your own for so long.'

She stood up. The checkerboard and the book still lay on the bed. She turned and smiled.

'It's the same poem, isn't it? "Kisses are a better fate/ than wisdom",' she said.

In the morning I walked alone to the western tip of the island. It was a lovely place to wake up in, with its tidy *fales* and a loose breeze and the sun pouring through the trees. At the sides of the track there were deep stands of swamp taro and immaculate groves of pandanus. Cairns of coconut husks covered with dried leaves had been placed between the houses; in one of the houses the wooden window-screen was up, propped open by a rusty shotgun.

To the right, beyond the breadfruit trees, the lagoon chimed like a chandelier. Outriggers threaded over its surface. A dog barked. Ahead the track narrowed to a path and the houses thinned out: everything – the madness of the range, Majuro, fatigue, the endless one place after another, the doughnuts, videos and garbage that had enriched the dignified tedium of these lives – falling away. There was no peace anywhere – Greene had said that in *The Lawless Roads* – but sometimes you stumbled on quiet sectors of the battlefront. I walked past smouldering copra-driers and through groves of palms cleared and replanted, the undersides of their leaves stickled with light thrown up from the mirror of the sea.

Where the apron of land ended a long sandspit wandered into the sea. A colony of black-naped terns stalked about on its tip. I walked to the frontier of sand, teased by glassy bubbles. The force of the light bouncing off the water revealed the limitations of the human eye, the sensation not so much visual as visceral. Beyond the distant tumbling masonry on the reef, there was no sound. Like standing at the stern of the ship, or trying to go back as far as I could, to the quiet sectors of childhood or the beginning of my memories, I couldn't go any further.

The boom-boom was promised for midday. Nobody paid any attention when it failed to appear. Airi was more interested in my camera, and made come-hither noises about that and my flashlight. I fobbed him off by buying a mat his wife had made and sat by a tree and watched the bright-teethed children looping naked off a jetty of coral into the water.

Then, at half past one, Airi came flailing his arms, squeaking that the boom-boom was leaving any minute. It wasn't true, of course. A boxy plywood boat lay to in the shallows, being bailed without a break. The island's mayor was travelling and he handed up his baggage: a water canister, bags of rice and breadfruit cheese, a small boy, kerosene and, with infinite care, a shiny plastic briefcase.

Eventually the marinised Toyota diesel was choked and we turned across the frictionless water. Cathy was sitting under the thatched shelter with the women and didn't wave. Further out the waters lifted. We passed islet after islet, following the inner curve of the lagoon and engulfed by new bursts of mineral and petrol blues with every variation in depth. A cup of perfect coffee appeared from nowhere. I counted the pace of the bailing: the rolling boat was shipping 300 litres an hour. Thirty porpoises surfaced at the bow, arcing out of the water in threes and fours; the helmsman put down his cigarette-holder and whistled them to stay with us. In the mid-afternoon fish came in on the lure and were gutted, cut, and dropped raw like chewy iron on a bowl of cold rice. Squalls came and went, then a thrashing storm. Below the scene was of meditative calm: the helmsman hardly looking at the smudged view ahead; the mayor wordlessly handing round more coffee; the boy bailing swiftly. I crouched and took the scoop from him, and while the sinking boat rolled on through the swells and the skies cleared, I sat by the clattering diesel, bailing with one hand, pushing fish and balls of sweet rice into my mouth with the other.

Bibliography and some sources

The tree of life
Nicholas Halasz, *Alfred Nobel*, London 1962.
I am indebted to M. Roland Bourdeix, and to the Institut de
Recherches pour les Huiles et Oléagineux on Espiritu Santo, for
their history of the coconut economy in the Pacific.

The invasion of the South Pacific
J.C. Beaglehole, *The Exploration of the Pacific*, London 1934.
Douglas L. Oliver, *Native Cultures of the Pacific Islands*,
Hawaii 1989.
Marshall Sahlins, *Islands of History*, London 1985.
Thomas Williams, *Fiji and the Fijians*, vol. 1, London 1858.

Marshall Islands
Peter Hayes, Lyuba Zarsky and Walden Bello, *American Lake:
Nuclear Peril in the Pacific*, London 1987.
Giff Johnson's *Collision Course at Kwajalein*, Hawaii 1984,
contains the full background picture to US missile testing in the
Pacific. An account of an observer at Operation Crossroads, the
Atom Bomb Test at Bikini atoll in 1946, appears in James
Cameron's autobiography *Point of Departure*, London 1986.
Richard Rhodes, *The Making of the Atomic Bomb*, London
1988.

Captain Cook
J.C. Beaglehole (ed.), *The Journals of Captain James Cook on his Voyages of Discovery*, Cambridge 1956.
Alan Moorehead, *The Fatal Impact*, London 1966.
Patrick O'Brien, *Joseph Banks: A Life*, London 1987.

Stories of New Caledonia
Lt Biseuil, *Notices historiques et anecdotiques sur la Nouvelle Calédonie 1774-1878*, Paris 1898.
George Griffith, *In an Unknown Prison Land*, London 1901.
Clovis Savoie, *Histoire de la Nouvelle Calédonie et ses dépendances sous les gouverneurs militaires 1853-1884*, Paris 1907.
Barbara Tuchman sheds a lot of light on New Caledonia's past in her chapter on the fabulous degeneracy of the reign of Pope Alexander VI in *The March of Folly,* London 1984. For details of recent events in New Caledonia, I used David Robie's *Blood on their Banner*, Sydney 1990, and others.

The New Hebrides and Vanuatu
R.W. Adams, *In the Land of Strangers: A Century of European Contact with Tanna 1774-1874*, Canberra 1984.
Asterisk (Robert Fletcher), *Isles of Illusion*, London 1923.
John Beasant, *The Santo Rebellion: An Imperial Reckoning*, Melbourne 1984.
Bernard Deacon, *Malekula: A Vanishing People in the New Hebrides*, London 1934.
Margaret Gardiner, *Footprints on Malekula*, Edinburgh 1984.
Tom Harrisson, *Savage Civilisation*, London 1937.

Nationalism and coups d'état
Robert T. Robertson and Akosita Tamanisau, *Fiji: Shattered Coups*, Sydney 1988.
Pacific Islands Monthly and Islands Business, May 1987 et seq.

I could not have written the sections on New Caledonia, Vanuatu and Fiji without the help of Nicholas Rothwell. And Dale Keeling, the editor of the independent journal *Fiji Voice*, was especially generous with his time, and shrewd in his analysis of the coups in Fiji, which most journalists had dismissed as straightforward nationalism.

The Polynesians
I.C. Campbell, *A History of the Pacific Islands*, Christchurch 1989.
P. Collinder, *The History of Marine Navigation*, London 1954.
David Lewis, *We, the Navigators*, Wellington 1972.
The story of the arrival of the first 'godly mechanics' in the Pacific is told in Norman Lewis's *The Missionaries*, London 1988.

The war in the Pacific
Peter Calvocoressi, Guy Wint and John Pritchard, *Total War Vol. II: The Greater East Asia and Pacific Conflict*, London 1989.
Ronald H. Spector, *Eagle Against the Sun: The American War with Japan*, London 1987.

Robert Louis Stevenson
Sidney Colvin (ed.), *Vailima Letters*, London 1899.
Nicholas Rankin, *Dead Man's Chest: Travels after Robert Louis Stevenson*, London 1987.
Robert Louis Stevenson, *In the South Seas*, London 1912.
        – *A Footnote to History*, London 1912.
        – *Island Nights' Entertainments*, London 1912.

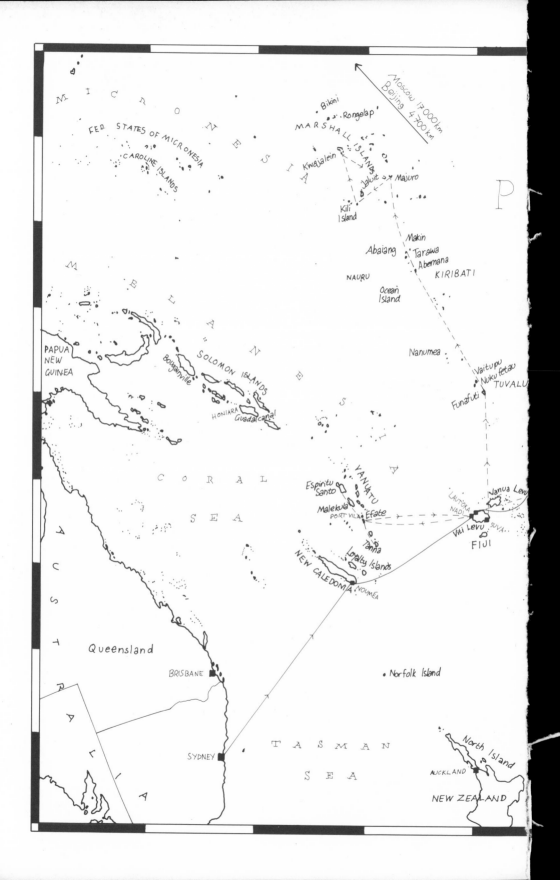